1 THESSALONIANS
2 THESSALONIANS

ABINGDON NEW TESTAMENT COMMENTARIES

1 THESSALONIANS
2 THESSALONIANS

VICTOR PAUL FURNISH

Abingdon Press
Nashville

1 THESSALONIANS, 2 THESSALONIANS

This book is printed on acid-free paper.

Library of Congress Cataloging-in-Publication Data

Furnish, Victor Paul.
  1 Thessalonians, 2 Thessalonians / Victor Paul Furnish.
     p. cm. — (Abingdon New Testament commentaries)
  Includes bibliographical references (p.   ) and index.
  ISBN 978-0-687-05743-6 (binding: pbk., : alk. paper)
     1. Bible. N.T. Thessalonians—Commentaries. I. Title. II. Title: First Thessalonians, Second Thessalonians.

  BS2725.53.F87 2007
  227'.8107—dc22

                                                                                        2007004723

All scripture quotations unless noted otherwise are taken from the *New Revised Standard Version of the Bible,* copyright 1989, by the Division of Christian Education of the National Council of the Churches of Christ in the United States of America. Used by permission. All rights reserved.

The Graeca® fonts used to print this work are available from Linguist's Software, Inc., PO Box 580, Edmonds, WA 98020-0580 tel (206) 775-1130.

07 08 09 10 11 12 13 14 15 16—10 9 8 7 6 5 4 3 2 1

MANUFACTURED IN THE UNITED STATES OF AMERICA

To D. Moody Smith
with appreciation and in friendship

CONTENTS

CONTENTS

CONTENTS

FOREWORD

The *Abingdon New Testament Commentaries* series provides compact, critical commentaries on the writings of the New Testament. These commentaries are written with special attention to the needs and interests of theological students, but they will also be useful for students in upper-level college or university settings, as well as for pastors and other church leaders. In addition to providing basic information about the New Testament texts and insights into their meanings, these commentaries are intended to exemplify the tasks and procedures of careful, critical biblical exegesis.

The authors who have contributed to this series come from a wide range of ecclesiastical affiliations and confessional stances. All are seasoned, respected scholars and experienced classroom teachers. They take full account of the most important current scholarship and secondary literature, but do not attempt to summarize that literature or engage in technical academic debate.

Their fundamental concern is to analyze the literary, socio-historical, theological, and ethical dimensions of the biblical texts themselves. Although all of the commentaries in this series have been written on the basis of the Greek texts, the authors do not presuppose any knowledge of the biblical languages on the part of the reader. When some awareness of the grammatical, syntactical, or philological issue is necessary for an adequate understanding of a particular text, they explain the matter clearly and concisely.

The introduction of each volume ordinarily includes subdivisions dealing with the *key issues* addressed and/or raised by the New Testament writing under consideration; its *literary genre, structure, and character;* its *occasion and situational context,* including its wider social, historical, and religious contexts; and its *theological and ethical significance* within these several contexts.

In each volume, the *commentary* is organized according to literary units rather than verse by verse. Generally, each of these units is the subject of three types of analysis. First, the *literary analysis* attends to the unit's genre, most important stylistic features, and overall structure. Second, the *exegetical analysis* considers the aim and leading ideas of the unit, deals with any especially important textual variants, and discusses the meanings of important words, phrases, and images. It also takes note of the particular historical and social situations of the writer and original readers, and of the wider cultural and religious contexts of the book as a whole. Finally, the *theological and ethical analysis* discusses the theological and ethical matters with which the unit deals or to which it points, focusing on the theological and ethical significance of the text within its original setting.

Each volume also includes a *select bibliography,* thereby providing guidance to other major commentaries and important scholarly works, and a brief *subject index.* The New Revised Standard Version of the Bible is the principal translation of reference for the series, but the authors draw on all of the major modern English versions, and when necessary provide their own original translations of difficult terms or phrases.

The fundamental aim of this series will have been attained if readers are assisted, not only to understand more about the origins, character, and meaning of the New Testament writings, but also to enter into their own informed and critical engagement with the texts themselves.

Victor Paul Furnish
General Editor

PREFACE

In the history of the interpretation of Paul's letters, 1 and 2 Thessalonians have often been consigned to second-class status. Many have dismissed 1 Thessalonians as pastorally rich but theologically thin, and 2 Thessalonians as so preoccupied with the Second Coming that it is theologically irrelevant. Anyone who has ventured, nonetheless, to consult a commentary on these letters probably anticipates that there is more to be said about them; and this commentary seeks to oblige.

If 1 Thessalonians is the earliest of Paul's letters, as most interpreters agree, it is also the earliest extant Christian writing. For this reason, it is a document of incalculable historical and theological importance. The apostle's statements about believing in Jesus as the Christ are the earliest affirmations of Christian faith. And the letter as a whole provides insight into Paul's life and thought during a formative period for both, at the beginning of his mission to Macedonia and Achaia.

If 2 Thessalonians is authentically Pauline, it comes from this same period and shows that developments in the Thessalonian congregation required the apostle to supplement—or perhaps even to re-conceive—his previous eschatological teaching. The present commentary, however, regards this letter as deutero-Pauline, composed by an unknown Paulinist several decades after the apostle's death. On this reading, the letter is significant for what it discloses about the reception of Paul's thought and the importance of the Pauline tradition in the late first-century church.

My indebtedness to the work of many other interpreters is apparent from the numerous references to secondary literature.

There are more of these than specified by the guidelines for this series. In part, these additional notes are necessary because much of the important, recent scholarship on the Thessalonian letters is accessible only in periodicals and scholarly monographs. In addition, I have thought it important to direct readers to more extensive discussions of the most controversial issues than a commentary of this length can provide, and to make sure that major, diverging points of view are represented.

I am also indebted to Perkins School of Theology, Southern Methodist University, for a Scholarly Outreach Award that helped me launch my research on the Thessalonian letters; to Kathy Armistead and the staff of Abingdon Press, who have supported this commentary series and my work as its General Editor in many ways; and, in particular, to Pheme Perkins, a member of the Editorial Board, from whose comments on the typescript of the present volume I have greatly benefited.

It is a special pleasure to dedicate this commentary to D. Moody Smith—a friend since we first met at Yale, half a century ago.

Victor Paul Furnish

LIST OF ABBREVIATIONS

1 Clem.	*1 Clement*
1 En.	*1 Enoch*
1QH*	*Thanksgiving Hymns**
1QM	*War Scroll*
1QS	*Rule of the Community*
2 Bar.	Syriac *Apocalypse of Baruch*
AB	Anchor Bible
ABD	*Anchor Bible Dictionary*
ABRL	Anchor Bible Reference Library
Ag. Ap.	Josephus, *Against Apion*
AGJU	*Arbeiten zur Geschichte des antiken Judentums und des Urchristentums*
Alex.	Dio Chrysostom, To the People of Alexandria
Alleg. Interp.	Philo, *Allegorical Interpretation*
alt.	alternate translation or reading
Am.	Pseudo-Lucian, *Amores (Affairs of the Heart)*
Ant.	Josephus, *Jewish Antiquities*
AT	Author's translation
B.C.E.	Before the Common Era (= B.C.)
Barn.	*Barnabas*
BBR	*Bulletin for Biblical Research*
BDAG	Bauer, W., F. W. Danker, W. F. Arndt, and F. W. Gingrich, *Greek-English Lexicon of the New Testament and Other Early Christian Literature*, 3d edition
BDF	Blass, F., and A. Debrunner, *Greek Grammar of the New Testament and Other Early Christian Literature*, trans. and rev. by R. Funk, 1961

BETL	Bibliotheca ephemeridum theologicarum lovaniensium
Bib	*Biblica*
BJRL	*Bulletin of the John Rylands [University] Library*
BZ	*Biblische Zeitschrift*
BZNW	Beihefte zur Zeitschrift für die neutestamentliche Wissenschaft
C.E.	Common Era (= A.D.)
CBQ	*Catholic Biblical Quarterly*
CGTSC	Cambridge Greek Testament for Schools and Colleges
chap(s).	chapter(s)
ConBNT	Coniectanea biblica: New Testament Series
Did.	*Didache*
Ebib	Études bibliques
EDNT	Balz, H., and G. Schneider, eds., *Exegetical Dictionary of the New Testament*, 1990–1993
EKKNT	Evangelisch-katholischer Kommentar zum Neuen Testament
Embassy	Philo, *On the Embassy to Gaius*
Ep.	Seneca, *Moral Epistles*
et al.	and others
Eth. Nic.	Aristotle, *Nicomachean Ethics*
ETS	Erfurter Theologische Studien
Flatterer	Plutarch, *How to Tell a Flatterer from a Friend*
Frag.	Musonius Rufus, *Fragments*, ed. and trans. by C. Lutz, 1947
Gk.	Greek
GNS	*Good News Studies*
GNT³	*The Greek New Testament*, 3d edition ed. by K. Aland *et al.*
Hist.	Tacitus, *Histories*
HNT	Handbuch zum Neuen Testament
HNTC	Harper's New Testament Commentaries
HTR	*Harvard Theological Review*
HUT	Hermeneutische Untersuchungen zur Theologie

IBC	Interpretation: A Bible Commentary for Teaching and Preaching
ICC	International Critical Commentary
Ign. *Eph.*	Ignatius, *To the Ephesians*
IVPNTC	IVP New Testament Commentary
J.W.	Josephus, *The Jewish War*
JBL	*Journal of Biblical Literature*
Jos. Asen.	*Joseph and Asenath*
Joseph	Philo, *On the Life of Joseph*
JSNT	*Journal for the Study of the New Testament*
JSNTSup	Journal for the Study of the New Testament: Supplement Series
Jub.	*Jubilees*
KEK	Kritisch-exegetischer Kommentar über das Neue Testament (Meyer-Kommentar)
L.A.B.	Pseudo-Philo, *Liber antiquitatum biblicarum*
LCBI	Literary Currents in Biblical Interpretation
LCL	Loeb Classical Library
LEC	Library of Early Christianity
lit.	literally
LXX	Septuagint
m. 'Abot	Mishnah, *The Fathers*
Mart. Isa.	*Martyrdom of Isaiah*
MM	Moulton, J. H., and G. Milligan, *The Vocabulary of the Greek New Testament Illustrated from the Papyri and Other Non-Literary Sources*, 1930
MNTC	Moffatt New Testament Commentary
Mof.	*The New Testament in the Moffatt Translation*
n.	footnote
NAB	*New American Bible*, revised edition
Names	Philo, *On the Change of Names*
NCBC	New Century Bible Commentary
Nestle-Aland[27]	*Novum Testamentum Graece*, 27th edition, ed. by B. and K. Aland *et al.*
NIGTC	New International Greek Testament Commentary
NIV	*New International Version of the Holy Bible*
NJB	*New Jerusalem Bible*

NovT	*Novum Testamentum*
NRSV	*New Revised Standard Version of the Bible*
NT	New Testament
NTD	Das Neue Testament Deutsch
NTR	New Testament Readings
NTS	*New Testament Studies*
Or.	Dio Chrysostom, *Oration*
OT	Old Testament
par., parr.	parallel, parallels
Planting	Philo, *On Planting*
Pol. *Phil.*	Polycarp, *To the Philippians*
PSB	*Princeton Seminary Bulletin*
Pss. Sol.	*Psalms of Solomon*
REB	*Revised English Bible*
repr.	reprinted
RNT	Regensburger Neues Testament
RSV	*Revised Standard Version of the Bible*
s.v.	under the word
Sacrifices	Philo, *On the Sacrifices of Cain and Abel*
SBLDS	Society of Biblical Literature Dissertation Series
SBLSBS	Society of Biblical Literature Sources for Biblical Study
SBLSP	Society of Biblical Literature Seminar Papers
SHCT	Studies in the History of Christian Thought
Sent.	*The Sentences of Pseudo-Phocylides*
Sib. Or.	*Sibylline Oracles*
SNT	Studien zum Neuen Testament
SNTSMS	Society for New Testament Studies Monograph Series
SP	Sacra Pagina
SPAW	*Sitzungsberichte der Preussischen Akademie der Wissenschaften zu Berlin*
Spec. Laws	Philo, *On the Special Laws*
T. Ash.	*Testament of Asher*
T. Benj.	*Testament of Benjamin*
T. Naph.	*Testament of Naphtali*

TDNT	*Theological Dictionary of the New Testament*, ed. G. Kittel, *et al.*
trans.	translation *or* translated by
TU	Texte und Untersuchungen zur Geschichte der altchristlichen Literatur
TZ	*Theologische Zeitschrift*
WBC	Word Biblical Commentary
WMANT	Wissenschaftliche Monographien zum Alten und Neuen Testament
WUNT	Wissenschaftliche Untersuchungen zum Neuen Testament
WW	*Word and World*
ZBK	Zürcher Bibelkommentare
ZNW	*Zeitschrift für die neutestamentliche Wissenschaft und die Kunde der älteren Kirche*
ZTK	*Zeitschrift für Theologie und Kirche*

Introduction:
1 Thessalonians

Assuming its authenticity, which is rarely questioned, 1 Thessalonians is almost certainly the earliest of Paul's surviving letters, and hence the earliest surviving Christian document. For this reason, one must read 1 Thessalonians in the first instance without presuming that Paul already held views that he expresses only in subsequent letters or that are attributed to him in Acts and other later writings. The same principle applies when estimating the literary character and features of this letter, for it may well be the apostle's first attempt to communicate with a congregation in writing (Koester 1979).

Epistolary Character and Aims

Formally, this letter (so designated in 1 Thess 5:27) opens and closes rather like others of the Hellenistic period (see commentary on 1:1 and 5:25-28). Even so, efforts to identify 1 Thessalonians with one of the specific epistolary types discussed in ancient handbooks (for these, see Malherbe 1988) have not been entirely successful. Some interpreters have classified it as a letter of consolation (e.g., Donfried 2000a, esp. 38-41, 48-49; A. Smith 1995, esp. 51-60); others as a letter of friendship (e.g., Schoon-Janßen 2000); still others as parenetic, a letter devoted to advice, instruction, exhortation, and encouragement (e.g. Malherbe 2000, 81-86). Clearly, 1 Thessalonians exhibits certain features of each of these types. Yet because the ancient epistolary categories were applied mainly to private correspondence between family members and friends, the letters of teachers to their students, business letters, and official (e.g., governmental) letters, they do not readily accommodate a letter like 1 Thessalonians. Paul was writing as one divinely commissioned with the gospel, and was addressing a community of fictive "brothers and sisters" who were bound together and bound to him primarily by their common faith in the God of Jesus Christ. This letter does indeed represent "an experiment in Christian writing" (Koester 1979, esp. 33-34).

Efforts have also been made to identify 1 Thessalonians with one of the classical rhetorical genres (for these, see Aune 2003, 418-20). It is sometimes characterized as an example of deliberative rhetoric, which aimed at either persuading or dissuading an audience concerning some future course of action (e.g., Kennedy 1984, 142; Johanson 1987, 188-90, but with reservations). More often it is described as reflecting the strategies of epideictic rhetoric, which was devoted to praise or blame (e.g., Wanamaker 1990, 48-50; Schoon-Janßen 2000, 182-93). Yet rhetorical genres were frequently mixed, particularly in letters (Reed 1997, 176). In 1 Thessalonians Paul employs a variety of rhetorical strategies in order to achieve his aims.

The aims of this letter are clearly *pastoral* (emphasized esp. by Malherbe 1987; 2000, 77-78 and throughout). This is the term, rather than any that can be drawn from the ancient handbooks, that best identifies its contents and describes its literary character. The occasion of the letter was Timothy's report to Paul about his visit to the Thessalonian congregation (see below, "The Letter's Composition and Dispatch"). His reason for writing was consonant with his reason for having sent Timothy back to Thessalonica (3:1-10): "to strengthen and encourage" the new converts in their faith, lest they be tempted to forsake the gospel because of the anxieties and difficulties their conversion had brought them. As through Timothy's visit, so now through this letter Paul exercises his "pastoral care" of the congregation.

Given what he has heard from Timothy, the apostle's specific aims in writing are (a) to commend the congregation for its unwavering "faith and love," which include its continuing affirmation of himself and his mission (3:6-7); (b) to motivate its continuing fidelity to the gospel he proclaimed (3:8), no matter the opposition and harassment that it may experience as a result (see 1:6; 2:2, 14; 3:3-4; 4:10b-12); and (c) to instruct and encourage it concerning matters about which it needs to be informed or reassured (3:10).

The first two aims are especially apparent in chapters 1–3. There Paul's reminders and assurances are incorporated within a narrative of the congregation's founding and of his continuing concern for it. This narrative serves to nurture the cordial relationship that already exists between the missionaries and their converts and to encourage them in their faith. The third aim is especially apparent in chapters 4–5. There he urges his converts to fulfill their holy calling of "pleasing God" (4:1-8), to conduct themselves responsibly in society as well as within the church (4:9-12; 5:12-22; cf. 5:1-11), and to understand that believers who have died will experience the Lord's return no less than those who survive to the end (4:13-18). Consistent with his pastoral aims and rhetorical strategy, Paul opens the letter by *praising* his converts for their faith, love, and hope (1:3), and closes it by *summoning* them to "put on the breastplate of faith and love, and for a helmet the hope of salvation" (5:8).

Also consistent with the pastoral character and aims of 1 Thessalonians is the prominence of terms and images drawn from family life (Malherbe 1995; see esp. Aasgaard 2004, 121-22, 152-66, 287-89; Harland 2005; cf. Burke 2003). God is identified as "[the] Father" (1:1, 3; 3:11, 13) and Jesus as "his Son" (1:10). Repeatedly, and in proportion to length significantly more often than in any other letter, Paul addresses his converts as "brothers" (NRSV: "brothers and sisters"; see below, "The Thessalonian Converts"). He also portrays them as "infants" (2:7b, NRSV n.), with himself as the nursing mother to whom they are "very dear" (2:7b-8); as "children" (*tekna*) who know him as their "father" (2:11) and from whom he now feels orphaned (2:17); as a household which, if it is unprepared for the Lord's return, will suffer the pain experienced by a woman in labor (5:2-4); and as "sons of light and sons of the day" (*huioi*, 5:5; NRSV: "children"), people whom the Lord has already claimed as his own. Collectively, these images vividly express the affection and responsibility that Paul feels for his converts, and his awareness of the bond that unites them to him and to one another. His intent is to deepen their sense of belonging to a "household of faith" (an expression he uses in Gal 6:10 AT), whose members share a common calling and destiny.

Another special literary feature of this letter is the exceptionally high density of second person plural verbs and pronouns. Especially the high incidence of the latter reflects the apostle's concern to present himself as personally and seriously interested in how the members of his young congregation are faring. This concern may also account in part for the unusually high number of *first* person plural verbs and pronouns. Primarily, however, the extensive use of the first person plural prompts the question whether the colleagues Paul names in the prescript had some role in the writing of this letter. The reasons for believing they did not are indicated below (see "The Letter's Composition and Dispatch").

The literary structure of 1 Thessalonians has been variously analyzed (see Jewett 1986, 216-21). Although Paul generally followed epistolary conventions in opening and closing the letter, the structure of the letter-body is somewhat unconventional. A few interpreters have concluded that our 1 Thessalonians is actually a composite of two separate Pauline letters, or that one or more passages are later, non-Pauline interpolations. All of these theories have to be argued on the basis of internal evidence, however, because the textual tradition offers no support for the view that there were two predecessor letters, or that certain passages were added later.

Almost no support has been forthcoming for the suggestion that 5:1-11 is a later addition (Friedrich 1973; 1981, 207), intended to preclude his audience from taking 4:13-17 as evidence that Paul expected the Lord to return very soon. Textual evidence is lacking, there is no real tension between the two passages, and the non-Pauline elements in 5:1-11 are plausibly explained as Paul's incorporation of traditional expressions and motifs (see commentary). The passage most widely regarded as an interpolation is 2:14-16, but this commentary accepts those verses, too, as belonging to the original letter (see commentary for arguments pro and con).

Several interpreters agree in identifying 1:1–2:12 + 4:3–5:28 and 2:13–4:2 (give or take 2:14-16) as two originally separate letters

(Schmithals 1964, 1972; Richard 1995, 11-14; Murphy-O'Connor 1996, 104-14), but there is disagreement about which of these was earlier (according to Schmithals, 1:1–2:12 + 4:3–5:28; according to Richard and Murphy-O'Connor, 2:13–4:2). Most interpreters, however, remain unconvinced by such partition theories and regard them as unnecessary. The letter taken as an integral whole makes good sense, as various studies of its rhetoric (esp. Johanson 1987) and numerous commentaries (e.g., Malherbe 2000) have clearly shown (R. F. Collins 1979; 1998, esp. 398-402).

Beyond the fundamental issue of the letter's integrity, the main question about its structure has been what portion constitutes the letter-body. Many identify this as 4:1–5:22 (or 5:24), taking the whole of 1:2–3:13 as an extended "thanksgiving." Although Paul Schubert (1939, 16-27) is regularly cited in support of this analysis, he himself regarded 1:2–3:13 as the "main body" and 4:1–5:22 as the conclusion (ibid., 26). The present commentary follows a somewhat middle course, holding that there are two distinct thanksgiving paragraphs in this letter, and that both of them stand *within* the letter-body (for the overall results of this analysis, see table of contents). The first thanksgiving appears in 1:2-10 (cf. Hooker 1996, 444), the second in 2:13-16. A third expression of thanksgiving, "How can we thank God enough for you...?" (3:9) is best regarded as spontaneous, prompted not by epistolary convention but by the immediate context (for spontaneous thanksgivings in papyrus letters, see Arzt 1994, 33-35). It is no argument against this that thanksgiving paragraphs in other Pauline letters can be viewed as *preceding* the letter-body (esp. 1 Cor 1:4-9; Phil 1:3-11). In this respect as in others, 1 Thessalonians represents an early stage in the development of Paul's epistolary habits.

Historical Occasion and Context

Thessalonica

After the death of Alexander III ("the Great"), Macedonia became an independent kingdom ruled by Cassander (358–297 B.C.E.), who in 315/316 B.C.E. founded the city of Thessalonica, naming it for his wife, Alexander's half-sister (historical surveys in Hendrix 1992; vom Brocke 2001, 12-20). It was situated on a naturally protected harbor and along the Via Egnatia, which was the major highway across Greece, linking the Adriatic Sea on the west to the Hellespont on the east. Thessalonica thus became one of the two most important trading centers in Roman Greece (the other being Corinth; Charlesworth 1926, 126-27). It was also, still at the time of Paul's arrival, the capital of the Roman province of Macedonia.

The population in Paul's day has been estimated at around 30,000, made up mostly of Greeks, including many native Macedonians (vom Brocke 2001, 71-73, 86-101). There is firm evidence of a sizeable Jewish community from the end of the second and on into the third and fourth centuries C.E. There is, however, little evidence for a Jewish presence in the first century (vom Brocke 2001, 207-33; Ascough 2003, 191-212), and it is only literary, not archaeological. According to Acts 17:1-8, Paul preached in "a synagogue of the Jews" there, making some Jewish converts but also facing substantial Jewish opposition. The only other first-century evidence comes from the Jewish philosopher Philo of Alexandria (d. ca. 50 C.E.), whose claim that Jewish communities had spread throughout the empire had an apologetic aim. Moreover, he referred only to Jewish colonies in the province of Macedonia, not mentioning Thessalonica by name (*Embassy* 281-82). The first certain archaeological evidence of Jews in the city is provided by a sarcophagus inscription from the third century C.E. Thus, despite the impression given by Acts 17, the Jewish community at the time of Paul's mission was probably neither large nor influential.

There is, however, substantial evidence of the pagan cults that the apostle would have found in Thessalonica (e.g., Edson 1948; Donfried 1985; Hendrix 1992; vom Brocke 2001, 114-42). As in other urban centers, they were of diverse origins—Egyptian, Roman, and Phrygian, as well as Macedonian and Greek. One of the two most important was the imperial cult, attested in Thessalonica from the time of Augustus but probably rooted in earlier cults to Roma and the Roman benefactors. It is well attested that an especially prominent aspect of the city's life was its rendering of civic honors to the "divine Caesar," for whom a temple had been erected.

Of equal prominence was the mystery cult of Cabirus, the deity most often represented on the city's coins. Apparently distinctive to the Cabirus cult in its Thessalonian manifestation was its devotion to just one of the several legendary Cabiri, and its revering him as the "holiest" of all the deities of the city (vom Brocke 2001, 117, 120-21). Almost nothing is known, however, about the actual practices of the cult in Thessalonica.

Paul's Thessalonian Mission

Paul's mission in Thessalonica followed one in Philippi where he had been "shamefully mistreated" (1 Thess 2:1-2; cf. Acts 16:11–17:1). He remained in Thessalonica long enough both to need and to be able to work at his trade (1 Thess 2:9), and for the Philippian congregation to send him financial assistance on at least two occasions (Phil 4:15-16). This suggests a stay of several months, substantially longer than the few weeks implied by the account in Acts ("three sabbaths," 17:2). His arrival in the city is plausibly dated to the spring or summer of 49, and his departure to the autumn or early winter of the same year (cf. Malherbe 2000, 71-74).

Paul was probably accompanied from Philippi to Thessalonica by Timothy as well as Silvanus, although Acts 17:1 mentions only the latter (calling him "Silas"; Timothy's presence in Philippi is suggested by Phil 1:1; 2:22; Acts 16:1, 3). Subsequently, even Acts notes that Timothy as well as Silas was in Beroea (17:14), and it is certain that both were with Paul in Corinth (2 Cor 1:19; cf. Acts 18:5). That they had both participated also in the Thessalonian mission is further suggested by the apostle's joining of both names with his own in 1 Thess 1:1 (see commentary), followed by his use of the first person plural throughout most of the rest of the letter.

Given Paul's remark, "we worked ... while we proclaimed" (1 Thess 2:9), and that most of his converts were artisans (see below, "The Thessalonian Converts"), it is possible that a Thessalonian workshop was the principal site of the missionaries' preaching and teaching. The fundamental points of their message can be inferred from several statements in 1 Thessalonians. At its core, it must have affirmed that there is one living and true God (1:9b), whose Son, (the Lord) Jesus, resurrected from the dead, will reappear on the eschatological day to rescue the elect from God's wrath (1:10; 5:9-10; cf. 2:19; 3:13; 4:6); and further, that those who have come to know this one true God (cf. 4:5) are God's elect (1:4), "destined for salvation" (5:9), called into God's kingdom (2:12b; cf. 5:24), and continuing beneficiaries of the powerful working of the Holy Spirit (1:5, 6; 4:8).

From the beginning, apparently, the missionaries had been explicit about the consequences of accepting this gospel. Abandoning all other gods (1:9b), converts were to conduct their lives in a manner that was worthy of the God who had called them in holiness (2:12a; 4:7-8), whose will was their sanctification (4:3a), and by whose faithfulness they would be established in holiness at the last day (3:13; 5:23-24). Along with this, they seem to have been instructed about specific ways they "ought to live and to please God" (4:1, 3).

While this message was received by some as truly "God's word" (2:13), there is no doubt that both the missionaries and their converts experienced a considerable amount of active opposition. Paul may overstate its extent and severity when he refers to "much affliction [*thlipsis*]" (1:6, AT) and a "great struggle [*agōn*]" (2:2, AT). But it was serious enough to have forced him to leave Thessalonica sooner than he had planned (1 Thess 2:17).

Indirectly, and with no mention of the Jewish involvement that is portrayed in Acts 17:5-8, Paul identifies the perpetrators of the suffering as Gentile residents of Thessalonica (2:14, see commentary). It is possible that the missionaries' proclamation of "one God" had put them at risk, especially from the officials and adherents of the city's important imperial cult. At least in principle, their converts could no longer swear the required oaths to Caesar (cf. Acts 17:7, "the decrees of the emperor"; de Vos 1999, 156-57), and this would have left them open to the charge of being "atheists" and a threat to the public order. In addition, they must have faced other difficulties on a daily basis: the risk of being held up to public shame and humiliation, the possible loss of their livelihoods, the taunts and insults of strangers, and not least, painful estrangement from their non-believing family and friends. These are likely the tribulations (not martyrdom, for which there is no evidence) to which Paul has reference when he speaks of the "persecution(s)" (1:6; 3:3-4), "great opposition" (2:2), and suffering (2:14) in Thessalonica.

The Thessalonian Converts

According to Acts, one of Paul's converts in Thessalonica was Jason (whether he was a Jew or Gentile is uncertain; vom Brocke 2001, 234-40), who subsequently became Paul's host in the city (17:5-9). Other Thessalonian Christians mentioned in Acts are Aristarchus (20:4; 27:2; cf. 19:29) and Secundus (20:4), but they seem not to have been associated with the apostle until some years after his evangelization of the city (Malherbe 2000, 66-67). Neither in 1 Thessalonians nor elsewhere does Paul himself identify any of his Thessalonian converts, or any who later became members of the congregation or served as its leaders. Estimates of the number of converts range from twenty to seventy-five (de Vos 1999, 154), but these remain highly speculative.

One can be quite certain, however, that most if not all of Paul's converts in Thessalonica were Gentiles. This is clear from his statements that they "turned to God from idols, to serve a living and true God" (1 Thess 1:9b), and that their suffering has been inflicted by their fellow Gentiles (the required meaning of "your own compatriots" in 2:14; see commentary). Moreover, the moral instructions in 1 Thess 4:3-5 would be less apt for Jewish believers than for Gentiles who have recently come to "know God" (v. 5). Finally, the letter is silent on topics that might have been of specific importance to converts from Judaism (e.g., whether or to what extent they remain obligated to the Law of Moses).

According to Acts 17, the Thessalonian converts included not only Jason, a citizen of considerable means and standing who seems to have become Paul's patron (vv. 5-7), but also some of the city's "leading women" (v. 4). On the evidence of 1 Thessalonians alone, however, the infant congregation must have been made up mostly of persons at the lower end of the socio-economic scale. The apostle's instruction to "work with your hands" (1 Thess 4:11) suggests that most of the converts were artisans, as he was. While their work required manual skills, it would have brought them only modest income and contributed nothing to their social status.

Although the remark about "leading women" in Acts 17:4 is a formula with minimal evidentiary value (cf. 17:12), it is probable that some women were among the first converts in Thessalonica (acknowledged even by Fatum 1997, 192, who, however, questions whether women really "counted" in the Christian community there). The conversion of entire households that Paul himself attests for Corinth (1 Cor 1:16; 16:15) must also have taken place elsewhere, as well as the conversion of women whose husbands remained unbelievers (the situation presupposed in 1 Cor 7:8-16). Thus, when the apostle addresses this and other congregations as *adelphoi* (lit. "brothers") he is employing the term inclusively, for "brothers and sisters" (a usage documented in a family letter from the second century C.E.; White 1986, 159-60 [Letter A; lines 14, 19-20 compared with lines 4-6]).

The Letter's Composition and Dispatch

Paul most likely wrote 1 Thessalonians within a few months of his departure from Thessalonica, and fairly early in his Corinthian mission, which began early in the year 50 (e.g., Malherbe 2000, 71-74). The apostle could hardly write as he does in 2:17-19 had any great amount of time elapsed since the founding of the Thessalonian congregation. Moreover, it would appear that Timothy, just returned from there, has provided Paul with his first definite news of how the new converts are faring (3:1-10). That the letter was dispatched from Corinth is almost certain. Paul's phrasing of the reference to Athens in 1 Thess 3:1 suggests that he is no longer there, and his mention of Silvanus and Timothy as co-senders (1:1) corresponds with the sure evidence that both men were with him in Corinth (2 Cor 1:19; Acts 18:5).

Some interpreters take the predominance of the first person plural (in places like 1:2, 4-5, 9; 2:2-6) as an indication that Silvanus and Timothy collaborated with Paul in writing the letter, and are therefore to be regarded as "co-authors" (e.g., Murphy-O'Connor

1995, 19-20; Stirewalt 2003, 37-44; more cautiously, Byrskog 1996, 236-38). But this letter reads much more like the product of one person than like a collaborative effort (note, e.g., the eruptions of the first person singular in 2:18; 3:5; 5:27). It is more plausible to explain (most of) the first person plurals as "authorial" (or "literary"), a stylistic device employed in antiquity as well as today (e.g., R. F. Collins 1980-81, 178-80; M. Müller 1998, esp. 188-89; Malherbe 2000, 87-89). This seems confirmed by the fact that "we sent" in 3:2 and "I sent" in 3:5 both refer to the same event, namely, Paul's dispatch of Timothy back to Thessalonica. The letter's recipients probably would have understood the plurals in question as evidence that Silvanus and Timothy continue to be as committed as Paul to their well-being.

The occasion of this letter was Timothy's report to Paul about his return visit to the congregation (3:6), an assignment that he had undertaken at the apostle's behest (3:1-2). It is not impossible that Timothy also brought back a letter from the congregation to Paul (thus Malherbe 2000, 208-10), but there is no certain evidence of this. Paul had charged Timothy to "encourage and strengthen" the new converts (3:2), whom he knew (or supposed) were still experiencing the afflictions that had begun with their conversion (1:6). With Timothy's return, Paul learned that the congregation remained faithful to the gospel and well disposed toward the missionaries (3:6-9). He also learned, however, that in certain respects its faith needed to be encouraged and deepened (3:10). Judging from the contents of 1 Thessalonians, which Paul wrote in response, he understood the converts to need instruction on two points above all: how to conduct themselves in a manner that is worthy of God (2:12; 4:1-12), especially when faced with adversity (e.g., 3:3); and why they need not despair over some fellow believers who, against all expectations, have died without experiencing the Lord's return (4:13–5:11).

The apostle probably dictated this letter to a scribe (see commentary on 5:27), but there is no indication of who that might have been. Nor is there any indication of who carried the letter to Thessalonica, although it could well have been some Corinthian believer who had business in that Macedonian city (Nicholl 2004, 192).

THEOLOGICAL AND ETHICAL ORIENTATION

Because the aims of this letter are pastoral, it does not yield either a systematic theology or a comprehensive ethic. It has, nonetheless, an evident and important theological and ethical orientation. In characterizing this orientation, one must not assume that the views and convictions expressed in Paul's later letters are already present, or even anticipated here. It would also be wrong to suppose that the letter's theological and ethical orientation can be determined simply by identifying the various pre-Pauline theological and ethical traditions that it occasionally echoes (e.g., in 4:14; 5:9-10; 5:12-21). The critical matter is how these traditions serve Paul's aims in writing. Thus, when examining its theological-ethical orientation, one must give attention to this letter *alone and as a whole,* taking care not to import views that the apostle expresses only in subsequent letters (an approach well exemplified by Schnelle 2005, 176-91).

The theological-ethical orientation of this letter is consistent with what can be inferred about the cardinal points of the gospel Paul had proclaimed in Thessalonica a few months earlier. Here as in his missionary preaching he speaks of the coming judgment of God, God's saving purpose, the empowering activity of God's Holy Spirit, the future return of God's Son, and—by no means least—the divine election and calling by which believers have been given a new existence in holiness and a sure hope for its fulfillment. The apostle's thinking about all of these topics has been significantly informed by the Jewish scriptures, even though 1 Thessalonians is one of the three certainly Pauline letters that contains no quotations from Scripture or specific appeals to its authority (the other two are Philippians and Philemon). The apostle has drawn on many scriptural idioms and images, however, and there are a number of allusions to scriptural passages (especially in chaps. 4, 5). From a theological standpoint, the most significant allusions occur when Paul speaks of the giving of the Holy Spirit (4:8, echoing Ezekiel); of being taught by God (4:9, echoing Isaiah and, perhaps, Jeremiah); and of donning the armor of faith, love, and hope (5:8, adapting an image from Isaiah).

The first direct theological assertion of the letter is about *election,* which Paul implicitly presents as an expression of God's love (1:4). He subsequently refers to this as God's *call* (2:12; 4:7), emphasizing the divine faithfulness (5:24). Because he is addressing Gentile believers, it is clear that he understands God's love and faithfulness to be universal in scope, inclusive of humankind as a whole. Conversion (accepting the gospel) means accepting not only one's election by the "living and true God" (1:9), but also God's call to holiness (2:11-12; 4:7; 5:23-24). Paul views both of these—conversion and the sanctified life—as empowered, like the gospel itself, by God's Holy Spirit (1:5, 6; 4:7-8).

The new existence of God's elect is eschatological existence, because they are already being called into God's kingdom (2:12) where their sanctification will be fulfilled (5:23). Meanwhile, the distinguishing characteristics of this new existence are faith, love, and hope. Paul's highlighting of these near the beginning of the letter and then again toward its close seems deliberate (1:3; 5:8).

Faith, as he speaks of it in this letter, is first of all the believers' trusting acceptance of their election by God. It is therefore itself a manifestation of God's love, and thereby also an affirmation of the "living and true God" (1:8, 9). At the same time, faith affirms the Son whom God raised from the dead (1:10; 4:14; cf. 5:10). Thus, to "continue to stand firm in the Lord" (3:8, referring to Christ) is an alternate expression for persevering in faith (3:2-3).

Paul links faith with *love* not only in the triadic formulations of 1:3 and 5:8 but also when he notes that Timothy has commended the converts' "faith and love" (3:6). In experiencing their faith as a manifestation of God's electing love, the "beloved" (1:4) are called to be agents of God's love in the world, for love is the outworking of holiness (cf. 3:12-13). And their love is to be no less inclusive than God's own (3:12; 4:10b-12; 5:15).

A further mark of the believers' new existence is their *hope* of "salvation" (5:8), the consummation of which will be inaugurated at the expected return of their Lord (e.g., 2:19; 3:13; 4:15). As Paul speaks of it here, salvation will have both a negative and a positive aspect. Negatively, it will mean being found "blameless" at the final judgment (3:13; cf. 4:6), and thus spared God's wrath

(1:10; cf. 5:9). Positively, it will mean being fully established in the holiness for which they have been called (5:23-24), and sharing "forever" in the life of their resurrected Lord (4:17; 5:10).

The specifically *theo*logical orientation of this letter is noteworthy. The theme of God's electing love underlies everything that Paul says about the believers' new existence. It also underlies what he says about Jesus, whom Paul most often refers to in this letter as the "Lord" (or "Lord Jesus," "Lord Jesus Christ"). Having been raised from the dead, he is destined to come again to rescue believers from wrath (1:10), gathering them to himself that they may share his life (4:14, 17; 5:10). Yet he will not be acting as an independent agent, but as God's "Son." It is *God* who raised Jesus from the dead (1:10), it is *God* who will be in command of the end-time events (4:14), and it is *God* who will fully sanctify the elect (5:23). Thus everything depends on the faithfulness of *God* (5:24).

Although believers will experience the fullness of salvation only when they are finally gathered up to be with the Lord (4:17), as God's elect who are already graced with faith, love, and hope, they "belong" even now to that day and are "children of light" (5:4-8). Accordingly, they are not to view the present only as a time for waiting. They are to embrace it as a time to "serve ... God" (1:9) in their daily lives—by conducting themselves in a manner that will be "worthy of God" (2:12), that will "please God" (2:4; 4:1), and that will be in accord with "the will of God" (4:3; 5:18). Again in these phrases the specifically *theo*logical orientation of Paul's thought is apparent. There is only a hint of the idea, prominent in his subsequent letters, that the present life of faith is life "in Christ" (e.g., "in the Lord," 3:8; 5:12).

Readers who are familiar with the apostle's subsequent letters will have no difficulty identifying a number of themes that seem to be "missing" from 1 Thessalonians. For example, in this letter Paul never mentions the Law, the tyranny of sin and death, or life according to the flesh; and he also says nothing about God's justice (righteousness), justification, the cross, reconciliation, or freedom. Claims that some or all of these are implicit or anticipated in the letter are not convincing. There is no need to try to read between the lines, for in what Paul *explicitly* says one can discern a coherent theological point of view. Moreover, those to whom he sent this letter could have compared it only with his missionary preaching to them, and insofar as that message can be reconstructed, its theological-ethical orientation seems to have been essentially the same.

COMMENTARY:
1 THESSALONIANS

PRESCRIPT (1:1)

In accord with the epistolary conventions of his day, Paul begins all of his letters with a prescript that includes the names of the sender(s) (superscription), those of the addressee(s) (adscription), and a greeting (salutation). The prescript here is the most conventional of any in the Pauline Corpus.

◊ ◊ ◊ ◊

That Paul's name stands first marks this letter as principally from him, but he does not identify himself as an apostle, as he does in every subsequent letter except for Philippians (and 2 Thessalonians, should it be authentic). Silvanus and Timothy, who had participated in the founding of the Thessalonian congregation, may be regarded as co-senders but hardly as "co-authors" (see Introduction and comments on v. 2). The mention of them here marks this letter as part of the apostle's continuing mission to his Thessalonian converts, and suggests that they endorse what he now writes (one function of the co-senders named in some Hellenistic letters; Stirewalt 2003, 37-42).

Silvanus is doubtless the same person whom the author of Acts knew as Silas and identified as a prominent member of the Jerusalem church (Acts 15:22, 27, 32). Timothy was one of Paul's most trusted associates, whom Paul variously describes as a "co-worker" (3:2; Rom 16:21), "brother" (3:2; 2 Cor 1:1; Phlm 1), "beloved and faithful child in the Lord" (1 Cor 4:17), and "like a son" (Phil 2:22). The only other mention of Silvanus in a certainly Pauline letter is in 2 Cor 1:19, where Paul indicates that both Silvanus and Timothy had participated in the mission to Corinth (cf. Acts 18:5), the city from which Paul now writes (see Introduction).

In all of the other Pauline letters the adscription identifies the community being addressed by referring to its location (e.g., Rom 1:7: "in Rome"), but here, "To the church composed of Thessalonians" (AT) identifies the community with reference to its members. The Greek term *ekklēsia*, often translated "church," was used both of formal political assemblies (e.g., Acts 19:39) and of informal public gatherings (e.g., Acts 19:32). Its application to communities of Christians, as in the phrase "church(es) of God" (e.g., 2:14; 1 Cor 1:2; 11:22), may reflect a usage of sectarian Judaism, which described the eschatological community as "[God's] assembly" (1QM IV, 10; 1Q28a II, 4; *EDNT,* 1.411 [J. Roloff]). By identifying the Thessalonian converts as constituting an *ekklēsia* "in God the Father and the Lord Jesus Christ" (1:1), Paul effectively distinguishes their assembly from all others in the city, formal or informal.

Paul rarely uses the phrase "in God" (elsewhere, only in 2:2; Rom 2:17; 5:11). If the present instance is interpreted spatially, he means that the church lives by remaining in communion with God and Christ (e.g., Holtz 1998, 38 n. 34). If it is interpreted instrumentally, he means that the Thessalonian congregation has been brought into being by God's action through Christ (e.g., Best 1972, 62). Either way, the identification of God as "Father" and of Jesus Christ as "Lord" may well echo confessional formulations already current in the church (cf. 3:11, 13; 1 Cor 8:6).

This is the only Pauline letter in which the salutation, "grace . . . and peace," is not elaborated with the phrase, "from God our Father and the Lord Jesus Christ." However, following the almost identical wording in the adscription, the use of the full formula would have been redundant (but see 2 Thess 1:1-2). The greeting itself is probably an adaptation of the Jewish formula, "mercy and peace" (Tobit 7:12 [Sinaiticus]; *2 Bar.* 78:2).

◊ ◊ ◊ ◊

In this prescript the emphasis does not fall on the identity of the senders but of those addressed. They are to understand themselves as an assembly of persons whose identity derives from their relationship to God and Christ. Similarly, the salutation presupposes that it is the "grace...and peace" they have known in God the Father and the Lord Jesus Christ (cf. 5:23, 28) by which their faith is constantly nurtured.

THANKSGIVINGS, REMINDERS, AND ASSURANCES (1:2–3:13)

In this first half of the letter Paul seeks to encourage the Thessalonian believers in their faith by reminding them about the circumstances of his mission and their acceptance of the gospel, and by emphasizing that he remains devoted to their spiritual well-being. This section is distinguished rhetorically by the presence of three expressions of thanksgiving. The first (1:2-5) is expanded by remarks about the Thessalonians' faith (1:6-10), which lead, in turn, to reminders and assurances in narrative form about Paul's mission (2:1-12). The second (2:13-16) is followed by further assurances, conveyed as a narrative of what has transpired for Paul since he was in Thessalonica (2:17–3:10). This, in turn, prompts a spontaneous expression of thanks (3:9-10). The whole section is concluded with a benedictory prayer (3:11-13) that also points ahead to the second part of the letter.

First Thanksgiving (1:2-10)

The Greek text of this paragraph divides into just two sentences, vv. 2-5 and 6-10. In the first, Paul follows his statement that he continually thanks God for the Thessalonian congregation (v. 2) with two reasons his thanksgiving is warranted (vv. 3, 4-5). In the second, which complements the first, he notes how the gospel had been received in Thessalonica (v. 6) and indicates the wider consequences of its reception (v. 7). He documents the latter with reference to what others have come to know and report about the Thessalonians' faith (vv. 8-10).

Thanksgiving Proper (1:2-5)

The first person plural, "We ... give thanks" (v. 2) is probably authorial, standing primarily for "I," and only secondarily inclusive of those named as co-senders in v. 1 (see Introduction). Here, as elsewhere, Paul indicates that he is thankful for what God has accomplished for and among the letter's recipients. The fulsome style is characteristic of Pauline thanksgivings: the apostle is "always" thankful for "all" of them, and "constantly" mentions them in his prayers (v. 2). Contrary to the NRSV, "constantly" almost certainly refers not to his remembering (v. 3) but to his prayers, as it clearly does in 2:13; 5:17; Rom 1:9 (for examples from non-Christian sources, Spicq 1994, 1.32-34).

Most immediately, Paul's thanksgiving has been prompted by his remembering the manifestations of faith, love, and hope with which God has graced the Thessalonian congregation (v. 3). This triadic formulation is also evident near the close of the letter when he calls on the congregation to put on faith, love, and hope like armor (5:8), and it may well be reflected in 3:10-13 (v. 10, faith; v. 12, love; v. 13, where hope is perhaps implied). Several of his subsequent letters offer further instances of the triad (1 Cor 13:13; Gal 5:5-6; Rom 5:2-5; cf. 1 Cor 13: 7), and it also appears in a variety of contexts in other early Christian literature (Col 1:4-5; Heb 6:10-12; 10:22-24; *Barn.* 1:4; 11:8; Pol. *Phil.* 3:2-3; cf. Eph 4:2-5; 1 Pet 1:3-8; 1:21-22). The formulation was likely Paul's own creation and a staple of his missionary preaching (Wischmeyer 1981, 147-58; Söding 1992, 38-64; Weiß 1993, 211-15). As such, it would have been familiar to the Thessalonian believers as their apostle's summary of what constitutes the new life to which they had been called.

Here the triad is combined with three further terms ("work," "labor," and "steadfastness"; cf. Rev 2:2; Wis 3:11) in order to highlight the vital, active character of the Thessalonians' commitment to the gospel. Grammatically, the result is a long string of genitive forms. The context makes it clear that the second noun in each pair is to be understood as a genitive of origin. Paul writes of work, labor, and steadfastness that derive from and are expressions of faith, love, and hope. The pronoun "your" (plural) appears only at the beginning of this series, doing service for all three pairs of terms and binding them closely together.

Interpreters differ on what to do with the last two phrases in v. 3, which NRSV translates, respectively (but in reverse order), "in our Lord Jesus Christ," and "before our God and Father." Some connect the latter with "remembering" at the beginning of the verse (which is difficult but not impossible) and take the former only with the immediately preceding phrase, yielding "steadfastness of hope in our Lord Jesus Christ" (thus, NRSV). However, it is better to understand both of these phrases, like the pronoun, as applying to the triad as a whole (e.g., Rigaux 1956, 367-68; Weiß 1993, 199), whereby "in our Lord Jesus Christ before our God and Father" (the Greek order) would point toward the defining event of the community's life. Paul understands the vitality of the Thessalonians' faith, love, and hope to be the result of their relationship to Christ (cf. 5:8-10) and their sense of being ultimately accountable to God (allowing *emprosthen* [NRSV: "before"] the forensic meaning it clearly has in 2:19; 3:13; cf. 3:9; 2 Cor 5:10).

There is no reason to suppose that Paul's use of the phrase "work of faith" would have sounded odd to the Thessalonians, because there is no trace in our letter of the contrast he draws in Galatians and Romans between faith and "works of the law." Indeed, the singular, "work," ordinarily has a good sense in Paul's letters, as when it refers to his own missionary activity (e.g., 1 Cor 9:1) or the ministry of others on behalf of or within his congregations (e.g., 1 Thess 5:13). In the immediate context, "faith" refers to the affirmation of God, hence, the trust in God with which the Thessalonians responded to Paul's preaching (vv. 8-10). If the apostle now has any specific "work of faith" in mind, it would likely be the congregation's continuing trust in God even in the face of hardships (1:6). In 3:6, as here, faith is closely associated with love, while in 4:14, to "believe" means to acknowledge and trust the saving reality of Jesus' death and resurrection (cf. 5:9-10).

In the phrase "labor of love," the meaning of the word "labor" largely overlaps that of "work" (the two are used synonymously in 5:12-13; 1 Cor 15:58). Used together, these terms reinforce the general point that faith and love are not only present but demonstrably active in the congregation. But here, as elsewhere, the word "labor" may have the additional nuance of strenuous exertion or arduous toil, even to the point of exhaustion (cf. 2:9, where Paul refers to his laboring for an income; also 2 Cor 6:5; 11:23, 27). Clearly, for Paul love (*agapē*) is not simply an inner feeling or kindly attitude that manifests itself spontaneously, but a total disposition of one's life that involves deliberate choices and determined effort. In this letter, he commends the love that is active within the believing community as mutual respect and caring for one another (3:12; 4:9; 5:13). But also, his prayer that the Thessalonians may "increase and abound in love for one another *and for all*" (3:12) shows that he envisions love's reach as extending beyond the Christian assembly itself (cf. 4:9-12; 5:15).

It is possible that Paul associates the Thessalonians' "steadfastness of hope" with their persevering in devotion to the gospel despite the affliction (*thlipsis*; NRSV: "persecution") they have experienced for having accepted it (1:6; cf. Rom 5:3; 12:12; 2 Cor 1:6; 6:4). There are echoes here of the Jewish theology of suffering as seen in 4 Macc 17:2-4, where the mother of seven martyred sons is memorialized for having displayed "the courage of [her] faith" (v. 2) and "an enduring hope in God" (v. 4). Yet for Paul, steadfastness is not just a matter of passively enduring. Especially here, where it follows the mention of "work" and "labor," it refers to persevering in one's commitments and responsibilities (see also, e.g., Rom 2:7 [cf. Sir 2:14]; 2 Cor 12:12), which includes but is by no means limited to constancy even when under trial.

Such perseverance is an expression of hope, which is an important theme in this letter (see also 2:19; 4:13; 5:8). The object of hope is, particularly, Jesus' return (2:19; 4:13-18; cf. 3:13; 5:23), which will mean deliverance "from the wrath that is coming" (1:10) and remaining "with the Lord forever" (4:17). In this thanksgiving there is no hint that the Thessalonians' hope is waning in any particular, although Paul will subsequently offer some instruction in order to strengthen it (4:14-18).

In Greek, the sentence begun in v. 2 continues with a participle (*eidotes*, v. 4; the form suggests "knowing with certainty") that introduces the ultimate ground for the apostle's thanksgiving: God has chosen the Thessalonians to receive and believe in the gospel. Paul is expressing himself in language and concepts that derive from the Jewish scriptures, according to which Israel is the elect people of God, uniquely favored with God's love (esp. Deut 7:6-11; Isa 44:2). Thus, instead of referring to the members of his congregation as merely "my beloved brothers and sisters" (as in 1 Cor 15:58 [NRSV shortens this to "my beloved"]), he identifies them as "brothers and sisters beloved by God." In employing the perfect passive participle (*ēgapēmenoi*), he is following the precedent of the LXX, where it is frequently used with reference to God's electing love (e.g., Deut 32:15; 33:5, 26; Jer 11:15; 12:7; Hos 2:23, quoted in Rom 9:25; Bar 3:37[36]). Because the perfect tense suggests (as the adjectival form, *agapētoi*, cannot) that this love is experienced as both a past and ongoing reality (cf. Spicq 1965, 15-16; Best 1972, 71), one may paraphrase: "having once and always been loved by God."

It is a radical departure from the Jewish view of divine election, according to which Israel alone constitutes God's people, when Paul identifies this *Gentile* congregation as beloved and chosen of God (*tēn eklogēn hymōn*, v. 4; lit. "your election"). Indeed, the appearance of the term *eklogē* with reference to Gentiles is striking even in a Pauline letter. Otherwise, the apostle uses it exclusively of Israel's election (Rom 9:11; 11:5, 7, 28)—although he does employ the related verb (*eklegeomai*) to describe God's choosing of the believers in Corinth, who, like those in Thessalonica, were mostly Gentiles (1 Cor 1:27-28). This theme of election underlies the thought of the letter as a whole (see Introduction). It surfaces again in references to the Thessalonians as called by God (2:12; 4:7; 5:24), and when the apostle declares that they have been destined for salvation (5:9).

Adelphoi (lit. "brothers") is the expression Paul usually employs when addressing his congregations, and he does so frequently in this letter (only in 1 Corinthians, a much longer letter, does it occur more often). The NRSV's paraphrase (here and usually), "brothers and sisters," reckons with the fact that the Pauline congregations included women as well as men (see Introduction). The figurative use of the term as a designation for fellow believers was widespread in the church, perhaps from the very beginning (there are analogues in Jewish [Wanamaker 1990, 77] and other non-Christian sources [MM, *s.v.*]; see also Harland 2005). Such usage was consistent with the community's sense of being "children" of one God (the "Father," e.g., 1 Thess 1:1, 3). Paul's converts may have found it especially appropriate, given that they assembled in private houses. (For the significance of the kinship language and images of this letter, see Introduction.)

As evidence of the Thessalonians' election, Paul notes that the gospel came to them not only through the missionaries' proclamation ("in word"), but also with the power of the Holy Spirit and "full conviction" (v. 5a). He specifies "*our* gospel" (see also 2 Cor 2:4; cf. "my gospel," Rom 2:16), not in order to distinguish it from other "gospels" or because he claims to have originated it (note Gal 1:11), but to identify it as the gospel that God has "entrusted" him to proclaim (2:4). Elsewhere he refers to "the gospel of God" (2:2, 8, 9; cf. "the word of God," 2:13) and "the gospel of Christ" (3:2; cf. "the word of the Lord," 1:8).

The NRSV paraphrases *to euangelion hēmōn* (lit. "our gospel") as "our *message* of the gospel," but this obscures the very point that Paul wishes to emphasize: the gospel did not come to the Thessalonians only as a message (*logos*) but also with power. He attributes this power to the working of the Holy Spirit (see also v. 6; 4:8; 5:19; 1 Cor 2:4-5; cf. 1QH* XV, 6-7), which he further characterizes as involving *plērophoria pollē* (NRSV: "full conviction"), a phrase best rendered as "great fullness of divine working" (*TDNT,* 6.311 [G. Delling]). All three expressions describe the manner of the gospel's coming to Thessalonica, not how it was received there (which is first indicated in v. 6). Paul does not identify his gospel primarily with the particular message that he conveys, but with the saving power of God to which his Spirit-enabled ministry bears witness (cf. 2:13; Rom 1:16; 1 Cor 1:18).

In Galatians and 2 Corinthians Paul refers to the "powers" (*dynameis*, which NRSV variously translates "deeds of power," "mighty works," "miracles"), and in Romans to "the power of signs and wonders" that accompanied (or occurred in the wake of) his missionary preaching (Gal 3:5; 2 Cor 12:12; Rom 15:19;

cf. 1 Cor 12:10, 28, 29). However, such phenomena are probably not in view when he mentions "power" and the "Holy Spirit" in 1 Thess 1:5a—or in 1 Cor 2:4 where, similarly, he refers to the "demonstration of the Spirit and of power" that attended his preaching in Corinth. In these instances, the respective contexts as well as the use of the singular form, "power" (without the kind of further specification found in Rom 15:19), suggest that he is thinking of the divine power that is manifested when the gospel is proclaimed and believed.

The remark in v. 5b both rounds off the thought of vv. 4-5a and anticipates later comments about how Paul had conducted himself in Thessalonica (2:1-12). Because of the power that attended the preaching of the gospel, Paul knows with certainty (*eidotes*, v. 4) that his converts belong to God's elect, just as the Thessalonians, for their part, know (*kathōs oidate*, v. 5b) that his mission among them was entirely for their sake. This is the first of several instances where the Thessalonians are reminded of what they should be able to affirm about Paul's character and veracity on the basis of their own experience (see also 2:1, 2, 5, 9, 10, 11; cf. 3:3, 4; 4:2; 5:2).

The Thessalonians' Faith (1:6-10)

Here Paul shifts his attention from how the gospel came to the Thessalonians to how they received it ("And you" [*kai hymeis*], v. 6, is emphatic). His two main points are, first, that they became "imitators" of himself and of the Lord (v. 6), and second, that they in turn became "an example" for other believers (v. 7). Hellenistic teachers typically commended their own conduct as exemplary for their students (e.g., Seneca, *Ep.* 6; further, Malherbe 1986, 135-38), and Paul himself often does something similar (e.g., 1 Cor 4:6; 7:7a, 8; 8:13; chap. 9; Gal 4:12; Phil 4:9). In Paul's case, however, there is a critical difference, because he understands his conduct to derive from and disclose the gospel of Christ, whom he serves as an apostle. This christological dimension is evident in places where he specifically calls for "imitation," quite explicitly in 1 Cor 11:1, and implicitly in 1 Cor 4:16 and Phil 3:17. Thus, when in our passage the Thessalonians are commended for having become imitators "of us and of the Lord," the second phrase is not an afterthought (as some claim in view of the Gk. word order, "imitators of us you became, and of the Lord") but essential to the meaning (Holtz 1998, 48 n. 107; cf. Gaventa 1998, 16).

The concept of imitation that is operative here and in the other Pauline passages is best considered with reference to the word *typos* in v. 7 (see also Phil 3:17), for which "example" (as in NRSV) can be a misleading translation. A *typos*, literally, was a form that had been molded or cast, and which could in turn be used as a mold or to make an impression—like a stamp or seal, or a die for the minting of coins (*TDNT*, 8.246-47 [L. Goppelt]; *EDNT*, 3.373 [G. Schunack]). Thus the imitation to which Paul refers does not involve the idea of either himself or Christ as a model whose particular actions are to be *copied* as closely as possible. For such a notion the word *hypodeigma* ("example," as in John 13:15; Jas 5:10, etc.)—a term that the apostle never uses—would have been more suitable than *typos*. Paul can present himself as a *typos* for his congregations (Phil 3:17) because his own life has itself been *stamped* by the Lord, whom he knows as the resurrected-crucified one who will come again (1 Thess 1:10; 4:14; 5:9-10); and they can be a *typos* for other believers (1:7; cf. 2:13) because, through the agency of Paul's apostleship, they, too, have been actually *formed* in Christ (cf. *TDNT,* 8.249-50; *EDNT,* 3.373; Marxsen 1979, 38-39).

Paul sees this faith-formation manifested particularly in the Thessalonians' having "received the word with joy inspired by the Holy Spirit" (cf. Rom 14:17; Gal 5:22), even though doing so has caused them to suffer (v. 6b). The "word" is the gospel (v. 5a) that he has proclaimed and they have believed (v. 8). Even if Paul exaggerates a bit when he writes of "*much* affliction" (AT; NRSV omits the adjective), there is no doubt that he is referring to more than inner distress or uncertainty, because he subsequently remarks on their having suffered at the hands of others (2:14; cf. 2:2). His letter discloses almost nothing about the nature of this, however (see Introduction). Most likely because the converts had abandoned their former gods and religious practices (vv. 9b-10), they were perceived by others as a threat to the social and political well-being of the city. This would have resulted in such difficulties as their alienation from unbelieving family members and friends; the curtailment of their opportunities to maintain, let alone to improve, their current economic and social status; the restriction of their access to the city's political and social institutions; and their constant subjection to harassment and public insults. The theme of joy in suffering, which has a background in Judaism (e.g., 4 Macc 10:20; 17:2-4; *2 Bar.* 52:6-7), surfaces again in 3:7-9 and frequently in Paul's other letters (e.g., 2 Cor 6:4-10; 7:4; 8:1-2; Phil 2:17), as well as elsewhere in the NT (e.g., Matt 5:11-12 par. Luke 6:22-23; Col 1:24; Jas 1:2; 1 Pet 1:6; 4:13).

Speaking with hyperbole, Paul claims that the Thessalonians' faith has such resonance that they have become a *typos* (NRSV: "example") for other believers in Macedonia, Achaia, and even beyond (vv. 7-8). Practically speaking, the news of their faith could have been spread by believers from Philippi (Meeks 1983, 27), who were probably the Macedonians who supported Paul's ministry in Corinth (2 Cor 11:9) even as they had supported it in Thessalonica (Phil 4:15, 16). But Paul hints at a theological explanation when he says that the gospel itself ("the word of the Lord"; a LXX idiom, e.g. 3 Kgdms [1 Kgs] 12:22; Ps 32[LXX: 33]:4; Isa 1:10) had "sounded forth" from them. This expression describes sound or noise that reverberates in all directions (Richard 1995, 50), and it corresponds to Paul's view of God's word as working with a divine power that transcends the efforts of any merely human agency (2:13; cf. Ware 1992, 128, 130). Thus, despite a certain syntactical awkwardness, vv. 7-8 convey essentially just one point. Because the Thessalonians' faith manifests so clearly the impress of God's working in their lives, they have become a *typos* that strengthens the faith of believers far and wide.

Paul concludes the paragraph by indicating that his Thessalonian converts now serve the only true God and await the return of God's Son. The accent here falls on what the converts have newly embraced (their abandoning of "idols" is mentioned only secondarily), and on the theological and christological aspects of the gospel they have accepted. Paul's reference to the Thessalonians' having turned away from idols is evidence that essentially all of them were Gentiles (see Introduction). It is not evidence, however, that his preaching to the Gentiles consisted of the two separate phases that some interpreters discern in Acts 17:22-31: first, winning hearers over to a theoretical monotheism, and then proclaiming Christ to them. The present formulation suggests, rather, that the Thessalonians' service (thus also, knowledge; see 4:5) of "a living and true God" was inseparable from their accepting the good news that God's Son, Jesus, whom God had raised from the dead, would return to rescue them from "the wrath that is coming."

A number of interpreters have argued that in vv. 9b-10 Paul is citing a widely used, formulaic summary of (Hellenistic) Jewish-Christian missionary preaching (e.g., Wilckens 1963, 80-91; Neyrey 1980, 220-21; cf. Best 1972, 85-87). An alternative hypothesis, that he has incorporated an early Hellenistic Jewish-Christian hymn, perhaps from a baptismal liturgy (Friedrich 1965; 1981, 215-16), has won less support. But the presence of several terms found only here in the certainly Pauline letters does not suffice to demonstrate a pre-Pauline formulation, and other early Christian sources yield no clear parallel to the alleged formula (in this respect, both Acts 14:15 and Heb 6:1-2 fall short). It is more likely that Paul himself composed this statement making use of missionary terminology that was current in both Hellenistic-Jewish and Hellenistic Jewish-Christian circles. Much of this terminology derived, in turn, from scriptural concepts and idioms. Thus:

- "turning" to God/the Lord (as Israel's repentance, Deut 30:2; Joel 2:12-14; Sir 5:7; as the conversion of Gentiles [from false gods], Tob 14:6; *Jos. Asen.* 11:7-11; subsequently, Acts 11:21; 14:15; 26:18, 20);
- "serving God/the Lord" (Judg 10:6-16 [B]; 2 Chr 30:8; Tob 4:14; subsequently, Matt 6:24 par. Luke 16:13; Acts 20:19);
- God as "living" and "true" (*Jos. Asen.* 11:10 [Jer 10:10]; "living," 1 Sam [1 Kgdms] 17:26, 36; Jer 23:36; Bel 5; *Sib. Or.* 3.763; subsequently, 2 Cor 3:3; 6:16; Matt 26:63; Acts 14:15; "true," Exod 34:6; 2 Chr 15:3; 3 Macc 6:18; Philo, *Spec. Laws* 1.332; *Embassy* 366);

- to "wait" for deliverance (Isa 59:11; Jdt 8:17; Sir 2:7);
- "rescue" with reference to God's action (Ps 21 [Hebrew: 22]: 4, 8, 20; Wis 16:8; 19:9; subsequently, Matt 6:13; 27:43; God as *ho rhyomenos* ["Redeemer"], Isa 47:4; 48:17; 59:20, etc.);
- the threat of God's *orgē* ("wrath"; Ezek 7:19; Zeph 1:15, 18; 2:2-3; 3:8; Sir 5:6-7; subsequently, Matt 3:7 par. Luke 3:7).

It is clear that the statement in vv. 9b-10 yields important clues about the content of Paul's own missionary preaching, especially in Thessalonica. But in this epistolary context, where the subject is how the Thessalonians *responded* to his preaching (Hooker 1996, 442), it serves a twofold function.

First, it provides an appropriate climax to Paul's thanksgiving by specifying what the Thessalonians' faith involves: their wholehearted serving of God, which means acknowledging God's exclusive claim over their lives (e.g., 1 Sam [1 Kgdms] 7:3), and their waiting, obediently and trustfully (e.g., Sir 2:7), for the return of God's Son from heaven. In a syntactically awkward addition Paul makes a point of identifying God's Son as Jesus, "whom [God] raised from the dead" (cf. Rom 10:9; Acts 4:10; 13:30, etc.). The title "Son" appears only here in this letter, as compared with 23 instances of "Lord" (esp. in connection with the *parousia*, e.g., 3:13; 4:15-17). As in 4:14 and Rom 8:11, the name "Jesus" gives historical concreteness to the formulaic mention of his death and resurrection. The promise of "rescue" from God's wrath should be read in connection with 5:9-10, where the focus is more on the positive hope of salvation, and where the saving event is identified as Christ's death (cf. Rom 5:9). The present participle, "who rescues," perhaps reflects Paul's view that believers are already enabled to live as "children of light and . . . of the day" (5:5). However, the emphasis here is on the eschatological future (cf. 2:19; 3:13), when the agents of evil will be called to account at the bar of God's righteous judgment (in the phrase "coming wrath" the present participle has a future reference; BDF §323), and subsequently destroyed (cf. Rom 2:5, 8; 3:5; 9:22).

Second, along with what is said about the Thessalonians' faith, love, and hope (vv. 3-4), vv. 9b-10 point forward to the appeals and assurances in chapters 4 and 5. There Paul will indicate that the sure hope of the Lord's return already qualifies and claims the present (e.g., 5:4-10), encouraging the ever greater service of God (e.g., 4:1-12) and bringing consolation to those who grieve (4:13-18). Thus, this thanksgiving paragraph, like those in the other Pauline letters, anticipates some matters that the apostle will be emphasizing and some appeals that he will be issuing as the letter proceeds.

◊ ◊ ◊ ◊

This thanksgiving accomplishes several things simultaneously. It encourages the addressees both to continue manifesting what is commended and to respond favorably to what will be said as the letter proceeds, and in the process it introduces some of the letter's themes. Viewed theologically, it yields three points that deserve special notice.

First, its most fundamental theological claim is that the members of the congregation are "loved" and "chosen" by God. This and similar statements in Paul's letters, including references to believers as "called" by God (e.g., 1 Thess 2:12), do not derive from speculation that some individuals may not be loved, chosen, and called. They express, rather, Paul's belief in the historical reality of God's love as it has been manifested in God's Son and experienced in the believing community. Believers may therefore live with the confidence that "salvation," not "wrath," is definitive of God's purposes for humankind (5:8, 9).

Second, even allowing for some degree of exaggeration in Paul's praise of the congregation, the points he singles out for commendation provide important clues about his understanding of what it means to be God's elect. Specifically, the triadic formulation in v. 3 (repeated in 5:8) identifies faith, love, and hope as constitutive of the believers' new existence, and thus of the church's life. It is theologically significant that everywhere this triad surfaces in Paul's letters faith is mentioned first, despite some variation in the order of love and hope. As the community's trusting response to the reality of God's electing love, faith provides an opening in the world for that love's transforming power, and for the hope it nurtures. Given the context provided by vv. 3-4, and subsequent references to faith (e.g., 3:2, 6, 10), love (e.g., 3:12; 4:9-12), and hope (e.g., 4:13-18), the explication of turning to God ("faith in God," v. 8) as serving him and waiting for his Son from heaven (vv. 9b-10) may perhaps be taken as a variation of the same theme. That is, believers serve God as they become agents of God's love (4:9, "taught by God to love one another") and wait in hope for the return of God's Son.

Finally, the concluding statement about the Son's return at the close of history should not be allowed to overshadow comments in vv. 3, 6 that presuppose a present, vital relationship between believers and their Lord. The community's faith, love, and hope derive from Jesus, who has been raised from the dead and has been made present to them already through the gospel. Paul's remark that the Thessalonians became imitators of himself and of the Lord has in view the formative power of precisely this relationship between Christ and the believing community. The Lord expected "from heaven" will not come as an arbitrary rescuer hitherto unknown, like a *deus ex machina* in the ancient theater. He will be the resurrected-crucified One who is already known to the community that bears the stamp of his lordship.

Reminders and Assurances (2:1-12)

In narrative form, Paul now reminds the congregation of the divine origin and difficult circumstances of his mission to their city (vv. 1-4) and assures them of his upright conduct (vv. 5-12). This section includes antithetical formulations (vv. 1-2, 3-4, 5-7a), repeated statements that the congregation itself can attest to what is being said (vv. 1, 2, 5, 9, 10, 11), and several striking metaphors (vv. 7b, 7c-8, 11). While it is rhetorically and thematically comparable to works in which Dio Chrysostom (ca. 40–112 C.E.) contrasts the ideal Cynic philosopher to charlatans and swindlers (*Or.* 12, 32, 33, 35; Malherbe 2000, 153-56), its own rhetorical climax is a statement about the congregation's need to respond appropriately to the call of God (vv. 11-12).

Interpreters have long debated whether these paragraphs are best characterized as *apologetic* or *parenetic*. Those who regard them as apologetic see Paul defending his integrity in the face of insinuations or outright charges that he operates from self-interest. Various suggestions have been offered concerning the identity of his critics, including: Jews outside the church (e.g., Milligan 1908, xxxi-xxxii; Holtz 1998, 94, 110-12); primarily Jewish but also Gentile unbelievers (Still 1999, 126-49); Jewish or Jewish-Christian Gnostics (Schmithals 1972, 123-218); millenarian radicals within the church (e.g., Jewett 1986, 102-104, 159-78). Those who describe these paragraphs as parenetic understand Paul to be offering himself as a model for conduct, much as contemporary moral philosophers like Dio Chrysostom did for their students (e.g., Richard 1995, 88-89; Malherbe 2000, esp. 154-56; cf. 84-85).

Neither of these assessments, however, does full justice to the character of this passage. Especially, the statements some take as apologetic provide no specific evidence that Paul's character, motives, or tactics had come under fire in Thessalonica, either within the church or from outsiders. They have more the aspect of assurances given in order to strengthen the resolve of the congregation to stand firm in its commitment to the gospel despite the opposition it continues to face from a hostile society, just as Paul fulfills his mission despite opposition and hardships (2:2, 9; cf. Vos 2000, esp. 82-83, 87-88). There is more to be said for viewing the passage as parenetic. Having just heard about the congregation's faith (3:6a) and goodwill (3:6b), Paul now writes to reinforce that faith and to nourish the presently healthy relationship he has with the congregation. He no doubt wishes also to *preclude* any willful comparing or naive confusing of himself with charlatan philosophers (Winter 1993, 71-72), and there are some *implicit* appeals here. Yet the function of this passage is best described as *paracletic*—a term that comes from the vocabulary of the letter itself, and embraces the ideas of encouragement, assurance, consolation, and exhortation (see commentary on 2:3).

◊   ◊   ◊   ◊

The Divine Origin of Paul's Mission (2:1-4)

Formally, Paul's reference to the God-given courage that he had in the midst of difficult circumstances (vv. 1-2) is supported by his subsequent claim that the mission to Thessalonica had been divinely authorized (v. 3). While there is no doubt that he attributes his courage to God, what starts out as a supporting remark develops into the apostle's most critical point: he was motivated by nothing else than a commitment to do the will of the One who had entrusted him with the gospel (v. 4).

As he does frequently, Paul prompts the Thessalonians to verify what he says from their own knowledge (vv. 1a, 2; see also 1:5, with comment). They can attest that his Thessalonian mission had indeed produced good results ("was not in vain"; similarly, 3:5), and that Paul, who had already suffered abuse in Philippi, did not turn back when he was faced with opposition again in Thessalonica (vv. 1b-2). Elsewhere, Paul refers to the "struggle" he had in Philippi (Phil 1:30). His present expression is "shamefully mistreated," which can indicate either verbal or physical abuse. He apparently means this to describe the "great struggle" in Thessalonica (1 Thess 2:2, AT) no less than the struggle in Philippi.

This "great struggle" is surely the same conflict mentioned in the opening thanksgiving (see commentary on 1:6, and Introduction). Paul still says nothing about its origins or character. For him, the important point is that God is the source of the courage to carry on despite adversity. The verb "having courage" is related to the noun *parrēsia*, by which Cynic philosophers commonly meant the harsh "boldness of speech" they thought they had earned the right to use in haranguing an audience (Dio Chrysostom, *Or.* 32.10; Fredrickson 1996). Paul, however, rejects such tactics in favor of a more affirming and nurturing approach (vv. 7-8). In the lexicon of his apostleship, *parrēsia* means the confidence by which those who trust in God are enabled to proclaim the gospel fearlessly in any and all circumstances (esp. 2 Cor 3:12; Phil 1:20).

In the present context, "our appeal" (v. 3), like "gospel" (vv. 2, 4; see commentary on 1:5), refers to the apostle's missionary preaching. This noun (*paraklēsis*), along with the related verb (variously translated, in 2:12; 3:2, 7; 4:1, 10, 18; 5:11, 14), is uniquely expressive of Paul's understanding of the gospel as involving both a gift and a claim. While in some instances he employs these terms when formulating rather specific appeals

(4:1, 10; 5:14), in other places they bear general meanings like "support," "encourage," and "comfort" (3:2, 7; 4:18; 5:11). Correspondingly, his missionary preaching had both indicative and imperative aspects. It presented, simultaneously, God's gracious invitation into the kingdom and the summons to conduct one's life in ways that are appropriate to that call (thus 2:12, where "urging" translates the participle, *parakalountes*).

The motives Paul disavows here are all self-evidently unworthy, but the terms he employs for them cannot be pressed for specific meanings. Thus *plane* ("deceit") may or may not refer to moral error, *akatharsia* ("impure motives") could well describe impurity in general (as it may in 4:7 and certainly does in Rom 6:19), and *dolos* ("trickery") is just as broad a term here as it is in Rom 1:29 (NRSV: "deceit"). In the present context these words are associated with currying the favor of others by using flattery or other deceptions (esp. vv. 5-6). Over against this, Paul insists that the aim of his mission is "not to please mortals, but to please God" (v. 4). The expression "to please God" (see also 2:15) derives from the LXX (e.g., Num 23:27; Isa 59:15), and means to do what is "acceptable" to God (e.g., Rom 12:2; Phil 4:18; Gen 5:22; Wis 4:10) by living in accordance with God's will (1 Thess 4:1-3). Here and in Gal 1:10 (cf. 1 Cor 7:32-34), "pleasing mortals" is construed negatively, as valuing human approval more than God's and therefore failing to please God.

The sense of divine vocation reflected here has two components. First, Paul's statement about having been "approved by God to be entrusted with the gospel" (AT) expresses the conviction that his labors for the gospel are divinely authorized and empowered (similarly, Gal 2:7; 1 Cor 9:17; 2 Cor 2:17; cf. Dio Chrysostom Or. 32.12; 34.4). Second, and equally important, Paul's reference to God as one "who tests our hearts" (a biblical idiom, Jer 11:20; 12:3; 17:10) expresses the conviction that he is continually accountable to the one by whom he has been entrusted with the gospel.

The Apostle's Upright Conduct (2:5-12)

Interpreters differ on whether the sentence begun in v. 5 concludes with v. 7a (after "apostles of Christ"; e.g., Nestle-Aland[27] and NRSV) or with v. 7b (after "among you"; e.g., *GNT*[3]; Holtz 1998, 81; Wanamaker 1990, 100-101). The latter is more likely, given that the assertion in v. 7b, "[b]ut we were..." (*alla egenēthēmen*), responds to the three negative statements in vv. 5-6, "we never came with words of flattery..." etc. (*oute gar pote...egenēthēmen*).

In vv. 5-7b, Paul confirms what he has just said about his motives in going to Thessalonica by noting how he presented his message while he was there. He is confident that both the Thessalonians (cf. vv. 1, 2) and God (from whom nothing is hidden, v. 4) can attest that in his preaching he neither resorted to flattery (cf. v. 4) nor otherwise dissembled (cf. v. 3). In v. 10 he makes a more general statement to the same effect, once more invoking the double testimony of the Thessalonians and God. Calling on God as a witness (also, e.g., Rom 1:9; 2 Cor 1:23; Phil 1:8) has scriptural precedents (e.g., 1 Sam 12:5, 6; 20:23; Jer 42:5; Wis 1:6).

Flattery (v. 5a) was often criticized by Hellenistic writers, who typically contrasted it with true friendship, characterizing it as mere display because it was the bestowing of excessive praise for the sake of the flatterer's own benefit (Aristotle, *Eth. Nic.* 2.7.13; 4.6.9; 8.8.1-2; 10.3.11; Philo, *Alleg. Interp.* 3, 182; *Planting* 104-6; *Migration* 111-12; Dio Chrysostom, *Alex.* 26; Aelius Aristides, *Discourses* 4 [in Boring 1995, no. 814]). They also regularly listed greed (v. 5b) among the most obvious of vices (e.g., Philo, *Sacrifices* 32), just as Paul himself does in 1 Cor 5:10, 11; 6:10 (the related verb appears in 1 Thess 4:6). Paul seems to expect the congregation to agree that his mission had not been a "pretext for greed" (v. 5b)—or, "an occasion for greed," if the word *prophasis* has its neutral sense here (cf. Spicq 1994, 3.205 n. 6; Wanamaker 1990, 97; Richard 1995, 98). He should therefore not be compared with the many itinerant teachers of the day who, as portrayed, for example, by Dio Chrysostom (*Or.* 32.10-11), were intent on lining their own pockets.

Similarly, the Thessalonians will know that Paul had not been striving for human "praise" (*doxa*, v. 6; Dio Chrysostom, *Or.* 32.10-11, also associates striving for *doxa* with seeking monetary gain). This underscores the point of v. 4 that he had aimed to please God, not human beings, and it reflects his view that the only praise that matters comes from God (cf. vv. 12 and 20, where *doxa* is appropriately rendered "glory," and Rom 2:29, where "praise" translates *epainos*). It is impossible to know who the "others" were from whom, in addition to the Thessalonians, Paul might have sought praise. Perhaps he himself had no specific people in mind.

The remark in v. 7a is parenthetical, but nonetheless significant for being the earliest surviving reference to Christian "apostles" and for providing a hint of how Paul, at this juncture in his ministry, viewed the authority of an apostle. Some interpreters hold that he means the plural, "apostles," to include both of the letter's co-senders (Best 1972, 100; Richard 1995, 109-10; Byrskog 1996, 238), or at least Silvanus (Schmithals 1969, 65-67; Wanamaker 1990, 99). But if it is correct to interpret most instances of the first person plural in this letter as authorial (see Introduction), then here, too, Paul likely has himself only—or primarily—in mind (e.g., Holtz 1998, 77-78; Reinmuth 1998, 126; Malherbe 2000, 144). It is significant, nonetheless, that he does not single himself out as "the apostle" in distinction from his missionary associates.

Paul's comment that he "could have thrown [his] weight around" (v. 7a, AT) implies that he regarded apostles as invested with some measure of authority. In the thanksgiving he has suggested the significance of authority for the present faith of his converts (1:5). Now he indicates both its source and purpose when he describes himself as "approved by God to be entrusted with the gospel" (v. 4, AT). It is difficult to know whether his conception of apostleship is already formed as fully as it is in his subsequent letters (1 Cor 9:1-12; 15:7-10; 2 Cor 11:4-15; Gal 1:1, 15-17; Rom 1:1-6), in part because the word "apostle" appears nowhere else in 1 Thessalonians. However, his comments elsewhere about not wanting to make arbitrary or self-serving use of his authority (1 Cor 7:6, 35; 2 Cor 1:24; 3:7; 8:8; Phlm 8-9) are consistent with both the remark in v. 7a and the imagery he employs in vv. 7b-8.

The interpretation of vv. 7b-8 hinges on a much-debated textual question in v. 7b. The NRSV translation, "we were gentle among you," follows Greek manuscripts that read *egenēthēmen ēpioi,* but also provides a footnote that takes account of other manuscripts that read *egenēthēmen nēpioi,* "we were infants among you." Although good evidence and plausible arguments have been offered in support of "gentle," there are slightly better reasons for adopting "infants" as the original word. The main considerations may be summarized as follows.

(a) There is agreement that "infants" is attested by a substantial majority of the earliest (and diverse types of) manuscripts, both in the East and in the West (Fee 1992, 175-79; B. Metzger 1994, 561-62). This is strong, objective evidence that "infants" was the original reading.

(b) Despite this, it has been urged that both the immediate context and Pauline usage point to "gentle" as the original reading (e.g., B. Metzger 1992, 232). On the one hand, characterizing himself as "gentle" provides a meaningful contrast to the preceding remark about the authority he might have exercised (v. 7a), and leads naturally to the following comparison of his conduct with that of a nurse caring for "her own children" (vv. 7c-8; cf. Malherbe 1989, 35-48). On the other, everywhere else in Paul's letters "infant[s]" connotes immaturity or some kind of insufficiency (1 Cor 3:1; 13:11; Gal 4:1, 3).

(c) "Infants" is undoubtedly the more difficult reading (the *lectio difficilior*), not only because a positive reference to infants would depart from normal Pauline usage, but especially because in this context the result would be a rather harsh mixing of images—likening himself first to an infant and then to a nursing mother (or wet-nurse). In accord with one of the standard principles of text criticism, this can be regarded as an argument *in favor* of the reading, "infants," because it is easier to understand why someone would have "corrected" the abrupt inversion of images by substituting the word "gentle" than why someone would have created it by substituting the word "infants." In fact, whenever a manuscript shows evidence of the text of this verse having been deliberately altered, the change (with but one exception) has been from "infants" to "gentle" (Fee 1992, 177).

(d) Sometimes textual variants originated unintentionally, when a scribe miscopied from the manuscript before him. Such a transcriptional error could have happened in this case, where the Greek phrases in question are almost identical; only the initial character (Gk. *nu*) distinguishes the noun "infants" (*nēpioi*) from the adjective "gentle" (*ēpioi*). Because the preceding word ends with this same character, and because in Greek manuscripts words are ordinarily run together without spacing, through the error of haplography (the inadvertent omission of something in the text) *EGENĒTHĒMENNĒPIOI*, "we became infants," might have been copied mistakenly as *EGENĒTHĒMENĒPIOI*, "we became gentle." Alternatively, the reverse error of dittography (the inadvertent repetition of something in the text) might have occurred, with the result that "we became gentle" was changed to "we became infants." Some believe the latter is more likely, because scribes would have been more familiar with "infants" than with "gentle" as a NT word (apart from the instance in question, "infant[s]" occurs 14 times and "gentle" only once). But this argument, by itself, carries little weight.

(e) Objections that the shift from "infants" to "nurse" is too harsh to be original also carry little weight. There is a similar instance in Gal 4:19, where Paul begins by portraying the Galatians as children for whom *he* has suffered the pain of childbirth, and ends up by speaking of Christ being formed *in them*. Moreover, when a full stop is placed after v. 7b, as the syntax of vv. 5-8 seems to require, the images do not clash as violently as when a full stop is placed after v. 7a.

If "infants" is the likelier reading in v. 7b, and if (as suggested earlier) the sentence begun in v. 5 runs through v. 7b, with v. 7a being parenthetical, then the NRSV rendering of vv. 5-8 needs some modest revision:

> [5]As you know and as God is our witness, we never came with words of flattery or with a pretext for greed; [6]nor did we seek praise from mortals, whether from you or from others ([7a]although we might have made demands as apostles of Christ), [7b]but we were infants among you. [7c]Having as much affection for you as a nurse who tenderly cares for her own children, [8]we are determined to share with you not only the gospel of God but also our own selves, because you have become very dear to us.

On this construal, Paul characterizes the conduct of his mission with two different images, one that emphasizes how he acted when he was in Thessalonica, and another that affirms his continuing affection for the congregation.

First, in contrast to wily charlatans who flatter their audiences for the sake of money and status (vv. 5-6), when in Thessalonica Paul and his associates had conducted themselves like "infants" (*nēpioi*)—innocents who are utterly incapable of dissembling or chicanery (v. 7b; cf. Pss 116:6; 119:130 [LXX 117:6; 118:130]). Paul employs the related verb (*nēpiazō*) in a similar way when he counsels the Corinthians to "be infants in evil" (1 Cor 14:20, noted by Gaventa 1990, 196).

Second, Paul's relationship to his converts is as deeply affectionate, responsible, and caring as the relationship between a "nurse" and her suckling children (vv. 7c-8). While this shift of images from "infants" to "nurse" is somewhat abrupt, he will shortly alter the imagery yet again to speak of himself as the congregation's "father" (v. 11). Whether his present thought is of a nursing mother (Rigaux 1956, 520; Marshall 1983, 71) or of a wet-nurse with "her own children" (Malherbe 2000, 146), the main point is clear enough. His affection for the Thessalonians has forged an unbreakable bond, and involves not only his imparting "the gospel of God" (cf. 1 Thess 2:2) but also putting *himself* (*tas heautōn psychas*) at the disposal of his children in the faith. In 2 Cor 12:14-15a Paul speaks, similarly, of "spend[ing] and be[ing] spent" for his congregation ("for you," v. 15a, translates *hyper tēn psychōn hymōn*), as parents should for their children. He also portrays his converts as his children in 1 Thess 2:11; 1 Cor 4:14; 2 Cor 6:13; Gal 4:19. And again in 1 Cor 3:2 and Gal 4:19 he is thinking of himself as the mother of his congregations (esp. Gaventa 1996a; 1996b; 1998, 31-34).

Although metaphorical references to surrogate nurses and nursing mothers were at home in the Jewish tradition (e.g., Num 11:12; 1QH* XV, 20-21) as well as in the Hellenistic world generally (Dio Chrysostom, *Or.* 4.73-139; 33.10; Plutarch, *Flatterer* 69BC), Paul's use of the image probably owes more to the latter than to the former (esp. Malherbe 1989, 35-48). Here he employs it, much as contemporary moral philosophers sometimes did with reference to their students, to portray himself as "tenderly caring" for those who look to him for support and spiritual nourishment. The NRSV's rendering of the rare word, *homeiromenoi*, as "deeply... care" (v. 8) is suggested both by the image with which it is associated and the subsequent assurance that the congregation has "become very dear" to the one who brought them the gospel (cf. Koester 1985, 226).

In vv. 9-12 Paul asks the converts to remember, further (cf. vv. 1, 2, 5), that he had earned his own living while in their city (v. 9), and remarks that they can attest—as God does (cf. v. 5)—that he had conducted himself honorably (v. 10), with father-like devotion to them (vv. 11-12).

Paul nowhere indicates what he did to support himself, but his comment in 1 Cor 4:12 about working with his hands (as a craftsman) is consistent with Acts 18:3, where he is identified as a "tentmaker" (discussions of the term, *skēnopoios*, in Hock 1980, 20-21; Lampe 1987; Murphy-O'Connor 1996, 85-89). Because he believed that accepting financial assistance from those he was evangelizing would both hinder his efforts and compromise his gospel (1 Cor 9:3-23), he was committed in principle to earn his own living, even though he regarded such toil as a hardship (e.g., 1 Cor 4:12; 9:6; 2 Cor 11:27). Paul's trade would have brought him only a modest income, however, so he was often left hungry, thirsty, and ill-clothed (2 Cor 6:5; 11:27). First in Thessalonica, then later in Corinth (Phil 4:15-16; 2 Cor 11:9), he gratefully accepted support from his Philippian congregation.

In our letter, Paul refers to his "labor and toil" as worthy of honor, explaining that he had not wanted to burden others (2:9; cf. 2 Cor 11:8-9; 12:13-16). In claiming to have labored "night and day" he likely means that working at his trade and proclaiming the gospel, when combined, left little time for sleep. Because the sequence "night... day" was usual in both Greek and Latin (examples in Rigaux 1956, 423-24), Paul's formulation does not necessarily reflect the Jewish view that a day begins at sundown, and there is no particular reason to interpret it literally, as indicating that he worked from before sunrise until after sunset. The phrasing "we worked...while we proclaimed" (v. 9) does not necessarily mean that he proclaimed the gospel where and as he was working. This could very well have been the case, however, because a workshop was often the setting for instruction and philosophical conversations (Hock 1980, 31-42).

By speaking of his manual labor Paul may be intending, in part, to lay a foundation for the appeal he will presently make to the Thessalonians to "work with [their] hands...and be dependent on no one" (4:10b-12). But this remark also reinforces earlier comments about his exemplary conduct (vv. 3-8), which he summarily characterizes (v. 10) as "pure" (*hosiōs*, which can also be translated "pious" or "devout"), "upright" (*diakaiōs*, which can also be translated "just"), and "blameless" (*amemptōs*). The first two words (in one form or another) are often found paired (but not elsewhere in Paul's letters), sometimes with reference to God (e.g., LXX Deut 32:4; Ps 145 [LXX 144]:17; Rev 16:5) and sometimes, as here, with reference to human conduct (e.g., Luke 1:75; Eph 4:24). Although Plato had applied the first term to actions that are "holy" before God and the second to actions deemed "just" by society (*Gorgias* 507 AB), Paul's coupling of them is likely influenced by the LXX, where they occur with little difference in meaning. The third adverb, which in a sense sums up the first two, points toward the ultimate decision about blamelessness that will be rendered by the Lord himself at his return (cf. 3:13; 5:23).

To his earlier portrayals of himself as being like an infant (v. 7b) and "a nurse tenderly caring for her own children" (v. 7c), Paul adds a third image: "like a father with his children" (v. 11; for a similar mixing of maternal and paternal images, see the "wet-nurse" passage from 1QH* cited above). Given that in Roman imperial times the *pater familias* had, at least in theory, nearly absolute power over the entire household (even his adult children, and including his married daughters; Osiek and Balch 1997, esp. 54-64), this image would certainly evoke a sense of the authority that Paul could exercise over his congregation (e.g., 1 Cor 4:14-21). However, in this context it is used more particularly to accent the seriousness with which he has taken his responsibility to provide instruction and guidance (v. 12). He is emphasizing his pastoral *devotion to* his Thessalonian "children" (for the Pauline occurrences of this metaphor, see commentary on v. 7c), not primarily his *authority over* them; note his remark that he has been attentive to the *individual* situations and needs of his converts ("we dealt with each one of you," v. 11).

In particular, Paul is devoted to guiding the Thessalonians into a way of life that will be "worthy of God," in that it accords with the radically new reality they have experienced through their conversion to the gospel (v. 12). The apostle's identification of God as "the one who calls" (also, 5:24; Gal 5:8) reflects his Jewish religious heritage (Holtz 1998, 91-92), which associates God's calling with the bestowal of life, especially through creation (*2 Bar.* 21:4), and the constitution of a covenant people (Isa 48:12). Although the present tense, "calls," brings out the continuing reality of God's life-giving presence, this is scarcely less in view even where Paul employs the aorist (past tense), "called" (as in 4:7 and Gal 1:6; cf. esp. Rom 8:30).

The apostle understands this present and continuing call of God as a summons into God's kingdom (*basileia,* also translatable as "dominion" or "reign"), which he believes is yet to come. This is one of the relatively few places where he mentions the kingdom of God, and the only place in 1 Thessalonians, even though his thinking was significantly informed by apocalyptic interests and views (see esp. 4:13–5:11). The reference to God's "glory" (*doxa*) also reflects apocalyptic thought (contrast v. 6, where *doxa* means the "fame" human beings seek from one another), according to which the faithful are destined to share in the eschatological revealing of God's glorious presence and power (e.g., *4 Ezra* 7:88-98; cf. 1 Cor 2:7; Rom 5:2; 8:18, 21, 30; the terms "kingdom" and "glory" are also associated in Ps 145[LXX 144]:11).

Finally, Paul reminds the Thessalonians that he has taught them to "lead a life" (lit. "walk"; cf. 4:1, 12) that is "worthy" of God and thus pleasing to God (see 1 Thess 4:1). He characterizes this instruction by employing three participles. The first, "urging" (*parakalountes*), is formed from the verb *parakaleō*, which, as noted, is especially prominent in this letter (see commentary on 2:3). The two that follow draw out meanings that the first itself can bear, depending on the context in which it appears: "encouraging" (*paramythoumenoi*), formed from a verb that is again associated with *parakaleō* in 5:14 (similar associations in 1 Cor 14:3; Phil 2:1), and "pleading" (*martyromenoi*), formed from a verb that connotes authoritative insistence.

◊ ◊ ◊ ◊

Insofar as this passage reminds the Thessalonians of Paul's pure motives and upright conduct, it also represents him as an exemplary figure whose conduct is worthy of emulation—and therefore not like that of charlatans and swindlers who pass themselves off as philosophers. Yet the real center of gravity in Paul's argument lies elsewhere. Everything he says here about himself, as well as about the faith of the congregation, derives from the same fundamental conviction already evident in the letter's opening thanksgiving (1:2-10): the Thessalonian mission was ordained of God, and its success is a demonstration of the power of God's working. Accordingly, the congregation is to understand that Paul has been approved by God and entrusted with the gospel (2:3-4); that the gospel is the word of God (vv. 8, 9), which constitutes a summons into God's kingdom (v. 12); and that it was from God that Paul had received the courage to fulfill his mission even in the face of serious opposition (v. 2). Within this context, even the comment that the Thessalonians "have become very dear" (lit. "beloved") to him (v. 8) carries theological overtones: finally, what binds Paul and the congregation together is their shared experience of the larger and decisive reality of God's electing and saving love (cf. 1:4).

Consistent with this, the statement in vv. 11-12 that stands as the rhetorical climax of the passage functions also as its theological climax. Viewed rhetorically, it summarizes what has been said about Paul's conduct by adding a third image to those already used of him (infant, nurse): he has dealt with his Thessalonian converts like a father who is devoted to urging, encouraging, and pleading with each of his children to live responsibly. This statement immediately takes on theological importance when Paul specifies that living responsibly means leading a life that is worthy of God, conducting it in ways that are appropriate for those who are summoned into the realm where God's sovereignty is without challenge. For this is the hope of salvation that Paul has proclaimed in Thessalonica, participation in the coming reign of God, where God's people are sanctified entirely by God's saving power (5:23-24) and will be in everlasting communion with their Lord (4:17; 5:9-10). Still, the main point that is registered as this paragraph concludes is not what God has promised for the future, but that God's impending kingdom already qualifies and claims the present, and should therefore make a difference already in the daily lives of those who are called (cf. 5:4-8).

Second Thanksgiving (2:13-16)

This paragraph is best described as a renewal of the first thanksgiving (see Introduction), and employs several expressions already used there: the phrase "we...give thanks to God" appears in both, as does the qualifying adverb "constantly" (1:2; 2:13); in both Paul addresses the Thessalonians as "brothers and sisters" (1:4; 2:14); in both he states that they "became imitators" (1:6; 2:14); and in both he refers to some affliction they have had to endure (1:6; 2:14). However, in the present case the mention of suffering inflicted on the Judean churches by "the Jews" (v. 14b) leads to a series of very sharply worded indictments (vv. 15-16), which, to be sure, seem oddly out of place in a statement of thanksgiving.

In general, interpreters have not been persuaded by those who argue that this second thanksgiving marks the beginning of an originally separate letter (Richard 1995, 11-14, sees it extending through 4:2), which, at an early date, was combined with another to form the present 1 Thessalonians. However, more than a few believe that one must reckon here with a non-Pauline interpolation added by a later hand (annotated bibliography: Weima and Porter 1998, 161-73). Some view the whole passage as interpolated (e.g., Pearson 1997; Schmidt 1983; Walker 2001, 210-20), while others identify the interpolation as restricted to vv. 14-16 (e.g., Richard 1995, 123-27) or vv. 15-16 (e.g., Meeks 1983, 227 n. 117). Because there is no evidence that 1 Thessalonians ever circulated without these verses, the case for an interpolation has had to be argued on other grounds (surveys: R. F. Collins 1979, 97-114; Schlueter 1994, 17-29; Bockmuehl 2001, 5-17). Theological, historical, and literary arguments have been advanced.

Theological. The sharply worded indictments of (some) Jews and the claim that God's wrath has come upon them (esp. vv. 15-16) do not accord with Paul's statements elsewhere about the Jews as a people, particularly the confidence he expresses in Rom 9–11 that ultimately they will be saved. Moreover, the comment that the Thessalonians "became imitators" of the churches in Judea (v. 14) is unique, because in every other place where Paul invokes the idea of imitation (including 1:6 in this same letter) he has reference to the imitation of himself or of Christ.

Historical. The one event so traumatic for the Jews that it could have been plausibly identified as God's wrath visited upon them (v. 16bc) was the fall of Jerusalem to the Romans in 70 C.E., but that occurred after Paul's death. Also, it is questionable whether the churches of Judea had undergone any serious suffering at the hands of any Jews (v. 14) by the time this letter was written. Moreover, the statement that Jesus was killed by Jews (v. 16a) is both inaccurate (Paul would have known that crucifixion was a Roman, not a Jewish, means of execution) and incompatible with the apostle's statement that Jesus was crucified by "the rulers of this age" (1 Cor 2:8).

Literary. The remark about giving thanks (vv. 13-14) is redundant after 1:2-10, and along with the series of accusations against Jews (vv. 14, 15-16) interrupts the line of thought, which otherwise flows rather well from 2:12 to 2:17. In addition, the syntax of these verses has an un-Pauline character, and they contain several expressions that Paul does not use elsewhere, or that he uses differently elsewhere.

Although these arguments have been carefully developed by their advocates, in the estimate of most interpreters they fall short of demonstrating the plausibility of any interpolation hypothesis. The most important considerations advanced by those who maintain that the passage is Pauline and integral to the context are the following (for details: R. F. Collins 1979, 124-35; Wanamaker

1990, 29-33; Schlueter 1994; Johanson 1995; Still 1999, 24-45; Bockmuehl 2001, 7-31).

(a) Because Paul's style is demonstrably *not* monolithic and unchanging, but characterized by a certain amount of variation, the burden of proof lies heavily upon those who claim that the style of the passage is un-Pauline.

(b) The accusations against Jews have been formulated in part under the influence of a polemical tradition within Judaism itself, according to which the prophets of old had been killed by an unfaithful segment of God's own people (see commentary on v. 15). The influence of this tradition, which is also apparent in the Gospels, helps explain why the passage exhibits some linguistic and stylistic features that are either unusual or not found elsewhere in Paul's letters.

(c) The apostle's sharp invective also manifests the sort of hyperbole that Greco-Roman speakers and writers regarded as an effective rhetorical strategy in polemical situations (Schlueter 1994, esp. 65-123). Thus, any historical inaccuracies or ambiguities in the charges leveled in vv. 14-16 are sufficiently explained as due to polemical exaggeration, which involves, by definition, some distortion of the facts. This means, for example, that there is no need to identify one particular historical event as God's wrathful judgment against the Jews (although various events prior to the writing of 1 Thessalonians have been suggested as possibilites; e.g., Wanamaker 1990, 30; Bockmuehl 2001, 25-27).

(d) Some hold that the charges and claims made about Jews in this passage *are* consistent with the views Paul expresses in Rom 9–11 (see comments below). However, even if one finds the case for consistency unpersuasive, it does not necessarily follow that our passage must be regarded as non-Pauline.

First, it is important to take account of the different topics and aims of the two passages. On the one hand, the polemical hyperbole in 1 Thess 2:14-16 serves to accentuate the courage of the Judean churches, and thereby also the courage of the Thessalonians who "became imitators" of them. On the other hand, in Rom 9–11 the status of the Jews is actually the topic, and

Paul's comments about them are both more considered and more carefully articulated than in 1 Thessalonians.

Second, it is possible that Paul's views about the status of unbelieving Jews changed over time, whether because of further reflection and experience or—as some suggest—for the more specific reason that his lessening sense of an imminent return of the Lord allowed him to believe there was still time for them to repent. Clearly, it is wrong simply to *assume* that Paul was absolutely consistent in what he thought and how he expressed his thinking, or that his views on any given topic never changed or developed.

(e) While it is true that in Paul's letters the term "imitators" appears only here with reference to imitating ordinary believers (as distinct from the apostle), the *idea* that some believers will or should follow the example of other believers is quite at home in Paul's thought (see commentary on v. 14).

(f) Claims to the contrary notwithstanding, these verses are neither impossibly redundant nor seriously disruptive of the flow of thought. The thanksgiving proper (vv. 13-14), which includes a comment about the congregation's courage in the midst of suffering, complements the first thanksgiving in chapter 1; and although the charges in vv. 15-16 amount to a digression, this digression also serves to underscore the courage of the Judean churches, and thus of the church in Thessalonica.

Thanksgiving Proper (2:13-14)

In Greek, v. 13 begins, "And we" (*kai hēmeis*), the conjunction looking back to the first thanksgiving and the emphatic "we" perhaps helping to shift attention from the Thessalonians as witnesses, v. 10, to what Paul's thanksgiving attests. This second thanksgiving renews and complements the first, for statements in the first about the Thessalonians' election and the coming of the gospel to them with the power of the Holy Spirit (1:4, 5-10) are echoed and extended here: what they "heard" from Paul (cf. Rom 10:14-17 [Isa 53:1]; Gal 3:2, 5) they both "received" (cf. 1 Cor 15:1; Gal 1:9) as the authoritative word of God and "accepted" (cf. 1 Thess 1:6) as such, and the powerful working of that word continues to form them as believers (cf. Phil 2:13).

Paul underscores the authenticity of the Thessalonians' response by noting that it resulted in their suffering (v. 14), doubtless a further reference to the affliction that began during his mission (1:6; 2:2). Now he specifies that it was inflicted by the converts' "own compatriots," and that it involved "the same things" experienced by the Judean churches at the hands of Jews. For this comparison to work, "*your own* compatriots" must refer to fellow Gentiles (e.g., Still 1999, 218-24). In addition to identifying the source of their suffering, this is further evidence (see also 1:9b) that the Thessalonian congregation was composed primarily, if not entirely, of Gentile believers (see Introduction).

Although Paul implies that the Judean churches had experienced serious physical suffering, there is no firm evidence that this was the case. Acts indeed portrays Judea as the place where, as a Pharisee, Paul himself had persecuted Christians (9:1, 21; 22:4-5, 17-20; 26:9-11). But this seems unlikely, given his own remark (Gal 1:22-23) that the Judean churches only *heard* he had once persecuted believers somewhere (Paul never says where: Gal 1:13, 23; 1 Cor 15:9; Phil 3:6).

The apostle's vagueness about the nature and severity of the suffering undergone by the Thessalonians actually serves his aim. He wants not only to commend them for being steadfast but to urge their continuing perseverance, no matter how formidable the opposition might become. Both objectives are served by his nonspecific statement that in their suffering of the "same things" they became imitators of the churches in Judea. Elsewhere Paul speaks, as in 1:6, of believers "imitating" himself and Christ, not other churches; yet the *idea* that believers can be examples for fellow believers is present in 1:7, as well as in 2 Cor 9:1-2 and Phil 3:17.

Most English translations place a comma after "the Jews" (v. 14), as if the apostle is indicting the Jewish people as a whole, but this reading is not supported by either Greek grammar or Pauline usage. The very next words (v. 15a) constitute a restrictive clause, showing that Paul is thinking specifically of "the Jews *who killed both the Lord Jesus and the prophets*" (Gilliard 1989). Nonetheless, the charges leveled in vv. 15-16 are so sweeping that they verge on being a wholesale condemnation.

Jewish Opposition (2:15-16)

The scathing accusations in vv. 15-16a, along with references in v. 16bc to a dreadful punishment, are the more prominent for being so out of place in a thanksgiving. Formally, they constitute a digression; functionally, whether Paul intended it or not (some interpreters infer an emotional outburst), this digression emphasizes the remarkable courage of the Judean believers—and thus, of their Thessalonian imitators—by associating the Jews who opposed the Judean churches with an alleged pattern of Jewish opposition to God's purposes.

There are five accusations, of which the first and last are the most specific. In part, Paul is drawing on a Jewish polemical tradition rooted in the Hebrew Bible, which charged that the unfaithful within Israel had killed the prophets (e.g., 3 Kgdms [1 Kgs] 19:10, which Paul cites in Rom 11:3). He also borrows a slander that was abroad in Gentile circles (see commentary on v. 15), and in general follows the rhetorical convention of polemical exaggeration (Schlueter 1994, esp. 65-123). These considerations explain the presence of some un-Pauline terms and stylistic features, and why the charges are so sweeping and, at points, historically ambiguous or even distorted.

The first charge (v. 15a) links the death of Jesus to the death of Israel's prophets (the unusual Gk. word order would allow the translation, "killed both the Lord—that is, Jesus—and the prophets"). The wording of this charge is derived from the Jewish polemical tradition (e.g., 2 Chron 24:20-21; 36:16; Neh 9:26; Jer 2:30; 26:8, 20-23; *Mart. Isa.* 5; *Jub.* 1:12), which may lie behind Paul's use of the verb "killed" in referring to Jesus' death (see esp. 3 Kgdms [1 Kgs] 19:10, 14). The same tradition is reflected elsewhere in the NT, most prominently in the parable of the wicked tenants (Mark 12:1-9 and parr.) and in Matthew's denunciations of the scribes and Pharisees (23:29-36). Other NT passages that implicate the Jews in Jesus' death include Mark 8:31 (and parr.); John 5:18; Acts 3:12-15; 13:27-28. Like Paul, Acts 7:52 attributes Jesus' death to the descendants of those who had killed the prophets.

The second charge (v. 15b) is less specific, for it is unclear who the victims are (does "us" refer just to Paul? to all apostles? to all believers?), whether they were driven out (NRSV) or systematically "persecuted," and whether the aorist tense ("drove") points to one specific past event. The compound form of the verb (*ek-diōxantōn* for *diōxantōn*) intensifies it, and within this polemical context, with its rhetorical exaggeration, suggests at the very least violent expulsion. The other two ambiguities contribute further to the rhetorical force of the indictment by allowing it to be understood quite expansively (cf. Schlueter 1994, 72-73). Interpreters who believe that this particular charge confirms Acts 17:5-10, which has Paul leaving Thessalonica because of trouble stirred up by Jewish agitators, must still reckon with the probability that in Paul's day the Jewish community in the city was not very large or influential (see Introduction).

Viewed together and without reference to what follows, the third and fourth charges (v. 15c) amount to a sweeping indictment. To "displease God" means to act in any way that is contrary to God's will (see commentary on 2:4), and to "oppose everyone" means to act malevolently against the rest of humankind. The latter calumny appears often in the anti-Jewish writings of Paul's day, for example, Tacitus, *Hist.* 5.5: "The Jews are extremely loyal toward one another, and always ready to show compassion, but toward every other people they feel only hate and enmity [*sed adversus omnes alios hostile odium*]" (LCL; additional examples in Boring 1995, no. 815). Moreover, this charge of misanthropy was sometimes coupled with the charge of atheism (attested by Josephus, *Ag. Ap.* 2.148), not unlike Paul's juxtaposing of accusations about displeasing God and opposing humankind.

These two charges are explained in the fifth and final indictment (v. 16a): Jews defy the will of God and act to the detriment of the rest of humankind by hindering Paul from taking the message of salvation to the Gentiles. That Paul had personally experienced the hostility of Jews, even if not in Thessalonica, is clear from 2 Cor 11:24, where he says—without indicating when or why—that he has five times received the traditional Jewish punishment of thirty-nine lashes. It is possible that these lashings occurred rather early in his ministry, even before the writing of 1 Thessalonians, when his contacts with Jewish synagogues were likely closer and more frequent than later on. As for what prompted them, given his charge that Jews have impeded his Gentile mission it could be that "a Jewish Paul was being punished or harassed for admitting Gentiles into a religious movement seen to be Jewish without demanding circumcision" (Schlueter 1994, 191).

Whatever specific events may lie behind it, this final charge is not simply about what the apostle has personally experienced. Its standpoint is theological and eschatological, not autobiographical. If, as Paul believes, God has entrusted him with the gospel and authorized him as an apostle in order that the Gentiles may be saved (2:4, 13; cf. 1 Cor 9:22b; Rom 11:14), then Jewish opposition to his Gentile mission is nothing less than opposition to what God wills for humankind (cf. Holtz 1998, 107; Davies 1999, 718). This is the only occurrence in 1 Thessalonians of the verb "to save" (but in 1:10 "rescue" is a synonym), and the noun "salvation" appears just twice (5:8, 9). Nevertheless, it is clear that in this particular letter Paul is thinking of salvation as primarily (but not only) future—as deliverance *from* God's wrath (1:10; 5:8-9) and *for* unending life with Christ (4:17; 5:10).

For those Jews who have impeded God's plan of salvation, however, there is no escaping the divine wrath. With this dire announcement (v. 16bc) the digression is concluded. Paul's claim that the Jews "have constantly been filling up the measure of their sins" echoes a biblical idiom (Gen 15:16; Dan 4:34; 2 Macc 6:14-15; Wis 19:3-5; cf. *L.A.B.* 26:13) used with reference to iniquities so excessive they can no longer be counted, hence—to borrow a different, more Pauline expression—"sinful in the extreme" (Rom 7:13 [Mof.]). The plural "sins" (there is no other instance of this term or its cognates in 1 Thessalonians), which occurs infrequently in Paul's letters, derives from the tradition. Here it refers to the whole series of transgressions just alleged, while the adverb "constantly" heightens the rhetorical exaggeration that characterizes the entire recital. In the NRSV, "Thus" at the beginning of the statement construes the Greek (*eis* + articular infinitive) as indicating result, which is probably correct, even though in Paul's letters the construction more often expresses purpose.

Those who opt for the latter usage here tend to be influenced by statements in Romans that God hardens the hearts of the Jews in order that the Gentiles might be saved (Wanamaker 1990, 116, cites Rom 11:7-10, 28, 32). There is, however, no hint of this idea in 1 Thessalonians.

Given the context, it is certain that in the final clause of v. 16 Paul is referring to "God's wrath" (NRSV), even though the best ancient manuscripts have only the word "wrath" (for the concept, see commentary on 1:10). Precisely what he is saying about this in relation to the Jews is less certain. Most interpreters take the aorist (past tense) form of the verb as indicating that Paul believes God's wrath has already befallen them. But since in 1:10 and 5:9 he associates wrath with the eschatological day (also Rom 2:5, 8; 5:9), others argue that the aorist more likely has a prophetic sense here, announcing as already realized what is actually conceived as future, because it is certain and imminent. Or does Paul mean that God's coming wrath toward the Jews is already *beginning* to be manifested (NAB: "the wrath of God has...begun to come upon them")? Because of the polemical and hyperbolic character of the rhetoric, it is best not to press for one specific meaning. The same applies in the difficult case of *eis telos*, which can be rendered "at last" (NRSV; NJB: "finally"), "completely" (NRSV alt.), or "forever" (NRSV alt.; Mof.: "to the bitter end"; Malherbe 2000, 171: "until the end"). Invective is not hospitable to the nuanced expression of considered judgments, and this digression is pure invective.

◊ ◊ ◊ ◊

Particularly if this is an authentically Pauline passage, but also even if it is not, interpreters have to confront the theological and ethical issues that are raised by the inventory of hostile actions alleged against the Jews in vv. 15-16. In reflecting on those, several matters are worth considering.

First, the aim of this passage is disclosed by the thanksgiving proper, vv. 13-14, not by the digression in vv. 15-16. Paul wishes to commend the members of his congregation for being steadfast in their faith, despite the affliction it has brought them, and to encourage them to remain so, no matter the continuing risks. The accusations in vv. 15-16 are secondary to this principal aim of commendation and encouragement.

Second, this passage is not, strictly speaking, "anti-Jewish," and it is certainly not "anti-Semitic." It is not anti-Semitic, because Paul—himself a Jew—is not indicting the Jews for *being* Jews; and it is not anti-Jewish, because he is not issuing a general indictment of the Jews as a class. He is alleging particular ways in which certain Jews have opposed the purposes of God: by hostility toward the Judean churches, killing the Lord Jesus and the prophets, and hindering his mission to the Gentiles.

Third, the passage nevertheless takes on an anti-Jewish aspect by reason of the vituperative hyperbole that characterizes its rhetoric. This includes the sweeping charges that Jews displease God and oppose humankind, and the pronouncement that they have sinned to the limit and become the objects of God's wrath. Although later, in Romans, Paul will refer to the Jews as "objects of [God's] wrath that are made for destruction" (9:22), in that context he envisions their ultimate salvation, while in the present context no such hope is held out, at least not explicitly (see the final point below).

Fourth, while the harshness of Paul's tone and the seriousness of his allegations are not to be minimized, several further considerations allow these to be seen in perspective. (a) The charges are formulated so sharply at least in part because they have been drawn from the "insider rhetoric" of his own Jewish polemical tradition. (b) Elsewhere he does not hesitate to employ stock Jewish allegations about Gentiles (e.g., 4:2-8; Rom 1:18-32; 1 Cor 6:9-11a; 5:1; 12:2; Gal 2:15). (c) In several letters he expresses his outrage at certain Jewish *Christians* in terms that are at least as harsh as those found here (e.g., 2 Cor 11:3-4, 13-15; Gal 4:21–5:1, 11-12; Phil 3:2). (d) Paul's denigration of those perceived as enemies by charging them with a long history of hostility serves the social function of strengthening his congregation's own sense of Christian identity (Wanamaker 1990, 118-19) and of belonging to a yet wider community of believers. This larger community, which includes Jewish Christians (the Judean churches), has faithfully endured—as the "suffering righteous" (Schlueter 1994, 75)—despite the execution of their Lord.

Finally, it is important to observe that in Rom 9–11 Paul affirms a vital role for unbelieving Israel in God's plan of salvation, concluding that the Jews will ultimately be saved (e.g., 11:25-32). Some interpreters believe that the sharp accusations and gloomy pronouncements in 1 Thess 2:13-16 contradict that view, or at least leave no room for it. Thus, if Paul himself is responsible for our passage, his thought on this topic would have to be judged as either inconsistent or having changed between the writing of the two letters. Other interpreters, however, believe that the accusations in 1 Thessalonians do not close out the possibility of repentance for the Jews, and that there are no *fundamental* differences between Paul's outlook here and in Romans, even though the tone is different. But a word of caution is in order. Given the aim and character of our passage, it cannot yield a considered view of the status and destiny of unbelieving Jews in God's plans. Whether or not the views that Paul expresses on this subject in Romans are coherent, they are at least considered, which is not the case in 1 Thessalonians. For this reason, all comparisons between the theological outlook of our passage and that of Rom 9–11 are problematic from the start.

Further Assurances (2:17–3:10)

The narrative of 2:1-12, following the first thanksgiving, reminded the congregation of how Paul had conducted his mission in Thessalonica. Now a narrative following the second thanksgiving notes the events that have led to the writing of this letter. As in the earlier narrative, the apostle is nurturing his relationship with the Thessalonians by assuring them of how much he is concerned for their well-being as a community of faith. His aim is to encourage them to remain steadfast in their commitment to the gospel. After emphasizing his eagerness but also inability to revisit the congregation (2:17-20), he indicates why he had sent Timothy, what joy he experienced upon receiving his envoy's report (3:1-8), and how much he still longs to be with his congregation (3:9-10).

Paul's Longing for the Thessalonians (2:17-20)

For the fifth time since the beginning of the letter Paul addresses the congregation as "brothers and sisters" (v. 17), further emphasizing the familial bond that unites him with his converts. Family language continues when he says, "we were made orphans," which expresses the desolation he feels because of his forced separation (note the passive voice) from them. Whether Paul is likening himself to a child deprived of his parents or to a parent deprived of his children is unclear (the verb *aporphanizō* was used in both ways). In either case, he wishes to think of this separation as both temporary and brief; "for a short time" seems to be his own *ad hoc* combination of two idioms, one ("for a time") connoting a limited period and the other ("for an hour") connoting brevity. Although he assures them that he is not absent from them in his "heart" (his truest self; cf. 2:4), his language shows that he also yearns desperately to see them again in person (see also 3:10), and hints that he may actually have made the effort. When he says that he had "more than once" wanted to return (v. 18, AT), he shifts momentarily to the first person singular ("certainly I, Paul") in order to accentuate the intensity of his feelings.

The apostle's statement that "Satan prevented us" (AT) from returning to Thessalonica is viewed by some interpreters as a demonizing of the Jews (cf. 2:16) who, according to Acts 17:5-10, had forced him to leave Thessalonica. Others read this as a demonizing of the city officials, mentioned in the same passage. More likely, and in accord with portrayals of the adversary of God (known by various names) in Jewish intertestamental literature, the apostle is thinking much more generally of all the forces of evil, ruled by Satan, that are at work to thwart God's will (cf. 1 Cor 5:5; 7:5; 2 Cor 2:11; 12:7; also 2 Cor 4:4; 6:15; 11:3, 14; 1 Thess 3:5). For this reason, and also because the focus here is not on external events but inner feelings, it is useless to speculate on what specific circumstance prevented the apostle's return to Thessalonica. Years later, when he writes of being hindered from getting to Rome (Rom 1:13; 15:22), he does not invoke Satan's name at all.

Paul explains the depth of his present yearning (vv. 19-20) by asking, rhetorically, what ground he has for "hope or joy or [a] crown of boasting," and by twice providing the answer (in the form of another rhetorical question, v. 19; directly, v. 20): it is the Thessalonian congregation. Here, as elsewhere (there are similar comments in Phil 2:16; 4:1; 2 Cor 1:14; cf. 1 Cor 9:2), he anticipates the accounting of his apostleship that he must give to the "Lord Jesus" (cf. 2:15) on the eschatological day of judgment (cf. 1 Cor 3:8, 12-15; 4:4). In the present context, "hope" has the sense of confidence. The "joy" and "crown" to which Paul refers are often mentioned in Jewish and early Christian texts in connection with God's ultimate blessing of the righteous (e.g., 1QS IV, 7; thus Phil 4:1). Joy, as Philo noted (*Names* 163), accompanies the arrival of the good that hope has expected (thus Rom 14:17; Heb 12:2); the bestowal of a crown betokens vindication and victory, as in an athletic contest (4 Macc 17:15; 1 Cor 9:25). The phrase translated "crown of boasting" could be rendered "crown of glorying" (boasting in a good sense, as in 1 Cor 15:31), and is equivalent to the more usual "crown of glory" mentioned in similar contexts (e.g., Wis 5:16; *T. Benj.* 4:1; 1 Pet 5:4).

Paul refers to the Lord's return as his *parousia* ("coming"), a term that in ordinary usage designates one's "presence" as distinct from one's absence. The use of it here for the triumphal advent of Christ at the close of history (see also 3:13; 4:15; 5:23) accords with occurrences in various Hellenistic texts, where it can designate either the official and celebrated visit of a king or emperor, or the appearance of a divinity (examples in BDAG, 780 *s.v.*, §2b). The religious and political associations that this term would have had for Paul's Gentile congregations may explain why, except for 1 Cor 15:23, he does not use it of Christ's return in any subsequent letter (see, however, 2 Thess 2:1, 8-9).

The formal answer to the rhetorical question of v. 19 employs the present tense: "Yes, you *are* our glory and joy!" (v. 20). This may be shorthand for "you are the ground of the glory and joy we will experience at the Lord's return." If so, the eschatological standpoint of v. 19 is continued, with the present tense now reflecting a sense of the certainty and imminence of the last day.

Timothy's Mission (3:1-10)

The apostle now expresses his confidence in the Thessalonian converts by recounting his dispatch of Timothy to visit them, and by attesting that his envoy's subsequent report has brought him great joy. While Paul says that he had sent Timothy to strengthen the congregation's faith (vv. 2, 5), there is no doubt that an equally important aim had been to nurture the relationship between himself and the congregation. In this respect, Timothy's mission was similar to that of Hellenistic diplomatic envoys, who were sent out "to confirm and reaffirm the affection and loyalty of each party to the other" (Mitchell 1992, esp. 659-60, 662). This passage is of particular importance for determining Paul's aim in writing the present letter (see Introduction).

The Dispatch of Timothy to Thessalonica (3:1-5): Although vv. 1-2 seem to indicate that Paul and Timothy were both in Athens when the apostle decided to send Timothy back to Thessalonica, the account in Acts presents a different scenario. According to Acts, Timothy and Silas (Silvanus) remained in Macedonia when Paul went to Athens, rejoining him only after he had moved on to Corinth (17:10-15; 18:5). The two accounts may not be utterly incompatible, however. It is possible that Paul means he was already "alone" in Athens when he decided to send Timothy—who was actually somewhere else—back to Thessalonica (argued esp. by Donfried 2002). In any event, 1 Thessalonians was written after Timothy had completed his mission and had reported to Paul in Corinth (see Introduction).

Confident that Timothy had been successful, Paul commends him as "our brother and *synergos tou theou*" (v. 2). Here "brother" likely means his "brother" in working for the gospel (cf. 2 Cor 1:1; Phlm 1). The phrase *synergos tou theou* can be translated either "co-worker for God" (NRSV) or "co-worker with God" (cf. REB). The former is supported by a number of passages in which Paul refers to one or more persons as co-workers with himself (or one another) for the gospel (Rom 16:3, 9, 21; 1 Cor 16:16 [the related verb]; 8:23; Phil 2:25; 4:3; Phlm 1 [Timothy], 24; cf. 2 Cor 1:24; perhaps also 1 Cor 3:9). But the widely attested textual variants "minister of God" and "minister of God and our co-worker" support the latter, for they are best explained as attempts by ancient readers who interpreted the phrase as "co-workers with God" to "correct" the synergism they found implied in it. Synergism is a false issue, however. If not in 1 Cor 3:9, which is also ambiguous, at least in 2 Cor 6:1 ("As we work together with him [i.e., God]"), Paul does not hesitate to speak of the work of ministry as jointly divine and human in the sense that *God* works *through* the apostles to effect reconciliation (2 Cor 5:18-20).

Paul had not sent Timothy to strengthen the congregation's faith (v. 2) because he doubted the authenticity of it, but because he feared that some might be "shaken by these afflictions" (v. 3a, AT); or, as he also puts it, may have succumbed to the wiles of "the tempter" (v. 5; i.e. Satan, as in 2:18).

The phrase "these afflictions" may be read as a reference to (a) Paul's own tribulations (as in v. 7), (b) the congregation's (as in 1:6), or (c) both the congregation's and Paul's. Option (c) is the most likely. Paul has just mentioned both the congregation's suffering (2:14) and his own (2:15); and from the beginning of the Thessalonian mission the missionaries and their converts had experienced the same afflictions (1:6; 2:2). He now reminds them that from the first he had spoken of believers as "destined" to suffer because of their commitment to the gospel (vv. 3b-4). It would appear that, despite Timothy's best efforts, even at the end of his visit the Thessalonian converts remained perplexed and anxious about the hostility directed against them. For this reason, and apparently as he had in person, Paul identifies suffering as integral to their election and God's saving purposes. This thought accords with Jewish apocalyptic expectations that disorder and sufferings will usher in the messianic age (e.g., Dan 12:1; *Jub.* 23:13-14, 16-31; *4 Ezra* 5:1-13; 6:18-28; 9:1-2; *2 Bar.* 25-27, 70; cf. Rom 8:18; 1 Cor 7:26-31).

Returning to his point that Timothy's mission had been to "find out about [the congregation's] faith" (v. 5), Paul mentions his concern that the sinister power of "the tempter" could have destroyed their faith, with the result that his "labor" would have been for naught. He refers to the missionary and now pastoral labor that he has expended for the gospel in Thessalonica (cf. 1 Cor 15:58; Gal 4:11; Phil 2:16). This seems to be an instance of how, when separated from a congregation, the apostle's concern, like that of parents separated from their children, could balloon into anxiety (cf. 2 Cor 11:28).

Timothy's Report and Paul's Response (3:6-10): Timothy's report about the congregation had dispelled Paul's anxiety (vv. 6-8). It is significant that Paul has used the verb *euangelizomai*—"brought us the good news"—rather than some neutral verb like "report," "tell," or "say" (note 1:9; 4:15; 5:3; 2 Cor 1:7; cf. Malherbe 2000, 200-01). Everywhere else in his letters the word refers to bringing the good news of God's saving work (e.g., 1 Cor 15:1-2), and this, one may infer, is what the news from Thessalonica has been for Paul. He rejoices that his converts continue to give evidence of "faith and love" (v. 6; cf. 1 Cor 13:2; 16:13-14; Gal 5:6; Phlm 5) and to "stand firm in the Lord" (v. 8; as in Phil 4:1; cf. Rom 14:4; also 1 Cor 16:13; Gal 5:1; Phil 1:27). The lack of a reference to hope, as well, is probably not significant. Paul has earlier commended the congregation for its hope (1:3), and his aim in 4:13-17 is not to instill hope but to expand it.

The remarkable clustering of first and second person pronouns in vv. 6-8 reflects the apostle's eagerness to affirm and deepen the bonds of friendship between himself and his congregation. This aim is also apparent when he interrupts his own sentence with an interjection—"just as we long to see you" (v. 6)—that elevates the Thessalonians' reported longing for him to the same level of intensity as his longing for them. Then, picking up the thread of his original thought, he once more emphasizes the closeness of their relationship. Just as he had sent Timothy to encourage the congregation in its faith (v. 2), so now Timothy's report about the congregation's faithfulness has encouraged Paul (v. 7). The phrase "our distress and persecution" probably refers in the first instance to the afflictions that Paul continues to experience, but it is broad enough to include the afflictions experienced by his converts. The two terms frequently stand together in the LXX (esp. in the Psalms), and Paul juxtaposes them again in a general catalog of his apostolic miseries, 2 Cor 6:4 (NRSV: "afflictions, hardships"). His statement that he will "live" if the congregation continues to "stand firm in the Lord" (v. 8) is both a commendation and an implicit appeal (here the "Lord" is Christ, as in Phil 4:1). Malherbe (2000, 202-3) observes that in the ancient world it was a commonplace to speak of friends living and dying together, and he rightly identifies 2 Cor 7:3-7 as a "significant parallel" to the present passage.

The expression of thanks with which Paul concludes this account (vv. 9-10) differs from the earlier, more formal thanksgiving paragraphs (1:2-10; 2:13-16). No other Pauline thanksgiving is as closely related to what immediately precedes, opens with a rhetorical question (let alone one that suggests the impossibility of giving adequate thanks), fails to mention that Paul is constant in his thanksgiving (e.g., "always" in 1:2; "constantly" in 2:13), or includes the kind of "prayer-report" (Wiles 1974, 51-53) found here in v. 10 (cf. Malherbe 2000, 204).

Paul's rhetorical question (v. 9), which presumes a negative answer, effectively emphasizes his inexpressible joy. He makes similar references to the joy brought to him by a congregation in two other thanksgivings (Phil 1:4; Phlm 7). But here he finds it impossible to "thank God enough" for the Thessalonian believers, because Timothy's report has engendered within him an overwhelming joy. In 2:19, 20, where Paul has also referred to this congregation as his "joy," he was thinking of the eschatological day when, standing "before our Lord Jesus," he would be held accountable for his work. He now speaks, however, of his present experience of communion with God, before whom he rejoices on account of the Thessalonian believers (cf. 1:3; contrast 3:13).

The prayer-report (v. 10) does not specifically carry forward the theme of thanksgiving, but gives renewed expression to Paul's longing to be with the congregation in person (cf. 2:17-20). Repeatedly ("night and day"; cf. 2:9) he "entreats [God] beyond any measuring" (AT) to see the Thessalonians again, that he might further enrich their faith. In this context, the phrase *katartisai ta hysterēmata* does not mean "restore whatever is lacking" (NRSV), as if some aspect of the congregation's faith has been lost or neglected. An equally permissible translation, and the one required here by the context, is "*complete* what is lacking." The apostle wants to deepen the Thessalonians' faith by leading them into a maturer experience and understanding of the gospel (cf. 2 Cor 10:15; 13:9).

◊   ◊   ◊   ◊

This passage affords some further indications of how, at this point in his ministry, Paul was understanding the character of faith (believing), as well as his role as a servant of the gospel of Christ.

The highest concentration of references to "faith" in the entire letter occurs here in 3:2-10. These are to be read, first of all, in the light of 1:8-10, where "faith in God" connotes trusting and serving the one "living and true God" of Paul's gospel. But the present references allow some additional observations about the view of faith contained in this letter.

(a) Paul equates a strong and vital faith with "stand[ing] firm in the Lord" (3:7-8). In affirming that "Jesus died and rose again" (4:14), the community of believers is attesting that the God in whom they have placed their trust is the God who has been revealed in Christ's death and resurrection. Thus "faith in God" involves a faith-relationship, as well, with Christ the Lord (perhaps a hint of this in 1:8-10).

(b) Faith is not to be taken for granted. It is not a situation in which believers, from the time of their conversion, can stand henceforth secure. Because fears and temptations may cause them to waver in their faith (3:3a, 5b), they have to be continually strengthened and encouraged in their believing (3:2b, 5a).

(c) Faith and love (*agapē*) go hand in hand (3:6). Paul has already linked these two, along with hope, at the beginning of the letter, and he will do so again near its close (1:3; 5:8). This linking makes it clear that he sees faith as always a "work in progress." Put another way, he does not think of "stand[ing] firm in the Lord" as simply "standing pat" on some past experience of grace or specified set of beliefs. Rather, he conceives of believers as those who "stand at the ready" to serve God and others in love, ever more intelligently and effectively, in all that they do.

Three further observations may be made about what this passage discloses concerning Paul's understanding of his ministry.

(a) It is evident that he was committed not only to the missionary task of winning converts but also to the pastoral task of nurturing and strengthening the faith of those already converted (3:2b, 5a). There is no evidence, from either this passage or the letter as a whole, that he distinguished in principle between his work as a missionary and his work as a pastor.

(b) Already in this, the earliest of his surviving letters, Paul has a clear sense that his apostolic service is destined to involve afflictions (3:3-4). It is noteworthy, however, that he does not take the step of offering any specific theological interpretation of them. That happens first in his letters to the Corinthians (esp. 2 Cor 4:7-12). It is also in the Corinthian letters that he begins to reflect on the meaning of the suffering experienced by believers in general, and on how that is linked to his own (e.g., 2 Cor 1:3-7; 4:17-18).

(c) In 2:17–3:10 Paul allows himself to be seen, even and precisely in his ministerial role, as no less acquainted with the experiences of loneliness, anxiety, vulnerability, joy, and affection than any other human being (2:17; 3:1, 5, 9). Like his congregation, he, too, needs to be encouraged and reassured (3:6-8). Moreover, while he takes his responsibilities as a servant of the gospel with the utmost seriousness (he expects to have to give an accounting of himself at the *parousia*, 2:19), he asks for no special esteem beyond that which is manifested in the congregation's good will toward him (3:6).

Benedictory Prayer (3:11-13)

Although this prayer follows from and confirms the prayer-report of v. 10, its most important function is to conclude the first, primarily narrative, section of the letter and to point ahead to the second, primarily hortatory, section of it. Despite several traditional elements and its overall traditional character, in subject matter it is closely related both to what has preceded and to what will follow.

This prayer opens by invoking not just God but also Jesus. The expression "our God and Father" is probably drawn from the liturgical tradition (see also 1:3; 3:13; Gal 1:4; Phil 4:20), while "Lord Jesus" is an especially prominent title in this letter (2:15, 19; 3:13; 4:1, 2). The striking invocation of Jesus along with God shows that Paul conceives of the two as closely related, yet the traditional and formulaic character of the language does not allow any firm conclusion about *how* he would describe their relationship. Nor is there any theological significance to his use of a singular verb ("direct") following the compound subject, for this is not uncommon in Greek (Bruce 1982, 71). It is nonetheless remarkable to find Paul assuming that Jesus along with God determines his apostolic itinerary, especially because in subsequent letters he often refers to his travels as subject to *God's* will alone (Rom 1:10; 15:32; 1 Cor 4:19; 16:7 [here "the Lord" is God], 12 [NRSV alt.]; Furnish 1989, 218-20).

The apostle continues his prayer by invoking just "the Lord" (v. 12), by whom he must still mean the Lord Jesus (vv. 11, 13). The only other instance of his addressing a prayer to Jesus is his report of having appealed to him to remove his "thorn . . . in the flesh" (2 Cor 12:7-9; Malherbe 2000, 212). In the present case, Paul first petitions the Lord on behalf of others: that the Thessalonians may "increase and abound in love [*agapē*]" (v. 12). The two verbs, which are essentially synonymous, suggest an exceeding or overflowing of ordinary limits or boundaries. Even though, or perhaps precisely because, Timothy has been able to assure Paul that his converts remain steadfast in love (3:6; cf. 1:3; 4:9), the apostle now prays that the Lord will cause their love to expand without limit (cf. Phil 1:9).

He prays initially for the overflowing of *agapē* within the community of faith, "for one another." This theme emerges again in 4:9-10, where believers throughout the whole of Macedonia are also in view; and in 5:15, where the appeal to do "good" (*to agathon*) to one another is simply an alternative formulation. Similar Pauline appeals for harmonious community relationships are found, especially, in Romans (12:10, 16; 14:19).

But Paul's prayer discloses a still larger vision of love's work. Because the overflowing *agapē* for which he prays knows no limits, it is the norm not only for relationships within the community of faith itself but also for the community's relationships with outsiders ("for all"). This same expansive vision is evident in 4:10b-12; 5:15 ("seek to do good to one another *and to all*"), and elsewhere in Paul's letters (e.g., Gal 6:10; Furnish 2002; 2005).

Nothing in this context restricts the meaning of "all" to *all believers beyond Thessalonica*. Had Paul meant this it is likely that he would have specified it, as he does in 1 Cor 7:17 (and elsewhere), "all the churches," and 1 Cor 14:33b, "all the churches of the saints" (cf. 1 Cor 1:2; 2 Cor 1:1). Nor does anything in this context support the view, held by a number of commentators, that he is thinking only of an unspecific love for humankind in general. His juxtaposition of "for one another" and "for all" suggests that, just as the first phrase has a local reference—the members of the Thessalonian congregation—so, too, has the second one; namely, *all unbelievers with whom the members of this congregation are in daily contact*. This would have included non-Christian family members, friends, and those with whom they necessarily had to deal in the workplace and wider community; those who might on occasion have visited their Christian assemblies (Malherbe 2000, 213); and even those who had harassed, oppressed, or were otherwise actively hostile toward them (note 5:15, repay evil with good).

In an aside, Paul compares the overflowing love for which he appeals with the love he himself has for his congregation (lit. "as, indeed, we for you"). Although this remark gives the petition in v. 12, if not the prayer as a whole, an implicitly imperatival aspect, it remains only an aside. It is not as such a call for the Thessalonians to follow Paul's example, but a further expression of his love and longing for them (similarly, 2 Cor 2:4; 11:11; 12:15).

The petition begun in v. 12 is continued in v. 13. Paul now anticipates that by enabling the Thessalonians to abound in love, the Lord (here, the reference is to God) will be strengthening their "hearts" to be "blameless in holiness" (AT); for at the *parousia* ("coming," as in 2:19) of the Lord Jesus they will have to stand before the judgment seat of God. In Hebrew anthropology, the heart is the seat of one's willing, motives, and most intimate thoughts—therefore of one's truest self (cf. 2:4, 17)—whose secrets God alone can discern (e.g., Ps 44:21; 1 Cor 14:25). Although Paul has previously implied that the "Lord Jesus" will preside at the final judgment (2:19), he now identifies God as the eschatological judge (perhaps implied in 1:10; see also Rom 14:10-11). This is consistent with the evidence from his letters overall, which suggests that he had no specific or firm conception of how justice would be administered on the last day (e.g., in 1 Cor 4:4-5 he identifies the returning Lord as rendering judgment [vv. 4-5a, cf. 2 Cor 5:10] and God as offering commendation [v. 5b; cf. Rom 14:10-11]). In this context, "blameless" means "unflawed" in the sight of God (cf. the related adverb in 5:23b), while "holiness" (*hagiosynē*) is the state of perfect sanctification for which believers hope, and which Paul attributes to God's sanctifying power (5:23a).

This is the only place in his letters where the apostle refers to the Lord's returning "with all his saints." On the basis of Pauline usage overall, one might suppose that these "saints" (lit. "holy ones") are believers (e.g., 1 Cor 1:1; 2 Cor 13:12; Phil 1:1; Rom 1:7) who are being returned from the dead (so interpreted already in *Did.* 16:7). However, this meaning is virtually excluded by the apostle's own subsequent portrayal of the expected end-time events (4:13-17), according to which the "dead in Christ" will be raised immediately *after* the Lord descends from heaven (v. 16). It is therefore probable that in this prayer, which resonates with traditional concepts and language, the "saints" are the "[holy] angels" who, according to a tradition evident elsewhere in the NT (e.g., 2 Thess 1:7; Mark 8:38; Matt 16:27; 25:31), will be accompanying Jesus when he returns. Behind this Christian tradition lies the affirmation of Zech 14:5 that "the LORD my God will come, and all the holy ones with him" (cf. *1 En.* 1:9 [cited in Jude 14]; Deut 33:2; Dan 7:18, etc.; J. J. Collins 1993, 312-18).

◊　◊　◊　◊

This prayer discloses the fundamentally theological standpoint from which Paul has written both the preceding narrative accounts of his ministry and the appeals and encouragement that will follow in chapters 4–5. The first petition (v. 11) shows that he considers the whole of his ministry subject to the will of God—*and* of the Lord (Jesus). Similarly, the second petition (vv. 12-13) shows that he looks to the Lord as the one who makes it possible for the Thessalonians' love to increase to overflowing, that they may stand before God, at the end, "blameless" and "in holiness." The first petition implicitly invites the congregation to view its relationship with the apostle in the light of God's larger purposes for his ministry. The second one hints that only the Lord can enable the congregation to heed the appeals that Paul will proceed to issue in 4:1-12. Indeed, the themes of love (v. 12) and holiness (v. 13) become, in reverse order, the two focal points of those appeals (vv. 1-8 and 9-12, respectively). An important presupposition of Paul's second petition is thereby brought to light: *because the present is already claimed by God, now is the time for abounding in love* (v. 12).

Although Paul's invocation of both God and Jesus (v. 11) shows that he conceived the two as closely related, this in itself reveals nothing about how he may have viewed the nature of their relationship. Just possibly, however, the apostle's language here reflects the same two-part creedal statement that he more fully employs in 1 Cor 8:6: "For us there is one God, the Father, from whom are all things and for whom we exist, and one Lord, Jesus Christ, through whom are all things and through whom we exist." If so, then here, as in 1 Corinthians, he may be presupposing that God is the Source ("Father") and Goal of all things, while the Lord (Jesus Christ) is God's agent in both creation and redemption. This necessarily remains a matter of speculation, however, and should not be permitted to distract one's attention from the content and function of the prayer itself.

PASTORAL INSTRUCTION AND ENCOURAGEMENT (4:1–5:24)

The expression that opens this section (*loipon oun*, 4:1) does not signal the close of the letter (despite the NRSV rendering, "Finally"), but introduces what follows as the point toward which Paul has been driving all along. Having reaffirmed his concern for the congregation's faith and well-being, the apostle now turns his attention to its present situation, of which he has just been apprised by Timothy. Paul speaks here as a pastor, mixing various assurances meant to encourage the Thessalonians in their faith with a number of practical directives concerning their conduct, both as individuals and as a congregation. The instruction and encouragement he offers in 4:1–5:11 address topics that seem to be of special concern to him, perhaps because of Timothy's report about the congregation, while the counsels in 5:12-22 are somewhat more general and formulated more succinctly. This second part of the letter, like the first, is concluded with a benedictory prayer (5:23-24), which draws together the section's two most important topics, holiness (cf. 4:1-8) and the return of Christ (4:13-17).

Matters of Special Concern (4:1–5:11)

The opening expression, "Consequently, therefore" (4:1, AT), looks back generally to the whole of chapters 1–3, where Paul has reminded the congregation of its origins, the meaning of its election, and its continuing relationship with those from whom it received the gospel. He has written in particular of his longing to pay another visit to the congregation (3:1), which was only intensified upon receiving Timothy's firsthand report (3:6, 10). Since Paul himself is still unable to visit, he now sends by letter the appeals and encouragement that he would convey in person, were that possible.

He has formulated counsels about sanctification (4:1-8), love (4:9-12), and the time of the end (5:1-11) as reminders, apparently believing that the congregation should already be knowledgeable about these matters (4:1, 2, 6, 9; 5:1, 2). What he says about those who have died (4:13-18), however, is presented as if it were new instruction ("we do not want you to be uninformed," 4:13). Beginning with the second, each topic is similarly introduced, using *peri* ("concerning" or "about"), and in three of the four cases the congregation is addressed as "brothers and sisters" (4:1; 4:13; 5:1). While some interpreters take the appeals in 4:1-2 as introducing all of the subsequent counsels, they are joined especially to those about sanctification (4:3-8).

Sanctification (4:1-8)

The initial appeal (vv. 1-2) is quite general, summoning the Thessalonians to excel even more than they do (see comment on 3:12) in a way of life (of "walking," as in 2:12; 4:12) that pleases God (cf. 2:4). Paul's tone is emphatic ("ask and urge," cf. 5:12, 14) but friendly and encouraging. He again credits the congregation with knowing what it means to be faithful to the gospel (see comment on 1:5).

The noun that the NRSV renders as "instructions" (*parangeliai*, v. 2; the corresponding verb appears in v. 11) could also be translated as "orders" or "commands" (cf. the force of the verb in 1 Cor 7:10). But in the present context it has the gentler meaning of "counsels" (note "ask and urge," v. 1), referring to the moral instructions that the Thessalonian converts had received (NRSV: "learned") from him (v. 1), perhaps in the form of baptismal catechesis. Just as those had been conveyed originally "through the Lord Jesus" (v. 2), Paul now urges "in the Lord Jesus" (v. 1; cf. Rom 14:14; Phil 2:19) that they be followed ever more diligently.

These two references to the Lord are essentially interchangeable, both of them signaling that Paul speaks with the authority of one who has been commissioned by God to proclaim the gospel (2:4, 7). There is no indication that he means to identify the instructions as having been drawn from the teachings of Jesus; and in fact, those that follow in vv. 3-8 have no counterparts in the Jesus traditions employed in the Synoptic Gospels (see commentary on v. 8a).

Paul carries forward the opening appeal by referring to God's will as the believers' "sanctification" (v. 3a). In distinction from that fulfillment of all "holiness" (*hagiosynē*) to which he has referred as a hope (3:13), "sanctification" (*hagiasmos*) describes the present situation of those who have been called by God through the sanctifying action of the Holy Spirit (vv. 7-8; cf. 1:5, 6). To make it clear that sanctification must be concretely evident in one's conduct, the apostle calls on believers to abstain from *porneia* (cf. Acts 15:20, 29). This term denotes not just "fornication," but any kind of sexual conduct that is viewed as aberrant (see also 1 Cor 6:18). In the Jewish scriptures and traditions, sexual immorality is closely linked with idolatry (e.g., Wis 14:12, 22-29). Although there is no indication that Timothy had reported sexual misconduct in the Thessalonian congregation, such a possibility cannot be ruled out.

The explication of sanctification continues in vv. 4-6a. In v. 4, the word *skeuos*, "vessel," is obviously used metaphorically, but for what? Some read it as a metaphor for "woman" (as it is in 1 Pet 3:7), others (esp. J. Smith 2001) as a metaphor for the male's "body" (cf. Rom 9:22 [NRSV: "objects"]; 2 Cor 4:7 [NRSV: "jars"]) or, more specifically, for the penis. Each of these interpretations has some ancient precedents (BDAG, 927-28 *s.v.*). Two less likely proposals are that "vessel" stands for a "virgin partner" (Bassler 1995, who refers to 1 Cor 7:36-38), or for any "morally neutral" sexual outlet, like a household slave (Glancy 2002, 59-63).

It is perhaps best to regard *skeuos* as a metaphor for "woman" (or "wife"), as does RSV, NAB, and TEV (also NRSV alt. and NIV alt.). This allows the accompanying infinitive, *ktasthai*, to have its usual meaning of "get" or "obtain." Thus interpreted, the phrase corresponds to a familiar idiom for acquiring a wife (e.g., LXX Ruth 4:5, 10; Sir 36:34; in Epictetus, *Discourses*, to a male's female lovers: I, 28.24; II, 24.22), and the reflexive pronoun, *heautou* ("for oneself") has a specific function. The interpretation represented in the NRSV, REB, and NIV translations, which takes *skeuos* as a metaphor for the male's "body," must read the infinitive as "take control of," for which there is scant lexical justification, and ends up with a reflexive pronoun that serves no real function.

If the counsel in vv. 4-5 is about acquiring a wife, then it is consistent with 1 Cor 7:2, where Paul directs that "because of cases of sexual immorality (*porneia*), each man should have his own wife and each woman her own husband." In the present passage, too, Paul indicates that a man avoids sexual immorality (v. 3b) when he acquires a wife (and continues to live with her) "in holiness [*hagiasmos*, as in v. 3a] and honor." It is otherwise, Paul notes, with those who "do not know God" (a conventional OT and Jewish characterization of Gentiles, e.g., LXX Jer 10:25), who marry "with lustful passion" (lit. "with the passion of desire").

Both the warning about passionate desire and the call for "honor" in marriage would have been widely appreciated in Greco-Roman society, which highly valued personal honor and regularly condemned unbridled passion. Honor, however, was related to one's standing in society as determined by the esteem accorded by others, whereas here Paul has linked it with the sanctifying action of God (*hagiasmos*) in the believer's life (cf. Malherbe 2000, 228-29). What, then, would it mean to take a wife "in holiness and honor" rather than with the passion of desire?

There is little chance that Paul is advocating marriages in which the partners permanently abstain from sexual intercourse. Almost certainly, such an extraordinary directive would have been explicitly stated and supported; moreover, in 1 Cor 7:1-6 the apostle emphatically opposes such arrangements. Nor is he advocating marriages that aim at affording the partners mutual sexual "fulfillment" or "pleasure." Such concepts do not surface either in the present passage or in 1 Cor 7. Because Paul's counsel is so general, it is difficult to decide between two remaining possibilities, although the second is perhaps likelier than the first.

(a) It may be, in accord with the views of certain pagan and Hellenistic-Jewish writers, that Paul regards the pure and honorable marriage as one from which all passionate desire has been *eliminated*, and sexual intercourse is to take place solely for the purpose of begetting children (e.g., Pseudo-Phocylides, *Sent.* 175-206; Musonius, *Frag.* XII 86.4-8; Pseudo-Lucian, *Am.* 19-20; cf. Philo, *Spec. Laws* 3.9; *Joseph* 43; argued by Martin 1995, 212-17; 1997; and Fredrickson 2003). One must acknowledge, however, that Paul says nothing either here or in 1 Cor 7 about procreation as the aim of marriage—which is understandable, given his expectation of the Lord's imminent return (note 1 Thess 4:15).

(b) A second possibility is that Paul views marriage as offering the one context in which sexual desire can be *responsibly exercised,* and thereby prevented from degenerating into wanton lust (i.e., *porneia,* v. 3b; cf. Best 1972, 164-65; Watson 2000, 159 [commenting on 1 Cor 7:2-6]). Evidence for this interpretation can be claimed from some of the same ancient writers cited in support of the first: the "desire" or "longing" that brings male and female together can be affirmed (Musonius, *Frag.* XIV, 92.11-14; Pseudo-Lucian, *Am.* 19); it is *"unbridled* sensuality" (Pseudo-Phocylides, *Sent.* 193) and *immoderate* appetites (for sex as well as for food; Philo, *Spec. Laws* 3.9) that are to be condemned.

Another difficult decision confronts interpreters in v. 6a, which can be read either as extending the advice about taking a wife (vv. 4-5) or as further explicating "sanctification" (v. 3b) by introducing another issue. The former reading (favored by most American and British commentators; see Malherbe 2000, 231-33) takes the expression, *to pragma,* as a reference to the subject in vv. 4-5, translating it as "this matter" (NRSV), or the like, and understands Paul to be using the infinitives *hyperbainein* (to "overstep") and *pleonektein* (to "defraud") of sexual transgression. One can understand how adultery with a fellow believer's wife could be viewed as overstepping one's proper relationship to the woman, and defrauding ("cheating") her husband (in this case, *adelphos* would be gender specific—"brother," not "brother and sister"). The alternative (favored mainly by German interpreters; but see also Richard 1995, 200-02) is to take *to pragma* as referring specifically to business matters, and to read the infinitives as designating commercial transgressions and fraud perpetrated against a fellow believer. Although a reference to misconduct in business would be somewhat intrusive in this context, which otherwise mentions only sexual misconduct (vv. 3b, 4-5), this cannot be ruled out. It is rather more likely, however, that v. 6a is to be read as an extension of the counsel of vv. 4-5.

In vv. 6b-8 Paul supports the preceding counsels, first, with a reminder that wrongdoers will experience the vengeance of the Lord (v. 6b). It may be that "the Lord" is to be understood as Christ (e.g., von Dobschütz 1909, 169; Rigaux 1956, 511; Best 1972, 166-67; R. F. Collins 1984, 269-71). This would agree with references in later letters to Christ as God's agent at the final judgment (1 Cor 4:4-5; 2 Cor 5:10). But it is also possible that, in the present instance, "Lord" refers to God himself (e.g., Richard 1995, 204; Holtz 1998, 164; Malherbe 2000, 233). If so, Paul would be echoing statements about the vengeance of the Lord in the Jewish scriptures (e.g., Ps 94[LXX 93]:1; Sir 5:3; cf. Josephus, *J. W.* 5.377), including Deut 32:35, which he quotes in Rom 12:19. In either case, he notes that the Thessalonians have heard him warn about God's vengeance before, presumably in the context of his missionary preaching.

A more fundamental and characteristically Pauline warrant is offered in v. 7. Here the apostle joins his present theme of sanctification/holiness (*hagiasmos*, vv. 3a, 4) with that of election and calling (1:4; 2:12; 5:9, 24): God has not called believers "to impurity" (*epi akatharsia*) but "in holiness" (*en hagiasmō*). With this, sanctification is identified as both the aim and the consequence of God's call (Schrage 1989, 225). To be called is to be set apart— thus, *already* "sanctified"—for the continuing service of God. Underlying both concepts is the belief, rooted in the Jewish scriptures, that God is holy and calls his people to be holy (e.g., Lev 11:44-45; 19:2; 20:7, 26). Perhaps some in the Thessalonian congregation had formerly been associated with the cult of Cabirus, who was revered in their city as "the holiest of all gods" (see Introduction). Whether that is in Paul's mind here (thus vom Brocke 2001, 120) is a possibility, but no more. The apostle's main point is clear: to be called into God's "own kingdom and glory" (2:12) means to be called, even now, into the domain of God's own holiness.

In Romans, where Paul will again contrast "impurity" and "holiness" (sanctification), "impurity" has a quite general reference, being associated with slavery to sin and wickedness (compare Rom 6:19 with Rom 6:13). In the present context, too, the reference is probably quite general, for despite the specific directives in vv. 3b-6a, the concluding, supporting statements in vv. 6b-8 are expressed as broadly as the introductory appeals in vv. 1-3a.

Although the declaration in v. 8a indirectly supports the appeals in vv. 3b-6a, its direct and primary function is to reinforce the affirmation about God's call to holiness (v. 7). Rejecting that call means rejecting not simply the human agents through which it has been communicated, but the God for whom they speak. Some interpreters believe that this reflects Paul's knowledge of a saying of Jesus found in Luke 10:16 par. Matt 10:40 (e.g., Rigaux 1956, 514; Allison 1982, 13, 20; Wenham 1995, 196). It is far more likely, however, that both Paul and the Gospel writers (see also Mark 9:37; John 12:44-45, 48; 13:20) are echoing the principle already present in 1 Sam 8:7 (cf. Exod 16:8), that to reject those whom God has sent is to reject God himself (Best 1972, 169; Tuckett 1990, 163-64).

The apostle's description of God (v. 8b) is an important part of his declaration, and can be adequately represented in English only by paraphrasing: the God who has called believers to holiness is the one "who indeed gives his Spirit—which is to say, the Holy Spirit—to you" (AT). Whereas Paul everywhere else refers straightforwardly either to "the Spirit" (as in 5:19) or the "Holy Spirit" (as in 1:5, 6), in the present case he accentuates the Spirit's holiness, and thereby the divine source of the sanctified life. His reference to God's *giving* (present tense) of the Spirit is noteworthy. On the one hand, it distinguishes this passage from others in which he uses past tense forms, associating the Spirit with the inception of faith (1:5, 6) and baptism (e.g., 2 Cor 1:22; 5:5). On the other hand, whether consciously or not, the apostle has transformed Ezekiel's representations of God's *promise* to give the Spirit (36:26-27; 37:6, 14) into a declaration that the Spirit is already *being given* to the believing community as God's sanctifying power. For Paul, this continuing gift of the Holy Spirit endows that community with an eschatological and charismatic character, and is the source of its life and hope until the Lord's return.

◊ ◊ ◊ ◊

Paul identifies sanctification (holiness) both as God's will and as the aim and consequence of the divine call to which people respond when they accept the gospel. Here, as often in his letters, he has presented the imperative—the truly "honorable" life is one lived in holiness—as inhering in the indicative of God's saving action. The holiness that is to be manifested in their lives is already given in and with the call to be God's people, set apart for his service. Therefore, the holiness to which Paul refers does not consist simply in "the avoidance of all forms of evil and impurity" (thus Betz 1989, 59). Just as he views election as a manifestation of God's love, so, too, he links being strengthened in holiness with abounding in love for one another (see 3:12-13).

Paul's understanding of the Holy Spirit as the present, powerful energy for holiness within the believing community (v. 8) is consistent with his subsequent direction not to "quench the Spirit" or to "despise the words of prophets" through whom the Spirit speaks (5:19, 20). In later letters, he will express his view of the Spirit's presence by describing the community as the "temple" of the Holy Spirit (1 Cor 3:16-17; in 6:19, also believers individually). He will also be more explicit about the Spirit's role in enabling conduct that is in accord with the will of God (esp. Gal 5:16-25; Rom 8:4, 12-17).

One must be cautious in drawing conclusions about Paul's view of marriage on the basis of this passage alone, for that is not his topic here. Three points, however, are reasonably clear. First, he seems to assume that most believers will be married; his advice about marriage amounts to a tacit affirmation of it. If he has yet pondered the advantages of remaining single, of which he will advise the Corinthians (1 Cor 7:7, 32-35), he does not mention them. Second, Paul is insistent that marriages be entered into and continued "in holiness and honor," not with the "passion of desire." This is consistent with 1 Cor 7:2, 9, where he seems to view at least one function of marriage as preventing lapses into sexual immorality. Finally, and more positively, the present appeal for "holiness" shows that Paul regards marriage as entirely compatible with the sanctified life in and to which believers are called. The marriage relationship is by no means excluded, therefore, when he prays that the Lord may strengthen believers in holiness, and enable them to "increase and abound in love for one another and for all" (3:12-13).

Love (4:9-12)

The expression that opens this paragraph ("Now concerning") typically introduces a new topic (cf. 4:13; 5:1), which in this case is *philadelphia* ("love of the brothers and sisters"). Even so, the call to sanctification continues insofar as Paul presumes a close connection between love (*agapē*) and holiness (3:12-13). Acknowledging that the members of the congregation already love one another (vv. 9-10a), he nevertheless urges them to do so all the more (v. 10b), and indicates what that will involve (vv. 11-12).

Here, consistent with the use of domestic imagery elsewhere in the letter, *philadelphia* (v. 9) refers to the love that the members of the family of faith are to have for one another. Thus, in Pauline usage (Rom 12:10 is the only other instance) *philadelphia* is functionally equivalent to *agapē*, the apostle's usual term for love, which appears later in this verse and elsewhere in the letter (1:3; 3:6, 12; 5:8, 13). Although *philadelphia* was also a topic commonly discussed by Hellenistic moralists (e.g., Plutarch, *On Brotherly Love*), there is no indication that the congregation had asked their apostle for such a discourse. It may simply be that he chose to speak of love in order to lay a foundation for the appeal in vv. 10b-11.

Paul's comment that there is no need for him to write about loving one another makes use of a conventional rhetorical strategy intended both to soften and to underscore a subsequent appeal on the specified topic (see also 5:1). The strategy is continued with the claim that believers have already been instructed concerning the matter. The striking expression "taught by God" (*theodidaktoi*, lit. "God-taught") seems to be Paul's own coinage, likely suggested by Isa 54:13 ("All your children shall be taught by the Lord"; cf. Jer 31[LXX 38]:33-34; Witmer 2006). If he has in mind any particular agent of God's instruction about love, it is less likely himself and other preachers of God's word (2:13) than the Holy Spirit (e.g., Aasgaard 2004, 159-60), to which he has just referred (v. 8) and which in subsequent letters he identifies closely with *agapē* (e.g., Rom 5:5; 15:30).

The remark that the Thessalonian believers' love for one another extends to their fellow believers throughout the province (v. 10a) may be compared with Paul's earlier comment that believers elsewhere in Macedonia and in Achaia had heard of this congregation's faith (1:7-8). He did not view these assemblies as isolated enclaves, but as a network of communities bound together by the faith and love they shared.

Acting in love is still the topic when Paul calls on the congregation to do so "more and more" (v. 10b; here and in 5:4, 14, 25, NRSV's "beloved" stands for *adelphoi*, which is more appropriately paraphrased, "brothers and sisters"; see commentary on 1:4). In form and content this appeal echoes his prayer that the Lord might enable love that *abounds* "for one another and for all" (3:12, using the same verb as here and in 4:1). As the apostle makes his appeal more concrete (vv. 11-12), it is evident that he is again calling for a love that overflows the boundaries of the congregation itself, shaping also the conduct of believers toward unbelievers. Three successive phrases specify what such love requires (v. 11).

In the first, the verb rendered by NRSV as "aspire" (*philotimeomai*) may also be translated, "make it [one's] ambition" (as the NRSV has it in Rom 15:20). This expression was often used by Paul's contemporaries to describe the striving of well-off citizens to win honor for themselves through philanthropy and public service (BDAG, 1059 *s.v.*). Paul's choice of the word here is therefore arresting (Malherbe 2000, 246-47), because he urges believers—the majority of them certainly not well-off financially—to "live quietly," and, in the second phrase, to "mind [their] own affairs." These are sometimes interpreted as counsels to avoid involvement in public life (e.g., Hock 1980, 46-47; de Vos 1999, 162, 175), for which the pairing of similar phrases by Dio Cassius (late 2nd–early 3rd cent. C.E.) can be cited as evidence (*Roman History* 60, 27). It is unlikely, however, that any of the artisan members of the Thessalonian congregation would have had sufficient means even to consider entering public service. Paul's subsequent reference to "outsiders" (v. 12) suggests that he is thinking more generally of the everyday conduct of believers in relation to unbelievers. His counsel is not to avoid or minimize one's contacts with outsiders, but to live as a responsible member of society, thereby gaining their respect (v. 12a).

In this context, the "quiet life" is perhaps to be associated with a lofty character, as it is by Philo (*On Abraham* 27). Although minding one's "own affairs" (*ta idia*, see 2 Macc 9:20; 11:26, 29) could refer to one's proper responsibilities before God, it more likely anticipates the following instruction to take responsibility for one's own livelihood ("work with your hands"). Paul had given at least this third instruction before ("as we directed you"), presumably as part of his missionary teaching (cf. 4:2), and he had demonstrated it in his own resolve to be self-supporting (2:9).

From the reference to manual labor one may infer that most of the believers in Thessalonica belonged to the city's working class. May one also infer that some had actually abandoned their life-sustaining occupations and were depending on others (whether believers or unbelievers) to support them (v. 12b)? As part of Paul's missionary instruction, the directive would have been general and precautionary, and this could be the case now as well (cf. Dibelius 1937, 23; Meeks 1983, 64-65): those who have been called into God's kingdom still have responsibilities to fulfill in this world. Most interpreters, however, hold that Paul knows of certain members of the congregation who have in fact given up gainful employment.

Some attribute this situation to a belief that Christ's return was immediately at hand (Marshall 1983, 117), others to a "millenarian radicalism" in the form of a "realized eschatology" that affirmed the day of the Lord was already present (Jewett 1986, 176-78). But had either of these beliefs been the root cause, it is strange that Paul's comments about "the times and the seasons" do not come right after 4:9-12 rather than in 5:1-11, and that even in the latter he does not specifically correct such an error. As it is, questions about the future are nowhere on the horizon in 4:9-12. Even if in 2 Thessalonians the idleness of some is blamed on overcharged eschatological expectations (esp. 3:6-12)—which is by no means certain—interpreting this letter on the basis of that one is problematic, not least because the Pauline authorship of 2 Thessalonians is seriously in question (see Introduction to 2 Thessalonians).

It has also been suggested that some members of the congregation were exploiting the generosity of fellow believers who, out of love, were willing to support them (e.g., Wanamaker 1990, 163). This, however, is purely speculative and doesn't account for why Paul, even in the face of such inactivity, would make it a point to commend the quiet life. A somewhat more plausible suggestion is that the problem was not idleness as such, but that some believers were so caught up in a zeal to evangelize that they were neglecting to care for their own and their families' needs (Barclay 1993, 522-25; Still 1999, 246). Such conduct would have been disruptive of domestic and congregational life, and also at odds with Paul's own practice (2:9). Moreover, it could have prompted unbelievers to make charges of personal irresponsibility not unlike those frequently leveled at Cynics and other philosophers (examples in Malherbe 1987, 99-101; 2000, 250).

Given Paul's understanding that the love that undergirds faith is expansive and inclusive (see commentary on 3:12), it is not surprising to find him gradually broadening his subject in this passage—from relationships within the Thessalonian congregation (v. 9a), to the congregation's relationships with believers throughout Macedonia (v. 10a), and finally to how believers should relate to unbelievers (v. 12a). His identification of the latter as "outsiders" (for this and related terms see Furnish 2002, 107-8) does not mean that he regards them as hopelessly beyond salvation, only that he recognizes important boundary markers by which the believing community is distinguished from the rest of society. Despite the boundaries, however, believers remain in almost constant contact with unbelievers, including members of their households, fellow workers, and friends or acquaintances. It is with this in mind that Paul has given the instructions in v. 11. Significantly, these pertain not just to conduct among believers that unbelievers can observe, but also to how believers should conduct themselves "*toward*" unbelievers (v. 12a). The apostle may hope that exemplary conduct will spare his congregation the suffering that some outsiders have caused it (1:6; 2:2, 14). There is, however, no indication that he is thinking of how such conduct, by engendering the goodwill of unbelievers, might make them more open to accepting the gospel (contrast 1 Cor 10:31–11:1, where an evangelistic motive is explicit).

◊ ◊ ◊ ◊

This passage documents the beginning of what would come to be called, centuries later, a "Christian social ethic." The apostle does not interpret God's call to holiness as a call to withdraw from society or to abandon one's ordinary tasks. So long as this age remains, believers are to conduct themselves as responsible members of society.

Recognizing that this will mean continuing, daily contacts with people who are indifferent, if not outright hostile, to the gospel that believers profess, Paul stipulates that the love that is normative for their life together should be the norm, as well, for their relationships with unbelievers. Here one sees the same expansive vision of love's scope that is evident in the appeals of 3:12 and 5:15. For Paul, any specific benefits that may accrue to believers when they "behave properly toward outsiders" are but incidental to the fundamental aim of his appeal, which is that they "please God" (v. 1) by serving as faithful agents of God's love in the world.

In this context, then, the content of "proper" behavior is to be understood with reference to the gift and claim of the gospel, not with reference to the prevailing norms and expectations of society at large. At the same time, however, and despite the sharp distinction he makes between the morality of believers and unbelievers (e.g., v. 5), the apostle is presupposing a certain measure of overlap between the norms of pagan society and the ethos that is engendered by the gospel (cf. Malherbe 2000, 260). This amounts to an implicit acknowledgment of the "moral significance of the public realm," and implies that it is both necessary and legitimate for believers to participate in "a public moral discourse" (Bockmuehl 2000, 135; cf. Furnish 2005).

Those Who Have Fallen Asleep (4:13-18)

This new topic, which has no apparent connection with the two that precede, is introduced as a matter on which the congregation needs to be enlightened ("we do not want you to be uninformed," v. 13). Taking as his starting point a creedal statement that he knows his audience affirms ("since we believe," v. 14a), the apostle posits a link between the destiny of those who have died before the Lord's return and Jesus' own death and resurrection (v. 14b). After elucidating this on the basis of a "word of the Lord" (vv. 15-17), he concludes with a pastoral appeal (v. 18).

◊   ◊   ◊   ◊

An Expression of Concern (v. 13): Translated literally, Paul's subject is "those who have fallen asleep" (vv. 13, 14b), a euphemism widely used in his day for "the dead" (v. 16). He is responding either to a report that the congregation is consumed with grieving for those who have not survived to experience the Lord's return, or to a specific question put to him about this by the congregation itself. In either case, the likely informant was Timothy. There was no need for the apostle to mention who or how many had died, for these matters were well known to his audience. He has also said nothing that would connect these deaths with the persecution of the church in Thessalonica, although numerous interpreters have suggested such a possibility.

The aim of Paul's instruction about the destiny of the deceased is to console those who grieve for them (cf. v. 18). Insofar as the reason for his congregation's grief can be determined, it must be inferred from what he says about the specific content of the hope that he offers (vv. 14-17). His reference to "others . . . who have no hope" is to unbelievers—whether Jewish or pagan, and whatever their own particular expectations about life after death—who do not share the specific hope that is grounded and realized in Christ

(v. 14a; cf. 1:3, 10; 5:9-10). Nonetheless, some of the formal conventions of Hellenistic letters of consolation are evident in Paul's own words to his grieving congregation (such letters survive from Seneca, Plutarch, and others; Stowers 1986, 142-51).

Jesus and the Dead (v. 14): While the "we" in v. 13 (and again in v. 15a) is authorial (= Paul), the "we" in v. 14a includes all who can affirm "that Jesus died and rose again." This has the ring of a traditional declaration of faith. (a) "We believe" marks what follows as a confessional statement. (b) The verb that is used here (and in v. 16) for rising from the dead (*anistēmi*) occurs nowhere else in Paul's letters except in quotations from Scripture (Rom 15:12; 1 Cor 10:7); the apostle himself employs a different verb (*egeirō*). (c) In all other references to Christ's resurrection, Paul indicates that it was the action of God (mostly by using the passive voice, "was raised," e.g., 1:10). (d) Paul himself seldom refers simply to "Jesus" when referring to Christ's role in salvation (elsewhere, 1:10; Rom 8:11; 2 Cor 4:14).

Unlike most other Pauline declarations about Christ's death and resurrection, the one in v. 14a does not in itself specify the soteriological significance of the event (contrast, e.g., 1:10, "rescues us"; 5:10, "for us"). This happens, instead, in the inference that Paul draws from the tradition (v. 14b). Although the construction of the sentence ("For since ... even so") points toward something like "even so, those who have died will rise again," the apostle does not refer explicitly to the resurrection of the dead. He focuses, rather, on God's bringing the dead to be with Jesus ("with him," v. 14b), elaborating on this in vv. 15-17. As he proceeds, however, it becomes clear that the verb "bring" (v. 14b) presupposes not only the Lord's return (*parousia*; see 2:19) but also the resurrection of the dead and their being taken up to meet the Lord as he descends from heaven (vv. 16-17; Becker 1993, 142-43).

The phrase "through Jesus" (v. 14b) goes either with "will bring," designating the agent through whom God acts (e.g., NRSV), or with "those who have died," identifying the deceased as belonging to Jesus (e.g., REB, "those who died as Christians"). If the latter, then the phrase would be equivalent to "in Christ" in v. 16. If the former, which is more likely, then it functions like a similar phrase in 1 Cor 15:51 (cf. 15:57; 1 Thess 5:9), where Paul also identifies Christ as the one through whom God will raise the dead.

The Lord's Return (vv. 15-17): Paul apparently believes that the Lord will return in the near future, for he speaks as if he and most believers will still be alive on that day (note "we who are alive," v. 15; cf. v. 17). This expectation, which was certainly shared by his Thessalonian converts, makes it all the more imperative that he address the fate of those who have died. Accordingly, he now elaborates on his general assurance (v. 14b) that, by reason of Jesus' own death and resurrection, the dead will not miss out on being "with him" when he returns. Paul explains that "first" of all "the dead in Christ will rise" (v. 16), and "then" those who are still alive "will be caught up ... together with them to meet the Lord" (v. 17a). He then recasts his original assurance into a claim about the destiny of all believers: "we will always be with the Lord" (v. 17b, AT; repeated and further amplified in 5:10).

Given this emphasis, it is apparent why the Thessalonian believers were so distraught about those of their number who had died (v. 13). Either they had failed to understand or the apostle had not previously specified that, because the resurrection will be the "first" of the end-time events, those who have died as well as those who survive will be gathered up to be with the Lord (a similar issue is similarly answered in *4 Ezra* 5:41-45). Indeed, Paul's emphatic claim that "we who are alive . . . will by no means precede those who have died" (v. 15b) seems aimed at countering a viewpoint that was current among the Thessalonian believers (Malherbe 2000, 272-73). His new instruction, then, is not that the dead will be raised (contrast Marxsen 1979, 65; Nicholl 2004, 35-38), but that the dead will be raised *first*, and will therefore be at no disadvantage in comparison with the living.

Paul expects three main events on that day (vv. 16-17a), each of which has at least partial parallels in Jewish apocalyptic traditions. First, the Lord will leave heaven and descend toward the earth (e.g., Dan 7:13, the descent of the Son of man; cf. *1 En.* 1;

Mark 13:26; 14:26 and parr.). The wait for God's Son "from heaven" (1:10) will then be over. Second, believers who have died ("the dead in Christ") will be resurrected (cf. Dan 12:1-3; *1 En.* 51; *4 Ezra* 7:26-32; *2 Bar.* 30:1-3; 50:2-3). Third, the resurrected and those who have not died will "together" be taken up to be with the Lord (cf. *1 En.* 39:6-8; 62:13-14; 71:16-17; *4 Ezra* 14:9).

Several details accentuate the divine power manifested in these events by giving them a military aspect (v. 16). Although less is spelled out than in the typical Jewish end-time scenario, here, too, God is envisioned as invading history and achieving the ultimate victory over evil. The shouted "command," the "call" of an archangel, and the blast from "God's trumpet" will announce these final events and set them in motion. Whether the command is to be issued by God or the returning Lord (v. 16) is not indicated. The unnamed archangel (Michael? cf. Dan 10:13; Jude 9) is presumably in charge of a retinue of angels (or "holy ones") who will accompany the Lord (cf. Deut 33:2-3; *1 En.* 1:9; 54:6; 60:1-2, etc.). Paul himself has referred to such in 3:13. The blowing of the trumpet (often said to be by angels, e.g., *Apoc. Zeph.* 9, 10, 12; Rev 8:13, etc.) will signal that the eschatological events are actually commencing (e.g., Isa 27:13; Zeph 1:15-16; *Apoc. Zeph.* 9:1-2; *4 Ezra* 6:23; 1 Cor 15:52; Matt 24:31).

Elements of the Jewish apocalyptic tradition are also evident in the reference to believers being "caught up in the clouds...to meet the Lord in the air" (v. 17a). The notion of a "rapture" to heaven of certain righteous individuals is found in various Jewish texts, both canonical and noncanonical (e.g., of Enoch: Gen 5:24; Wis 4:11; *1 En.* 71:1, 5, 14-17; *2 En.* 67:2 [A]; of Ezra: *4 Ezra* 14:9), and clouds are associated both with divine appearances (e.g., Exod 19:16; Ezek 10:3-4) and travel between heaven and earth (note esp. the descent of the Son of man, Dan 7:13; Mark 13:26 and parr., and the ascent to heaven of two faithful witnesses, Rev 11:12). According to the present scenario, however, the meeting with the Lord is to take place "in the air," the region which, according to ancient cosmology, is just above the earth (*2 En.* 29:4, 5).

What will happen to believers after they are gathered to the

Lord is not specified. Is it presumed that they will accompany him as he continues his descent to earth? Some interpreters think so, noting that the Greek word for "meeting" (*apantēsis*) was sometimes used for the formal reception by municipal officials of a visiting dignitary, who would then be ceremonially escorted into the city (e.g., Marshall 1983, 124-25; Turner 2003, 331). Or is it presumed that the believers, who have already been "caught up" from the earth, will subsequently be taken clear up to heaven by their Lord (e.g., Plevnik 1997, 65-98; 2000)? If this question held any interest for Paul, it is not evident here (Best 1972, 199-200; Malherbe 2000, 277-78). The one critical point is that believers will always be with the Lord.

Paul's claim that he is speaking "by the word of the Lord" (*en logō kyriou*, v. 15a; cf. REB, "This we tell you as a word from the Lord") is variously understood. One view is that it introduces what follows as incorporating the content, even if not the actual wording, of a saying of Jesus about the end-time. Some hold that Matt 24:30-31, especially, is evidence that such a saying was in circulation (e.g., Marshall 1983, 126; Wanamaker 1990, 171). Yet Paul's main point, that those who have died will share with the living in always being with the Lord, is found neither there nor in other alleged parallels in the Gospels (e.g., Matt 20:16; John 6:39-40; 11:25-26). An alternative suggestion, that Paul knew "a saying of Jesus unrecorded in the Gospels" (e.g., Morris 1991, 140-41; Holtz 1991, 385; 1998, 183-84), is little more than speculation, and therefore unverifiable (Malherbe 2000, 267).

The apostle's claim is best read against the background of several LXX passages where the exact expression he employs (which may also be translated "by word of the Lord") designates that what is said should be received as prophetic speech authorized by the Lord (e.g., 3 Kgdms [1 Kgs] 13:1-2, 5, 32; 21:35; 2 Chr 30:12; see esp. Hofius 1991, 338-40). This would mean that Paul is introducing his instruction either as a saying from the Christian prophetic tradition (e.g., Best 1972, 189-93; R. F. Collins 1980b, 159-60; Tuckett 1990, 176-82) or as his own prophetic word (e.g., von Dobschütz 1909, 193-94; Neirynck 1986, 311; Plevnik

1997, 81, 94). The latter is perhaps more likely, for Paul not only commends Christian prophets (e.g., 5:20) but sometimes speaks as one (1 Cor 15:51-52; cf. 1 Cor 14:37). In either case, he is claiming the Lord's authority for what he conveys.

For what in particular does Paul claim this authority? Some suggest that it is the end-time scenario presented in vv. 16-17, or at least in vv. 16-17a. Others take it to be the affirmation in v. 15b that those who remain alive until the end will have no advantage over those who have died. The latter is more likely, both because the status of the dead in relation to the living is exactly the point at issue, and because the statement about this comes immediately after Paul's reference to the "word of the Lord." It is possible, however, that he is introducing everything in vv. 15b-17 as spoken with the Lord's authority.

Pastoral Appeal (v. 18): The pastoral intent of the preceding instruction is evident as Paul directs the members of the congregation to "encourage one another with these words" (see also 5:11). By "these words" he probably means not only his assurances about the destiny of those who have died (vv. 14b, 15b, 17b) but also the creedal affirmation on which those are based (v. 14a) and his explanation of how the eschatological events will unfold (vv. 16-17a). Such encouragement necessarily carries with it a claim to believe what is said, for only then does it assuage grief and dispel hopelessness (Holtz 1998, 205).

◊　◊　◊　◊

For the Thessalonian congregation, the decisive point in this paragraph would have been the apostle's assurance that believers who die before the Lord's return will be at no disadvantage. Because they will be resurrected in time to be with the Lord, their salvation is not in doubt. Although Paul himself has not spoken of "salvation" here, he does use the word a bit later when he reformulates the present assurance as a statement about God's saving purpose: "God has destined us not for wrath but for obtaining salvation through our Lord Jesus Christ, who died for us, so that whether we are awake or asleep we may live with him" (5:9-10). In accord with earlier statements (1:10; 4:14a), but now more directly, Jesus' death-resurrection is identified as the event from which the "hope of salvation" (5:8) derives and through which it will be fulfilled.

While the declaration in 1:10 about rescue from the coming wrath (cf. 5:9) accentuates the "negative" aspect of Jesus' saving work, the emphasis in 4:14-17 (and again in 5:9-10) is on its positive aspect, namely, being always with the Lord. Paul says nothing about the character of this relationship, but he may well suppose that it will be realized in the context of "[God's] own kingdom and glory," into which believers are called (2:12). In several later letters he holds that inheriting this kingdom (1 Cor 15:40) and sharing in Christ's resurrection life (Phil 3:10-11; Rom 6:5-10) will involve the transformation of one's body into a new "spiritual" ("glorious") reality (e.g., 1 Cor 15:43-44, 51-54; Phil 3:21; 2 Cor 4:16-18; Rom 8:30). This idea, however, does not surface in 1 Thessalonians, even if Paul has already espoused it (contrast Plevnik 1997, 88; 1999, 544-45, who finds it implied in 4:17).

It is futile to query this passage on issues that Paul has not addressed. For example, he does not comment on the destiny of unbelievers, an issue that was not before him. He is silent even on the subject of a last judgment, despite several apparent allusions to such earlier in the letter (1:10; 3:13; cf. 2:16, 19). Other matters, too, are left open. What sort of existence did he conceive for the dead as they awaited resurrection? Did he expect the *parousia* to usher in an earthly reign of Christ, and if so, of what duration? Although comments in certain of his later letters bear on some of these matters, it is possible that he had not even reflected on such questions as early as the writing of 1 Thessalonians. What he offers here is not a comprehensive depiction of the end-time events, but pastoral instruction and assurance on one particular issue that was troubling his congregation.

The Times and the Seasons (5:1-11)

As in 4:9, Paul's phrasing ("Now concerning," v. 1) suggests that he is turning to a new topic, yet the question about the date of the Lord's return ("the times and the seasons") follows logically from what he has just said about the end-time events. Nothing requires one to suppose, however, that he is responding to another special issue or specific question that has arisen within the congregation. An introduction (vv. 1-2) is followed by a warning and an assurance (vv. 3-5), which are but preliminary to the exhortations in vv. 6-8. The exhortations are then supported by a theological affirmation (vv. 9-10), which in part recapitulates statements in 4:14, 17. Finally, a pastoral appeal (v. 11) echoes the one in 4:18, and along with the theological affirmation provides an appropriate conclusion, not only for this paragraph but for the whole of 4:13–5:11. There has been little support for the view that vv. 1-11 were added by a later writer who sought to correct any impression that 4:13-17 might leave of an imminent *parousia* (see Introduction).

Introduction of the Topic (vv. 1-2): Jewish apocalyptic eschatology generally held that God's plan of salvation would be unfolded according to a series of divinely appointed periods, each accompanied with appropriate signs (e.g., Dan 9:24-27; *4 Ezra* 4:33-52; *2 Bar.* 25-30). But even as Paul introduces this topic ("the times and the seasons" echoes the tradition, e.g., Dan 2:21; Wis 8:8; cf. Acts 1:7), he dismisses it as a subject about which his converts need no instruction (v. 1; cf. 4:9). They can understand that such speculation is useless, because they "know very well" (from his missionary preaching) that the Lord's appearance will be as sudden and unexpected as the coming of a thief at night (v. 2). This image, which does not appear in Jewish apocalyptic sources, was likely known to Paul from the Jesus tradition that lies behind the parable in Matt 24:43-44 par. Luke 12:39-40. There, too, it is emphasized that Jesus (the "Son of Man") will return "at an unexpected hour," like a thief in the night (cf. Rev 3:3; 16:15; 2 Pet 3:10).

In the present context, the phrase "day of the Lord" refers to the return of Christ and is thus equivalent to "the day of the Lord Jesus Christ" in 1 Cor 1:8 and similar expressions elsewhere in Paul's letters. The shorter phrase derives from Israel's prophets, who used it for the eschatological day when God will visit the earth with judgment and retribution (e.g., Isa 13:6, 9; 58:13; Jer 46:10; Amos 5:18, 20). This background is evident when Paul warns that those who are not vigilant will be unable to escape the coming destruction (v. 3).

Warning and Assurance (vv. 3-5): Some interpreters regard the cited claim about "peace and security" (v. 3a) as formulated by Paul on the basis of prophetic reproaches of people who cry "'Peace, peace,' when there is no peace" (Jer 6:14; cf. 8:11; Ezek 13:10, 16). If so, his warning (v. 3b) could have been prompted by issues within the believing community itself, perhaps by the unfounded speculations and assurances of certain Christian prophets (Malherbe 2000, 287, 291, 302). It is more likely, however, that Paul is quoting the Roman imperial slogan *pax et securitas* (e.g., *Pss. Sol.* 18:8; Josephus, *Ant.* 160, 247), which heralded the political and social stability that had been achieved and would be fulfilled through Roman rule (Bammel 1984, 375-79). There is good evidence that this slogan reflects the political ideology of the imperial cult in Thessalonica, which accorded lavish honors to Rome and Caesar (Hendrix 1991, 112-18; vom Brocke 2001, 167-85; Harrison 2002, esp. 86-87). Paul foresees ultimate destruction for those who, living in the darkness of unbelief, place their trust in the political might of Rome rather than in the saving power of God (v. 3b; Oakes 2005, 317-18). As formulated here, this warning echoes traditional apocalyptic motifs, including comparisons between the distress that will come to the unfaithful and the pain of a woman giving birth (Isa 13:6-9; *1 En.* 62:1-5; *4 Ezra* 4:38-43). Although some, citing Luke 21:34-36, believe that the warning derives from Jesus' own teaching (e.g., Wenham 1995, 314-16, 334-37), the evidence for this is not strong (Tuckett 1990, 173-76).

The assurances in vv. 4-5a exempt Paul's congregation from the preceding warning, and simultaneously lay a foundation for the exhortations that will follow in vv. 6-8. On the one hand, and unlike those who live in "darkness," believers are already "of light" and "the day" (i.e., of Christ), and will not be surprised or endangered by the Lord's return. On the other hand, precisely because they do not live in the darkness of unbelief, they are required to "keep awake and be sober" (v. 6). The images of "light" and "darkness" derive from the Jewish scriptures, where they are often employed, respectively, for what is and is not of God (e.g., Job 22:9-11; 29:3; Pss 18:28; 56:13; 74:20; 82:5; Isa. 2:5; 5:20; 30:26; 60:19-20). The expression "children [lit. "sons"] of light" is found also in the Dead Sea Scrolls (e.g., 1QS I, 9; II, 16; III, 13, 25; 1QM I, 1, 3, 9, 11, 13, 14), where it distinguishes those faithful to God from the unfaithful "sons of darkness" (e.g., 1QS I, 10; 1QM I, 1, 7, 10, 16), a phrase that does not appear in the NT. Believers are also identified as "sons of light" in Luke 16:8 (contrasted with "sons of this age") and John 12:26; and in Eph 5:8 they are called "children of light." Paul's further identification of believers as "children [lit. "sons"] of the day," perhaps his own coinage, joins the imagery of light to the concept of the coming day of the Lord, and points to the eschatological character of their present existence. The apostle employs similar imagery in Rom 13:11-14, where he bases his appeals on the imminence of the "day" of salvation. Here, however, his appeals follow from what he affirms about the believers' own present identity (Malherbe 2000, 294). In restating this (v. 5b), he shifts from the second to the first person plural (through v. 10), employing an ecclesial "we" that includes all believers (as in 4:14).

Exhortations (vv. 6-8): The apostle's call for wakefulness and sobriety (v. 6b) accords with his warning about the fate of those who speak complacently of "peace and security." While unbelievers (the "others"; cf. 4:13) continue to be heedless of what the future holds (vv. 6a, 7), those who "belong to the day" (v. 8) are to understand that they must stay awake and be sober (v. 6b). In v. 6b, the terms "awake" and "sober" are employed figuratively, the first for being attentive to what the time and circumstances require, the second for conduct that is reasonable and self-restrained (e.g., 1 Pet 1:13). This usage seems to have been at home in the church's eschatological traditions known to Paul (the terms are similarly paired in 1 Pet 5:8; one or the other is also used figuratively in Matt 24:42 par. Mark 13:35; 1 Pet 4:7; Rev

3:2-3). It is possible that the mention of those who get drunk in the literal sense (v. 7) is intended as an allusion to the drunken celebrations of the Dionysiac cult, which was especially prominent in Thessalonica (vom Brocke 2001, 128-29).

The general appeal (v. 6) takes a more specific form as Paul summons the Thessalonian believers to faith, love, and hope (v. 8). His use of this triadic formulation both at the beginning of the letter (1:3) and here toward the end seems deliberate, for it corresponds to the prominence of these three themes in the letter as a whole (faith, to believe: 1:3, 8; 3:2, 5, 6, 7, 10; 4:14; 5:8; love, to love or be loved: 1:3, 4; 2:8; 3:6, 12; 4:9; 5:8, 13; hope: 1:3; 2:19; 4:13; 5:8). Moreover, Paul has formulated this appeal in a way that highlights its fundamental character and importance, drawing on imagery found in Isa 59:17-19. The prophet portrays God as preparing for battle against iniquity and injustice by putting on the breastplate of "righteousness" and the helmet of "salvation." The apostle now adapts that imagery to the situation of believers, identifying "faith and love" as the "breastplate" and the "hope of salvation" as the "helmet" with which they must be equipped.

Instead of adding some third piece of equipment, the apostle identifies both faith and love with the breastplate, which allows him to identify hope alone with the helmet. This move, along with the altered syntax, "*for a helmet,* hope . . ." (Malherbe 2000, 298), and the fact that hope is mentioned last, gives hope a prominence that is in keeping with the context. Moreover, the consequent coupling of faith and love, whether deliberate or not, is typically Pauline (e.g., 3:6; Phlm 5; cf. 1 Cor 13:2) and in keeping with the apostle's view that faith and love are vitally related (Gal 5:6).

There is no significance in Paul's association of faith and love with the body's torso and hope with the head; he has simply correlated the sequence in his triad with the sequence in Isaiah's doublet, "breastplate . . . helmet." In contrast to Wis 5:17-20, which adds a shield and a sword to Isaiah's portrayal of the Divine Warrior, and Eph 6:14-17, which outfits the Christian soldier in full battle regalia, Paul is restrained in his use of the imagery, mentioning only the two most critical pieces of defensive armor. His focus remains on faith, love, and hope, through which the eschatological character of Christian existence is actualized already in the present, as believers await the Lord's return.

Theological Affirmation (vv. 9-10): The affirmation in vv. 9-10 provides a fundamental theological warrant for the preceding appeals, indicating why believers have been graced and claimed by faith, love, and hope. Here the theme of divine election, which underlies the whole letter, comes to the surface yet again (see also 1:4; 2:12; 4:7; 5:24). Now it is combined with a statement about the saving significance of Christ's death that probably echoes church traditions: God has not destined believers for destruction ("wrath," as in 1:10; 2:16; cf. "destruction," v. 3), but for the "salvation" that is mediated through Christ "who died for us" (vv. 9-10a; cf. esp. Rom 5:8). The translation "for *obtaining* salvation" is disputed by some, who argue that the Greek (*eis peripoiēsen sōtērias*) should be rendered "for the possession of salvation" (e.g., Rigaux 1956, 570-71; Holtz 1998, 228-29). But even if the former is correct, as most interpreters hold, it is clear that Paul views salvation as God's doing (note "destined us" and "through our Lord Jesus Christ..."), not the result of human striving (correctly, Gundry Volf 1991, 24-26).

In accord with his assurance that all believers can hope to be "with the Lord forever" (4:17b), Paul now describes salvation as *living* "with him" (v. 10). In this context, the aorist (past tense) verb (*zēsōmen*) has a future meaning: "that...we may *come* to live" with Christ, who has been raised from the dead (1:10; 4:14a). A few interpreters have argued that "awake" and "asleep" are metaphors for being, respectively, vigilant and negligent (e.g., Heil 2000), noting that the word for "asleep" is the same one Paul has used figuratively for inattentiveness (v. 6), not the one he has used as a euphemism for death (4:13, 15). On this interpretation, he would be referring to two contrasting types of conduct during the interim before the Lord's return. It is more likely, however, that the apostle is once again (despite the change of one term) speaking figuratively of the living and the dead. He is thus reaffirming his earlier assurance (4:13-17) that all believers will "together" (a word repeated in 5:10b from 4:17 but omitted by NRSV) be granted life with their Lord at his coming (cf. Rom 14:8).

Pastoral Appeal (v. 11): As in 4:18, Paul urges the members of his congregation to mutual encouragement, but now he enlarges the scope of the appeal by calling on them, as well, to "build up each other." In the earlier formulation, he summons them to use his words (in 4:13-17) to console one another about those who have died. Now, however, the task of encouragement includes whatever will benefit one's fellow believers. Paul uses the metaphor of "building up" frequently in later letters, and—in keeping with its scriptural use for God's building up of Israel (e.g., Jer 24:6; 42[LXX 49]:10)—always with an ecclesiological reference (e.g., 1 Cor 14:3-5; 2 Cor 10:8; 12:19; Rom 15:10). The same is true of the present appeal. While the phrase "each other" (*heis ton hena*) suggests that upbuilding will involve "one on one" relationships, Paul clearly views those relationships as nourished by the faith, love, and hope that the individuals share as members of a believing community (cf. Malherbe 2000, 301, 307).

◊ ◊ ◊ ◊

The questions Paul raises at the beginning of this paragraph follow from his preceding instruction. When will the Lord return and, by implication, what is yet to transpire before that occurs? But having introduced these questions he offers no answers, in effect dismissing the questions as unimportant. Rather, following the warning about succumbing to a false sense of security and the assurance that believers will not be caught off guard, he shifts attention to the status that believers already have, and to what is required of them in the present.

As Paul states it here, believers are "children of light and children of the day" (v. 5a) by reason of their divine election to the salvation that is mediated through Christ's death (vv. 9-10). Neither here nor elsewhere in the letter does he imply that election leads necessarily to salvation, or that there is a category of the "non-elect" from whom salvation will be withheld. He understands election to be an expression of God's love and saving purpose (1:4), which therefore does not operate coercively, but has the character of an invitation (cf. Richard 1995, 255). It is a "call" (2:12; 4:7; 5:24) that may or may not be accepted (note 1:6; 2:13), and that, after being accepted, is to be constantly reaffirmed in one's life (hence the exhortations in chaps. 4–5).

The declaration about Christ's death echoes in part the earlier one about his death and resurrection (4:14). Taken together, these two statements frame the whole of 4:13–5:11. It is not Paul's teaching about the end-time but his proclamation of God's acting in Christ for the world's salvation that represents the heart of his gospel and the basis for his appeals. His expectations about what God will do in the future are secondary to his conviction about who believers already are because of God's electing love and Christ's saving death. The declaration that Christ "died for us" (v. 10) attributes soteriological significance to that death, without, however, specifying *how* it brings salvation. If "for us" echoes Jesus' statement of self-giving, which Paul knew from the church's eucharistic tradition ("for you," 1 Cor 11:24; cf. Luke 22:19, 20), then he could be thinking of Christ's death as a sacrificial act of atonement for humanity's sins (esp. Gal 1:4; 1 Cor 15:3; 1 Cor 5:7b; Rom 3:25). The idea that Christ died *in place* of sinners (the "substitutionary" view of his death) seems to be ruled out, however, by the statement that Christ died "so that...we may live *with* him" (Hooker 1994, 28-29).

For Paul, the saving event of Christ's death (and resurrection) both graces believers with a new identity and endows the present with a significance that it does not have in traditional apocalyptic eschatology. As beneficiaries of Christ's death, believers are no longer enveloped by the darkness of this age, but have been empowered to live already as "children of light" who "belong to the day." In Paul's thought, therefore, the division between present and future that is typical of the apocalyptic worldview has broken down. Believers have been called not merely to prepare for a future salvation, but to allow the salvation that is bestowed in Christ to manifest itself already in their present lives as faith, love, and hope.

Counsels about the Congregation's Life (5:12-22)

The verb of entreaty that opens v. 12 (in Gk., the same as the first verb in 4:1) signals the beginning of a new series of counsels, all of which are stated more summarily than those in 4:1–5:11. These may be viewed as indicating what the instruction to "build up one another" entails (Malherbe 2000, 309). Although most are general and traditional (there are striking parallels in Rom 12:9-13), Paul has probably selected and, to some extent, tailored them to fit the situation of the Thessalonian congregation. A second verb of entreaty (in Gk., the same as the second verb in 4:1) makes the counsel in v. 14 formally distinct from those in vv. 12-13, and also from the uniquely formed directive in v. 15. The three appeals in vv. 16-18 exhibit a parallelism that sets them off both from what precedes and from what follows. This passage is thus formally divisible into five subunits.

Respect Those Who Provide Leadership (5:12-13)

First, Paul urges respect for those members who have emerged as congregational leaders. He refers initially to their "labor," using a term that is broad enough to include everything that they do for the congregation's well-being. Somewhat more specifically, he identifies them as those who "have charge of you in the Lord," which may also be translated "watch over you in the Lord" (AT). Here, "in the Lord" defines both the sphere within which and the norm according to which this function is performed. In a subsequent letter, Paul will include this activity among the "gifts" (*charismata*) that God distributes to the members of Christ's body (Rom 12:8; NRSV: "the leader"), but such terminology is not present in 1 Thessalonians. The verb employed for this function, both here and in Romans (*proistēmi*), need not mean to control or exercise authority over, but can also mean to "manage," "care for," "be protective of" (examples in BDAG, 870 *s.v.*, §2). It is possible that Paul is thinking of the congregation's patrons—for example, Jason, in whose house it reportedly assembled (Acts 17:5-9; cf. Phoebe, the "benefactor" [*prostatis*] of the church in Cenchreae, Rom 16:2). Yet the leaders who "admonish" their fellow believers, whom he goes on to mention specifically, also functioned as guardians of the community by urging its members to avoid improper behavior and guiding them into conduct appropriate to the gospel (see also v. 14).

Paul's request that the congregation be respectful of those who are leaders in these ways is not framed as a call to show deference to them, or to be subject to their authority. There is no indication that they have been specifically appointed to these tasks by Paul or anyone else, or that they hold any office or have special authority within the congregation. It is the service they render that has made them leaders and worthy of respect: "Esteem them very highly in love *because of their work*" (v. 13a). The adverbial phrase "in love" links the esteem for which the apostle now calls to his earlier counsels about loving one another (3:12; 4:9-10).

The counsel in v. 13b to "be at peace among yourselves" is grammatically independent of those in vv. 12-13a. It thus reinforces what "among yourselves" indicates, that the subject is not specifically being at peace with the leaders but being at peace with all members of the congregation (unlike v. 15, relationships with outsiders are not addressed here). Had Paul known of some special reason why his converts needed this counsel, he would probably have expressed it less generally. As it is, such appeals are frequent in the Jewish and early Christian ethical traditions (e.g., *m. 'Abot* 1:12; Matt 5:9; Mark 9:50; Heb 12:14; 1 Pet 3:11, which echoes Ps 34:14 [LXX 33:15]), and are echoed by Paul in Rom 12:18; 14:19; 2 Cor 13:11 as well as here. There is nothing distinctive enough about these Pauline formulations to support the view of some (e.g., Allison 1982, 14, 20; and Wenham 1995, 260, who refer esp. to Mark 9:50) that the apostle is drawing on a saying of Jesus (correctly, Tuckett 1990, 164).

Contribute to the Well-Being of Others (5:14)

A new verb of entreaty (note the identical introductory formula in 4:10b) distinguishes this counsel from those preceding, although the repetition from v. 12 of the direct address, *adelphoi* ("brothers and sisters"; in v. 14, NRSV renders this as "beloved"), shows that Paul continues to speak to the congregation as a whole. He now calls on its members to contribute to the well-being of their fellow believers, asking specifically that they deal constructively with the "unruly" (AT), the "fainthearted," and "the weak."

The meaning and reference of the first of these terms is disputed. Some translate the expression (*tous ataktous*) as "idlers" (NRSV), citing 2 Thess 3:6-11, where cognate terms are used of believers who have abandoned working for their own living, and also 4:11-12 in the present letter, where Paul urges that believers work to support themselves (cf. 2:9). If this is correct, it is possible that the idleness resulted from a distorted sense of how the imminent return of Christ impinged on one's present life. But this interpretation is no less problematic than the Pauline authorship of 2 Thessalonians on which it heavily relies. In the present context, and given the basic and usual meaning of the term that Paul uses (Spicq 1994, 1.223-26; Ascough 2003, 177-83), it is more likely that he is referring to those who, for whatever reasons and in whatever sense, are "out of line" and disruptive of congregational life. (Donfried 2000b, comparing Qumran usage, seeks to specify their disorderliness with more precision.)

Paul's reference to the "fainthearted" is also quite general. These would include believers who have become discouraged or disconsolate. It is unlikely that he is thinking again of those who grieve, because he has already addressed their situation (4:13-18), or of those who have been disheartened by his own afflictions, because Timothy's ministry to them has been successful (3:1-9). Similarly, there is no indication why the "weak" are so described. Nothing requires a specific reference to believers who are "weak in faith" (Rom 14:1) because they are not yet fully liberated from their prior religious beliefs (1 Cor 8:7-12). Here, as in 1 Cor 9:22 and 11:29, the apostle is probably using the term quite broadly, to include weakness of any kind.

Paul's intent is not primarily to identify needs within the assembly but to indicate that members should care for one another. Admonition is a responsibility not just of its leaders (v. 12) but of everyone. Encouragement is mentioned now for the third time as a congregational responsibility (the Gk. term for this in 4:18 and

5:11 is different, but synonymous with the one used here), and the appeal to "help" the weak employs a verb that connotes a proactive reaching out to uphold and support them.

This series of appeals is closed with a comprehensive call to "be patient with all." NRSV's addition, "of them," interprets Paul as referring particularly to those who need admonition, encouragement, and assistance, but in the context of vv. 12-14, "all" is better understood as "all members of the congregation." In the Jewish scriptures, where patience is attributed primarily to God, it is associated with slowness to anger, mercy, and kindness (e.g., Exod 34:6; Neh 9:17; Wis 15:1). This scriptural background is evident when Paul refers to God's patience (Rom 2:4; 9:22-23), and also when he identifies the patience that is required in the human sphere as an expression of love (1 Cor 13:4, "love is patient, love is kind") and a fruit of the Spirit (along with "love, joy, peace . . . , kindness, generosity," etc.; Gal 5:22). The patience he enjoins is to be expressed not just as forbearance, but as active goodwill toward all the members of the congregation.

Strive Mightily to Do Good (5:15)

This twofold counsel about nonretaliation (v. 15a) and doing good (v. 15b) follows with a certain logic after the preceding appeals to live in peace and be patient with all (vv. 13b, 14). The warning about retaliation is formulated more generally than any other counsel in this section ("See to it that *no one* renders evil for evil to *anyone*"; trans. Malherbe 2000, 310), and the appeal to do good ("always strive mightily to do good *for one another and for all*," AT) is the only one in the section that includes a reference to outsiders (cf. 3:12, and comments there).

As promulgated in ancient Israel, the principle of retaliation provided for a proportionate and therefore just response to evil (Exod 21:22-25; Lev 24:19-21; Deut 9:21), but beginning within Scripture itself one finds a developing critique of this principle on the grounds that vengeance belongs to God alone (e.g., Prov 20:22 [cf. 24:29; 25:21-22]; Sir 28:1-7; *Jos. Asen.* 28:14 [cf. 23:9; 28:5, 10; 29:3]; 1QS X, 17-18). The renunciation of the principle by Paul (also in Rom 12:17a; cf. vv. 14b, 21a) and others in the early church (e.g., Matt 5:39 par. Luke 6:29a; 1 Pet 3:9a) echoes this critique, and is consistent with arguments against retaliation in Greco-Roman philosophical traditions (Fitzgerald 1988, 103-7 notes, among others: Plato, *Crito* 49A-D; Seneca, *De Ira*; Musonius Rufus, *Frag.* X; Epictetus, *Discourses* I, 18; 28).

The warning about seeking revenge is in a sense only preliminary to the following positive appeal to do good (cf. Rom 12:17, 19-21; cf. v. 14; 1 Cor 4:12). This sequence itself has Jewish antecedents (e.g., Lev 19:18; 1QS X, 17-18; cf. Pss. 34:14 [LXX 33:15]; 37:27 [LXX 36:27]), and is present, as well, in 1 Pet 3:9 and Matt 5:38-39, 43-48 par. Luke 6:27-28, 32-36. But in the present case, unlike most of the parallels, Paul's follow-up appeal is not simply about responding to evil. More broadly and fundamentally, he urges believers to be striving "always" to do what is good "for one another and for all" (AT; in this respect, Rom 12:17 is comparable while Rom 12:19-21 is not).

The closely parallel appeal to "abound in love for one another and for all" (3:12), along with the emphasis on love throughout this letter, suggests (despite Malherbe 2000, 322) that "good" is here virtually synonymous with love (cf. also 1 Cor 14:1, where Paul's charge to "pursue love" uses the same Gk. verb that NRSV here translates as "seek"). This correspondence seems confirmed by the fact that Paul can use either term when urging believers to build up one another ("the good," Rom 15:2; "love," 1 Cor 8:1, etc.) and serve the neighbor ("the good," Rom 15:2; "love," Gal 5:14; Rom 13:10). What most distinguishes the apostle's present appeal from traditional Jewish teaching about nonretaliation is his insistence that even "outsiders" count as neighbors and are to be embraced in love. Because this more radical view is also present in the Jesus traditions that lie behind Matt 5 and Luke 6 (cited above), some interpreters hear in v. 15 an echo of Jesus' own teaching (e.g., Marshall 1983, 153; Holtz 1998, 255).

Rejoice, Pray, Give Thanks (5:16-18)

While his counsels in vv. 12-15 address primarily relationships among the members of the congregation, Paul now specifies three ways in which the congregation as such should be manifesting its calling.

Rejoicing is a prominent theme in Paul's letters, including this one (see also 1:6; 2:19-20; 3:9). The directive to rejoice "always" (*pantote*, also in Phil 4:4) suggests that the community's whole life is to be suffused with a joy in believing. This is consistent with what the apostle has said in 1:6, where he refers to joy as "inspired by the Holy Spirit" (cf. Gal 5:22; Rom 14:17; 15:33) and associates it closely both with faith (cf. 2 Cor 1:24; Phil 1:25) and with standing firm in faith despite affliction (cf. 2 Cor 6:10). Similarly, Paul looks forward in hope to the eschatological joy that he and all believers will experience when the Lord returns and the kingdom of God has come in its fullness (2:19-20; cf. 2:12; Rom 14:17; 15:13; Phil 4:1).

Prayer, too, is commended as definitive of the life of the believing community. In Rom 12:12 and Phil 1:4 (cf. 4:4, 6), as well as here, Paul associates it with rejoicing. What it means to pray "without ceasing" (*adialeiptōs*, often synonymous with *pantote*, used in the preceding instruction) may be inferred from Rom 12:12, where the instruction to "persevere in prayer" (cf. Acts 1:14; 2:42; 6:4; Eph 6:28; Col 4:2) urges the regular, diligent practice of it. Paul has previously mentioned his own diligence in prayer (1:2-3; 2:13; 3:10; cf. Rom 1:10; Phil 1:9; Phlm 4), and he will subsequently request the congregation's prayers on his behalf (5:25).

Thanksgiving, which is a specific form of prayer, has special prominence in 1 Thessalonians. Only this letter contains two thanksgiving paragraphs (1:2-10; 2:13-14), Paul remarks that he cannot thank God enough for the joy he feels for this congregation (3:9), and no other certainly Pauline letter contains a directive to give thanks. Rather than specifying any reason for thanksgiving, the apostle summons the congregation to give thanks "in all circumstances." He commends this not simply as a congregational "activity," but as an indispensable and continuing expression of his converts' faith in God (cf. Rom 1:21; 2 Cor 4:15).

The only theological warrant in 5:12-22 appears in v. 18b, where "this is the will of God...for you" is best understood as referring to all three appeals in vv. 16-18a. Those are closely connected in form and content. At the beginning of chapter 4, Paul referred to sanctification as God's will (4:3a), and then went on to specify several particular ways in which believers should allow God's sanctifying power to shape and guide their everyday lives. Now his identification of rejoicing, prayer, and thanksgiving as God's will suggests that he understands these to be essential to the identity of a community that has been called and set apart (sanctified) for the service of God. This is the only Pauline reference to God's will that includes the qualifying phrase "in Christ Jesus," and the phrase itself appears only one other place in 1 Thessalonians (2:14). It is less likely that Paul means simply "God's will for you as members of the Christian fellowship" (Bruce 1982, 125) than that he is broadening the warrant with a reference to the one through whom he believes God's will is disclosed and ultimately fulfilled.

Be Attentive to the Spirit (5:19-22)

The formally parallel prohibitions in vv. 19-20 pertain to the presence and working of the Spirit within the congregation (the absence of the designation "Holy," found in 1:5, 6; 4:8, is not significant). By itself, the directive not to "quench the Spirit" may be read as a general appeal to allow the Spirit that God has bestowed upon the congregation (4:8) to work freely within it ("quench" reflects a widespread association of God's Spirit with fire; e.g., Isa 30:27-28; Matt 3:11 par. Luke 3:16; Acts 2:3-4). The directive not to "disdain prophetic utterances" (AT) suggests a more specific reference. In accord with his Jewish heritage, which connected prophecy to the Spirit (e.g., Joel 2:28), Paul is saying that the congregation should not hinder the Spirit by demeaning Spirit-inspired prophecies. Significantly, he refers to prophetic speech, not "prophets." Nothing in this letter indicates that he regards certain believers as graced with a prophetic "office." Nor is there any indication that other spiritual "gifts," like tonguespeaking, were being exercised in this congregation. The situation that obtained later in Corinth (1 Cor 12–14) should not be assumed for Thessalonica.

If the subject of prophesying continues in vv. 21-22, as most interpreters believe, then it would appear that Paul knew of some in the congregation who actually were disdainful of prophecies, dismissing all of them out of hand. In this case, vv. 21-22 add an important stipulation: neither should the congregation *accept* all prophecies uncritically. It must subject all of them to evaluation (v. 21a), accepting those deemed to be "good" and dismissing those deemed to be "evil" (vv. 21b-22). Had Paul been confronting a major crisis about spiritual gifts, or had the prophecies in question pertained to issues that are actually documented for this congregation (e.g., undeserved suffering, grieving for the dead, uncertainty about the time of the *parousia*), his instructions here would probably have been more explicit and extensive. As it is, the details of the situation that may have prompted these counsels remain beyond the reach of historical research.

An alternative view, held by some, is that the directives in vv. 21-22 are not connected to those in vv. 19-20. Although NRSV interprets the Greek *de* ("but," v. 21a) as introducing a qualification of the preceding appeals, one could just as well put a full stop at the end of v. 20 and interpret the *de* as a transitional particle only, leaving it untranslated (in fact, a number of credible manuscripts omit *de*). In this case, the appeal in v. 21a would be for moral discernment *in general*, the verb "test" (*dokimazō*) referring, as it does in Rom 12:2 and Phil 1:10 (NRSV: "discern" and "determine"), to careful moral inquiry, reflection, and appraisal. The appeal in vv. 21b-22, which echoes in part a familiar Jewish idiom (LXX Job 1:1, 8; cf. 2:3; also 1QS I, 4), would then stand as a general follow-up exhortation about good and evil (cf. Rom 12:9b). Indeed, even if Paul's intention was in the first instance to stipulate something further about prophetic utterances, it is probable that also the broader application of vv. 21-22 would have been apparent to his congregation.

◊ ◊ ◊ ◊

Many of these counsels have parallels in non-Christian traditions, and Paul himself has provided few specifically Christian warrants for them. But when one considers them in the context of

4:1–5:24 and the letter as a whole, it becomes evident that they rest on several important theological presuppositions.

First, as God's elect (1:4; 2:12) the addressees belong to the Lord (v. 12), who "died and rose again" for their salvation and will come again that they may live forever with him (4:14-17; 5:8-10). This relationship defines who they are, their present calling, and their hope.

Second, God's Holy Spirit is a continuing creative presence in the congregation (v. 19), guiding and empowering believers into conduct that is worthy of the God who has called them, and that is an authentic manifestation of their sanctification (2:12; 3:13; 4:3-8).

Third, God's will for the elect is known and fulfilled through Christ Jesus (v. 18; 4:2-3; cf. 1:6). Given Paul's close association of Christ with faith, love, and hope (1:2-3; cf. 5:8-10), one may infer that he regards these three as particularly definitive of what life according to the will of God must involve.

Fourth, the sanctified life comes to expression as believers devote themselves, both individually and corporately, to do the will of God (v. 18). It is to this end that Paul counsels attentiveness both to the leading of the Spirit (vv. 19-20) and to the task of moral discernment (vv. 21-22). Although he identifies no specific criteria for distinguishing between true and false prophecies, or between good and evil in general, he likely intends for the congregation's judgments about these to be informed by the whole of the present letter.

Benedictory Prayer (5:23-24)

Although many interpreters take this prayer with what follows, as part of the closing section of the letter, the references to sanctification and Christ's return connect it more particularly to 4:1–5:22 where these topics are especially prominent. Just as the largely parallel prayer in 3:11-13 concludes the first main section of the letter, so this prayer concludes the second.

◊　◊　◊　◊

The effect of this benediction is to place all of the appeals and counsels of 4:1–5:22 under the heading provided by 4:3a, where Paul has declared that sanctification is God's will. Now, however, the focus shifts from what God's will requires of believers in the present to God's own sanctifying action on their behalf, which will be fulfilled at Christ's return (v. 23). The apostle's declaration that the God who has called them to holiness (cf. 4:7) is faithful and "will do this" (v. 24) makes explicit what his earlier prayer implies (3:13): the perfect sanctification for which believers hope will not be their own accomplishment, but God's. This sanctification will be "entire" in that the whole of one's being will be sanctified through the saving power of God.

Paul also prays that God will keep believers blameless until the return of Christ (v. 23b; cf. 3:13), referring in this connection to their "spirit and soul and body." Although he occasionally differentiates between the human "spirit" and "body" (e.g., 1 Cor 5:3; 7:34; cf. spirit/flesh, 1 Cor 5:5; mind/flesh, Rom 7:25), he uses this threefold formulation only here, where its function is clearly rhetorical. Along with the adjective "sound," which connotes wholeness and completeness, it reinforces the point that salvation will encompass every aspect of one's existence. The view that Paul was confronting a Gnostic-like dualism that viewed the body as inherently evil (Jewett 1971, 175-83, 250-51, 347; 1986, 107-8) is rendered problematic by the fact that no such issue is specifically addressed in this letter (even the word "body" appears only here).

Just as Paul regularly invokes God's "grace and peace" in the prescripts of his letters (see 1:1), he often refers to "the God of peace" (v. 23a) as he brings them to a close (also Rom 15:33; 16:20; 2 Cor 13:11; Phil 4:9; cf. Rom 15:13). In all of these instances, the term "peace," perhaps echoing the Hebrew *shalom*, refers to the fullness of salvation that comes from God. Similarly, Paul's affirmation that God is faithful (v. 24; see also 1 Cor 1:9; 10:13; 2 Cor 1:18; cf. Rom 3:3-4) corresponds to scriptural declarations about God's trustworthiness in dealing with his covenant people (e.g., Deut 7:9; 32:4; Isa 49:7). The association of God's faithfulness with God's call also occurs in 1 Cor 1:8-9, where, as here, Paul assures his congregation that God will enable believers to be found blameless at the return of Christ.

◊ ◊ ◊ ◊

At the beginning of chapter 4 and in most of what follows through 5:22 Paul has offered counsels on what is required if believers are to "please God" (4:1) and live the sanctified life to which God has called them (4:7). Now those imperatives are concluded, not with a summons to try harder to do the will of God, but with the prayer that the God who saves may "himself" accomplish the holiness and establish the blamelessness of those who have been called.

This excludes any notion of sanctification as a *process* that culminates in salvation. Paul's aim has not been to help his congregation *advance* in holiness toward salvation, but to help it "lead a life worthy of God" who is calling the elect into "his own kingdom and glory" (2:12). Holiness and blamelessness, like the kingdom and the glory, are not "goals" toward which believers are urged to direct their efforts, but gifts from God.

LETTER-CLOSING (5:25-28)

The closing of this letter conforms in general to the epistolary conventions of Paul's day. Several specific requests (vv. 25-27) are followed by a parting expression of best wishes, which in this case (as in other Pauline letters) takes the form of a grace benediction (v. 28).

◊ ◊ ◊ ◊

In requesting prayers (v. 25) on his behalf, Paul specifies nothing in particular for which they are to be offered. One may assume, however, that as in other letters he is requesting prayers for the success of his ministry (Rom 15:30-32; 2 Cor 1:11; Phlm 22; cf. Phil 1:19). Given earlier comments, the congregation may have supposed that Paul wanted them to pray that he be enabled to carry on his Gentile mission (2:16), to remain steadfast in the face of persecution (3:7), and to return to Thessalonica (3:10, 11; cf. 2:17-18). The wording attested by some ancient manuscripts, "pray for us *also*" (adopted by REB; cf. NAB), would be understandable following the benedictory prayer (vv. 23-24). But even if it is correct, it doesn't necessarily mean that Paul wanted the Thessalonians to pray for *his* sanctification as he has prayed for theirs.

It is unlikely that the request to "greet all the brothers and sisters with a holy kiss" (v. 26) is actually a request that they "greet *one another* with a holy kiss" (the wording in Rom 16:16; 1 Cor 16:20; 2 Cor 13:12; cf. 1 Pet 5:14), because "brothers and sisters" in the very next verse cannot possibly mean "one another." Rather, Paul seems to be asking the person(s) who will read this letter to the congregation (see comments on v. 27) to greet all of the other members on his behalf (von Dobschütz 1909, 232; R. F. Collins 1980a, 138; but Malherbe 2000, 341-42 thinks of believers in the environs of the city who had been converted after the missionaries had left). In Hellenistic society, a kiss was exchanged by family members or friends as an expression of their mutual respect and affection. Paul himself may have been responsible for introducing a "holy kiss" as the mode of greeting among believers. But even if he was not, this greeting (like the use of kinship language in this and other letters) was an appropriate expression of the sense of solidarity experienced by those who had come to regard themselves as "brothers and sisters" in a family of faith. By the middle of the second century such a kiss was a formal part of the church's liturgy (Justin Martyr, *Apology I*, 65), but there is no firm evidence that this was so already in the Pauline congregations.

The abrupt shift to the first person singular in v. 27 (cf. 2:18; 3:5) may indicate that the apostle has now ceased dictating to a scribe and taken up the pen himself (cf. 1 Cor 16:21; Gal 6:11; Phlm 19). The request he makes, however, is not only unique to this letter but strongly worded: "I put you under oath to the Lord that this letter be read out to all of the brothers and sisters" (AT). Here Paul anticipates the arrival of the letter in Thessalonica, when the bearer will hand it over to some responsible member of the congregation, perhaps one of those mentioned in 5:12-13a. That recipient, or at any rate the first reader, is to make sure that the letter is shared with "all" who are associated with the congregation. To do so would require reading it aloud to them, since the literacy rate among Christians was probably no higher than the 10-15 percent estimated for the Greco-Roman populace in general (Gamble 1995, 2-10). Yet while Paul's request as such is understandable, especially in a first letter to this congregation, why has he worded it so sharply? Did he have some reason to worry that otherwise it would not be heeded? However it is to be explained, the strong wording attests to Paul's belief that what he has written is highly important. No less, it is an implicit assertion of his authority over the congregation.

Paul's invocation of "grace" in the concluding benediction (v. 28), like his mention of the "God of peace" a few lines earlier (v. 23), echoes the letter's salutation (1:1). As in other Pauline benedictions (Rom 16:20; 1 Cor 16:23; Gal 6:18; Phil 4:23; Phlm 25; cf. 2 Cor 13:13), grace is identified specifically with Christ (see also 2 Cor 8:9; Gal 1:6). The final "Amen," although widely attested by ancient witnesses, was no doubt added by later copyists, influenced by liturgical usage (B. Metzger 1994, 566).

The pastoral character of this letter (see Introduction) is apparent even in these brief, closing lines. Paul twice addresses his converts as "brothers and sisters"; he asks that his greetings be extended to all with a holy kiss; he summons them to offer prayer for his ministry; and he urges that his letter be read to all, without exception. The apostle's instruction about disseminating this letter, like his decision to write it in the first place, may be seen as an exercise of pastoral authority. Yet he has chosen to close the letter as he had opened it, by accenting not his own status but the grace of the Lord Jesus Christ.

INTRODUCTION:
2 THESSALONIANS

Readers of 2 Thessalonians must take account of the fact that this letter presupposes and even reproduces some of the contents of 1 Thessalonians; and further, that it may not have been written by Paul. For the reasons specified below (see "Historical Occasion and Context"), this commentary presents 2 Thessalonians as a pseudonymous (i.e., "deutero-Pauline") writing, composed after Paul's death by an anonymous Paulinist. If this is correct, it contributes less to an understanding of the apostle's own thought than to an appreciation of the way he was regarded and his thought was interpreted toward the end of the first century.

EPISTOLARY CHARACTER AND AIMS

Whether written by Paul or not, 2 Thessalonians was composed as a *letter* and is so designated by its author (3:14, 17). It exhibits features common to Hellenistic letters in general, and shares many of the epistolary characteristics of 1 Thessalonians in particular. At the same time, however, it yields little about the circumstances that occasioned its writing or the situation to which it was addressed (see below, "Historical Occasion and Context"). If, in addition, it is pseudonymous, then it is probably best described as a *fictive letter*. That is, although the unknown author has addressed it to the church in Thessalonica, he seems to have intended it for circulation wherever Paul's letter to the Thessalonians was known.

The rhetoric of 2 Thessalonians may be classified as *deliberative* or *advisory* (e.g., Jewett 1986, 81-87; Holland 1988, 6-58; Hughes 1989, 51-74; Wanamaker 1990, 46-52), because the author employs strategies that are calculated to *dissuade* the recipients from certain beliefs and practices and *persuade* them of others. Above all, his aim is to dissuade believers from accepting false claims that the eschatological "day of the Lord is already here" (2:1-3a), and to persuade them of his own view of the character of the present time (2:3b-12; contrast Malherbe 2000, 351, 361, 390, who believes the letter is devoted primarily to consolation).

A secondary aim is to command good order and responsible conduct within the community itself (3:6-16). It is difficult, however, to agree with the judgment that this letter has the same "hortatory and pastoral" character as 1 Thessalonians (Malherbe 2000, 361). The appeals and counsels trade on Paul's *authority* (e.g., to "command" obedience, 3:4, 6-12; cf. 3:14), not—as in 1 Thessalonians—on the *trust* and *affection* that bind him to his addressees and they to him (e.g., 1 Thess 2:17–3:10). As a consequence, and despite the frequent use of "brothers and sisters" in direct address (1:3; 2:1, 13, 15; 3:1, 6, 13; cf. 3:6, 15), the familial images employed in 1 Thessalonians are missing. Here the author remains somewhat distant from the addressees, even when he mentions their suffering (contrast 2 Thess 1:4, 5-10 with 1 Thess 2:14) and reports his prayers for them (contrast 2 Thess 1:11-12 with 1 Thess 3:10).

To be sure, in other respects 1 and 2 Thessalonians have much in common. The use of the first person plural predominates in both; their prescripts (2 Thess 1:1-2; 1 Thess 1:1) and closing benedictions (2 Thess 3:18; 1 Thess 5:28) are nearly identical; and each contains two thanksgiving paragraphs (2 Thess 1:3-12 and 2:13-14; 1 Thess 1:2-10 and 2:13), a substantial section of eschatological instruction (2 Thess 2:1-12; 1 Thess 4:13–5:11), an affirmation of divine faithfulness (2 Thess 3:3; 1 Thess 5:24), a request for prayer (2 Thess 3:1-2; 1 Thess 5:25), ethical directives (2 Thess 2:15–3:16; 1 Thess 4:1-12; 5:12-22) that are closed with a prayer (2 Thess 3:16; 1 Thess 5:23), and an instruction to the addressees about the letter itself (2 Thess 3:14; 1 Thess 5:27).

Especially remarkable are the numerous instances of nearly verbatim correspondence between the letters. In addition to the prescripts and closing benedictions, the most striking of these are between 2 Thess 2:16-17 and 1 Thess 3:11-13; 2 Thess 3:8 and 1 Thess 2:9; and

2 Thess 3:10-12 and 1 Thess 3:4 + 4:1, 10b-12. On closer inspection, however, one discovers that in several places identical or similar wording is not matched by a correspondence of thought. For instance, although Paul's working to support himself is described in nearly the same words in 1 Thess 2:9 and 2 Thess 3:8, the explanations offered for that work are different. According to 1 Thess 2:9, he wanted to be able to preach the gospel without burdening his converts, but according to 2 Thess 3:9, he wanted to give them an example to imitate. These and other instances where the wording and thought of 2 Thessalonians either correspond or diverge from 1 Thessalonians are noted in the commentary. Taken together, they reveal an unusual and complex pattern of similarities and dissimilarities.

Because 2 Thessalonians manifests a high degree of rhetorical coherence and stylistic consistency, most interpreters affirm its literary integrity. The proposal that it is a composite of two Pauline letters (Schmithals 1964, 1972) is highly speculative, and raises more questions than it answers (cf. Jewett 1986, 33-36; Sumney 1990). The letter's literary structure is generally comparable to that of 1 Thessalonians. In addition to the fact that both contain two thanksgivings, both also contain a concluding section of directives concerning congregational life. The character of the respective preceding sections, however, is notably different in the two letters. Instead of the personal narratives that are the hallmark of 1 Thessalonians 1–3, the first section of 2 Thessalonians is dominated by instruction (1:5-10 and 2:1-12).

As in the case of 1 Thessalonians, detailed analyses of the letter's structure vary, depending largely on whether thematic, epistolary, or rhetorical categories are employed (examples in Jewett 1986, 222-25). The analysis in the present commentary makes use of all three (for an overview, see the Table of Contents).

HISTORICAL OCCASION AND CONTEXT

The Scarcity of Evidence

Second Thessalonians yields little information about the specific circumstances of its writing. This is especially true if it was written by someone other than Paul; but even assuming Pauline author-ship, the historical setting of the letter is difficult to reconstruct. Concerning *Paul's situation*, one learns only that Silvanus and Timothy are with him (1:1), that he faces continuing opposition from unbelievers (3:2; cf. 1:7), and that he has received a report about the situation in his Thessalonian congregation (3:11).

What little is disclosed about *the congregation's situation* is hardly more specific. While the members seem to be undergoing persecution (1:4-7), there is no indication of what form it takes, and the persecutors are identified only as "those who do not know God and . . . do not obey the gospel of our Lord Jesus" (1:8). More attention is paid to two issues that have arisen within the congre-gation itself.

First, the addressees seem to have been unsettled by claims that the eschatological day of the Lord is already present (2:1-12). Except for a hint that the unnamed proponents are repre-senting this as Paul's view (2:2), there is no indication of what evidence they offer in support of it. Nor is there any indication of the broader ideological framework within which such an idea had a place.

Second, there appear to be some believers who are unruly, not only refusing to work for a living but also disrupting the lives of other believers (3:6-12). Here, again, details are lacking. Is their unwillingness to work tied to a belief that the end-time is here, or is it a matter of simple laziness? And how are they disturbing oth-ers? By taking advantage of their beneficence? By seeking to impose their unusual views? The directives about dealing with these people are equally vague, and so ambiguous that it is unclear how and by whom they could have been administered. Are the perpetrators to be dismissed from the congregation (3:6, 14), iso-lated within it (3:10, 15), or merely admonished (3:12)? Is their eventual rehabilitation anticipated? It is also unclear whether the rule stated in 3:10 bans disorderly members from *communal* meals, only from eucharistic rites, or from both.

Identifying the circumstances in and for which this letter was written is further complicated by the lack of other sorts of histor-ical references. (a) Unlike 1 Thessalonians, little is said here about

Paul's time in Thessalonica. The major comment concerns his working to support himself (3:7-8), but this is an almost verbatim repetition of the statement in 1 Thess 2:9. Two other references are hardly more than incidental: "I told you these things when I was still with you" (2:5; cf. 2:15), and "even when we were with you we gave you this command: Anyone unwilling to work should not eat" (3:10). (b) There are no references to other specific congregations. In 1 Thessalonians there are specific references to "all the believers in Macedonia and in Achaia" (1:7) and "the churches of God...that are in Judea" (2:14), but here there is only a general mention of "the churches of God" (1:4). (c) Nothing at all is said about the apostle' s future plans, unless one counts the rather vague request to "pray for us, so that the word of the Lord may spread rapidly" (3:1).

What these scraps of evidence add up to depends in large part on whether 2 Thessalonians is read as Pauline or deutero-Pauline. For this reason, a consideration of the authorship of the letter must precede any proposal about the circumstances of its writing.

The Question of Authorship

Second Thessalonians was accepted and in circulation as an authentic Pauline letter by the middle of the second century, when Marcion (according to Tertullian, *Against Marcion* 5.16) included it in his list of scriptural writings (the pertinent evidence is thoroughly reviewed by Rigaux 1956, 112-20; briefly: Best 1972, 37-38). Since early in the nineteenth century, however, important questions have been raised about its authorship (annotated bibliography: Weima and Porter 1998, 51-64; history of the discussion: R. F. Collins 1988, 209-18), and by some estimates scholarly opinion has shifted to such an extent that most interpreters now view it as deutero-Pauline.

Reasons for Questioning Pauline Authorship

The most detailed and compelling challenges to Pauline authorship are those of William Wrede (1903) and Wolfgang Trilling (1972, 11-108; 1980, 21-26), whose arguments have been taken up by many subsequent interpreters. There are three types of arguments: literary, historical, and theological (in English, see esp. Bailey 1978–79; R. F. Collins 1988, 209-41; Menken 1994, 27-43).

Literary arguments: (a) The most important literary argument is that this letter appears, in certain respects, to have been written in imitation of 1 Thessalonians. The structural similarities and numerous instances of correspondence in wording noted above ("Epistolary Character and Aims") are best explained if a later author has used the earlier Pauline letter as a model. This would also account for the fact that correspondence in wording is not always matched by correspondence in thought.

(b) The style and syntax of 2 Thessalonians differentiate it from 1 Thessalonians and the other certainly Pauline letters (e.g., 2 Thess 1:3-12; see esp., Schmidt 1990; Ernst 1998).

(c) The tone of 2 Thessalonians is impersonal and formal. Unlike 1 Thessalonians, with its many familial images, its expressions of affection, and its patient counsels, this letter has an official, even authoritarian aspect: thanksgiving is presented as an *obligation* (1:3; 2:13); *commands* are issued (3:6-12); what the letter says must be *obeyed* (3:14).

Historical arguments: In several regards, 2 Thessalonians reflects circumstances or conditions that are unlikely to have occurred until after Paul's death.

(a) The emphatic assertion in 3:17 that the autograph greeting guarantees the authenticity of the letter is easier to understand if it is the claim of a later writer. The need to certify that the letter is genuine presupposes, if not the actual existence of forged letters, at least the possibility that such forgeries may be produced and circulated. (Whether the reference to a letter "as though from us" [2:2] points to the existence of a specific forgery is uncertain; see commentary.) Yet during Paul's lifetime, his views and even his apostleship were openly and directly challenged (esp. Galatians and 2 Corinthians offer clear evidence of this). His opponents had no need to misrepresent him by forging letters; and no letter of unquestioned Pauline authorship even hints that any such threat existed. In the three instances where the apostle himself calls attention to his handwriting (1 Cor 16:21; Gal 6:11; Phlm 19), his point is only to personalize what he is writing, not to prove the letter's authenticity.

(b) In 2 Thessalonians, Paul's "testimony" (1:10b), which is also referred to as his "gospel" (1:8; 2:14), is identified as the "truth" that one must love and believe in order to be saved (1:10b; 2:10, 12, 13-14). And it is specifically this Pauline gospel that is understood to constitute the core of the "tradition(s)" to which believers must hold fast (2:15; 3:6). Thus, unlike 1 Thessalonians where Paul indicates that he *transmits* the tradition (see commentary on 4:1-2), 2 Thessalonians regards Paul's gospel as *in itself* the saving truth that is definitive of the tradition (cf. Menken 1994, 42: "Paul's gospel is considered as autonomous and coherent divine revelation"). This conception of an identifiable *Pauline tradition* is evident only in the decades following the apostle's death (Menken, *ibid.*, cites Eph 3:1-19 and 2 Tim 1:8-14 as representative of this post-Pauline development).

(c) The image of Paul that emerges from 2 Thessalonians also renders its authenticity problematic. His role as founder and nurturer of the Thessalonian church is scarcely in view. The emphasis falls, rather, on his unquestioned apostolic status and authority; what he commands is to be obeyed (3:4, 6-12, 14). Moreover, this authority is understood to be exercised through the tradition, and his letters are viewed primarily as communicating that tradition (2:15; 3:14, 17; cf. 2:2), not as furthering specific pastoral aims. Indeed, from the standpoint of this letter, the apostle himself belongs to the tradition (see commentary on 3:1-5, and esp. 3:7-9). Also in these respects, 2 Thessalonians stands closer to the writings of the post-Pauline period than to 1 Thessalonians and the other unquestionably Pauline letters.

Theological arguments: There are a number of ways in which 2 Thessalonians diverges theologically from 1 Thessalonians (see below, "Theological and Ethical Orientation"). The most obvious of these, and the one most often invoked as an argument against Pauline authorship, is the letter's strikingly different eschatological outlook.

According to 2 Thess 2:3b-12, claims that the day of the Lord has already arrived (2:2) are quite wrong, because a number of events that have been ordained to precede it are still playing themselves out. The present time remains under the dominion of a "lawless one" whose "revealing" (2:3, 6, 8) has unleashed a satanic power that is spawning unrighteousness. Only with the "revealing" of the Lord Jesus, which is yet to occur (1:7), will the actual end-time events be set in motion.

There is no parallel to this scenario either in 1 Thessalonians or in any other certainly Pauline letter. Moreover, and even more important, the eschatological outlook that it reflects is seriously at odds with Paul's outlook as expressed in 1 Thessalonians. There the apostle refers to the *parousia* as if it is imminent (see commentary on 4:15), and insists that the Lord will come "like a thief in the night," suddenly and without warning (5:2-3).

Defenses of Pauline Authorship

Notwithstanding the difficulties involved, a number of interpreters, especially in the English-speaking world, remain convinced that 2 Thessalonians is a genuinely Pauline letter. In general, they argue that the literary, historical, and theological difficulties are not as serious as represented, and can, in any case, be satisfactorily explained without resorting to the view that the letter is deutero-Pauline (in English, see esp. Marshall 1983, 28-45; Malherbe 2000, 349-74; Nicholl 2004, 3-13, 183-221).

Literary arguments: (a) It is held that because 2 Thessalonians was written fairly soon after 1 Thessalonians, and to the same church on the same topic, it is not surprising that there are places where the wording of the letters closely corresponds. Some attribute this simply to Paul's memory of the first letter, while others suggest the possibility that he had retained a copy of it, which he then re-read before composing the second. But can this account for the instances of *verbatim* correspondence even where a different thought is expressed? And why would it be only in 2 Thessalonians that the apostle borrows from himself? There are, for example, no comparable parallels in his letters to the Corinthian church.

(b) The argument that the style and syntax of 2 Thessalonians are un-Pauline stands virtually unchallenged. It is true that the apostle himself sometimes writes long sentences (Malherbe 2000, 366 cites 1 Cor 1:4-8; Phil 1:3-11; 1 Thess 1:2-5 [or 7]); but the syntactical complexities in 2 Thessalonians also involve the types and relationships of their constituent clauses, and various points of grammar (Schmidt 1990; Ernst 1998).

(c) The formal tone of 2 Thessalonians is often explained as required by the threatening situation that Paul had to address; and it is argued, further, that this letter seems cool and impersonal only in comparison with 1 Thessalonians, which is *unusually* warm and friendly. There is, however, no certainly Pauline letter in which the apostle's response to a threatening situation has *such* a formal and official aspect, and is untempered by expressions of his personal feelings about the addressees (even Galatians is no exception; see 4:12-20!).

Historical arguments: (a) Some claim that the letter's handwritten greeting (3:17) is emphasized only in order to underscore its authority, and is comparable to 1 Thess 5:27, where Paul directs that the letter be read to all. But the comparison with 1 Thess 5:27 is quite unconvincing. When, more appropriately, 2 Thess 3:17 is compared with the autograph greetings in 1 Corinthians, Galatians, and Philemon, its distinctive *authenticating* function becomes clear. The further point, that letters falsely claiming to be Paul's are unattested during the apostle's lifetime and were in fact unneeded, is rarely addressed.

(b and c) Defenders of Pauline authorship disagree that 2 Thessalonians reflects conceptions of tradition and of Paul's status and authority that arose only after his death. They argue that the certainly Pauline letters also value the tradition(s) and also attest to Paul's exercise of apostolic authority. But while this is a correct observation, it falls short of engaging the two critical points, that in 2 Thessalonians the tradition is practically equated with Paul's gospel and his authority is understood to be exercised through the tradition.

Theological arguments: Most who maintain the authenticity of 2 Thessalonians contend that there is no basic difference in the eschatological outlook of this letter and 1 Thessalonians. They claim that it is not unusual for apocalyptic scenarios to anticipate both the suddenness of the end-time and that it will be preceded by signs. Thus, Paul is emphasizing the suddenness in one letter (1 Thess 5:1-3) and the signs in another (2 Thess 2:3b-12). It is said, further, that this shift of emphasis was prompted by an altered situation in the Thessalonian church: when Paul learned that 1 Thessalonians had been misunderstood (or deliberately misrepresented) as supporting a "realized" eschatology, he sought to correct that view in 2 Thessalonians by spelling out what must still occur before the Lord's return.

It is, however, very difficult to see how Paul's description of the manner of the Lord's coming (1 Thess 5:1-3) leaves any room for the extended scenario that is presented in 2 Thess 2:3b-12. And why is there no trace of this scenario in any subsequent Pauline letter, even in 1 Corinthians where the apostle is having to deal with some form of realized eschatology? Malherbe's reference (2000, 368-69) to 1 Cor 15:23-28 is not apt, for the events that Paul identifies there are not supposed to precede the *parousia* but to occur within the end-time itself (the comparable passage is therefore 1 Thess 4:14-17).

Other Proposals

Some defenders of Pauline authorship have suggested other ways of resolving, especially, the problems that are disclosed when 2 Thessalonians is read alongside 1 Thessalonians. Among the proposals:

(a) Paul wrote 1 and 2 Thessalonians at the same time, intending the former for the congregation as a whole and the latter only for the Jewish minority within it (von Harnack 1910; cf. Malherbe 2000, 350-56, who postulates a different "primary" audience for each, but does not define them as Gentile and Jewish, respectively).

(b) Second Thessalonians was not actually written to the congregation in Thessalonica, but to another (e.g., to the one in Philippi; Schweizer 1945).

(c) Second Thessalonians was probably written by one of Paul's close associates, either Silvanus or Timothy, so this makes it non-Pauline only "in the technical sense" (Donfried 1993, 86-87).

(d) Second Thessalonians was actually written *before* 1 Thessalonians, and when the letters are read in this sequence, "many of the problems associated with the relation between [them] are resolved" (Wanamaker 1990, 37-45; here, 37; see also Manson 1953).

All of these proposals, however, are highly speculative, create new problems that need resolution, and have won few adherents. There is no specific textual evidence for any of them; and (d) is further undercut by 1 Thess 2:17–3:10, which reads as if there had been no prior letter (Malherbe 2000, 363-64), and also 2 Thess 2:15, if it refers to 1 Thessalonians.

The State of the Question

The arguments advanced for the post-Pauline character of 2 Thessalonians have sufficient weight—not only collectively, but also, in several cases, individually—to render the letter's authenticity highly problematic. It cannot be claimed that these arguments *require* the conclusion that 2 Thessalonians is deutero-Pauline, but they strongly support this conclusion, and it is the one accepted in the present commentary. But whether one reads this letter as Pauline or as deutero-Pauline, it is important to keep the alternative view constantly in mind, and to give due consideration to any alternative interpretation that may follow from it.

The Letter's Composition

The Author and His Intentions

The author of 2 Thessalonians was steeped in the Jewish scriptures and influenced as well by both Jewish and Christian apocalyptic eschatology. While (like Paul in 1 Thessalonians) he never specifically quotes Scripture or refers to its authority, scriptural expressions, themes, and modes of thought permeate his writing (see, e.g., 1:5-10). Moreover, he has obviously been influenced by

Paul's thought as he knows it in the church's tradition and through the apostle's own letters. In addition to 1 Thessalonians, on which he specifically relies (see commentary), the author seems to have known other letters that were in circulation as Paul's (esp. 1 Corinthians and Romans). There are plausible echoes of these throughout 2 Thessalonians (identified in the commentary as they appear).

As indicated above ("Epistolary Character and Aims"), the author is concerned primarily to refute those who claim that the end-time events are already taking place (2:1-12), and, secondarily, to encourage responsible conduct within the believing community (3:6-12). He also wants to console the addressees as they continue to undergo persecution, but his consolation takes the form of instruction (1:5-10). It is possible that some believers regarded their persecution as the outworking of God's eschatological wrath (cf. 1 Thess 5:3), and thus a sign that the end-time had indeed arrived (e.g., Barclay 1993, 528-29). If so, then the author's own quite different interpretation of the church's afflictions (see below, "Theological and Ethical Orientation") contributes at least indirectly to his argument that the day of the Lord has not yet arrived, and thus anticipates the topic of 2:1-12.

Whether or not the "realized eschatology" opposed in 2 Thessalonians *originated* as a misunderstanding of 1 Thessalonians (e.g., 5:4-8), proponents are evidently citing that letter in support of their views (see commentary on 2:2). It would appear that our author, concerned to refute what he considers a perversion of Paul's thought, believes that this requires producing *another* "letter" from the apostle to the Thessalonians. In this way, he cloaks his response to the false teaching with the mantle of apostolic authority (for the ancient practice of pseudepigraphy see, e.g., R. F. Collins 1988, 242-63; Aune 2003, 387-88). Some have suggested that the author even wanted his letter to be accepted *in place* of 1 Thessalonians (e.g., Rist 1972, 82-83; Lindemann 1999). More likely, however, he wanted it to be received and read as a "clarifying" *supplement* to the eschatological teaching of that earlier letter.

In sum, one may reasonably infer that the author of

2 Thessalonians was a Hellenistic-Jewish Christian, that he was well-acquainted with the Jewish scriptures and apocalyptic traditions, and that he was concerned to uphold the Pauline tradition as he had received and understood it. Whether he had some leadership role within a local congregation, or perhaps some supervisory responsibility over a group of congregations, is impossible to determine.

Date, Place, and Destination

Since the author of 2 Thessalonians has masked his identity with Paul's, this letter provides no direct evidence about the date and place of its composition or the intended recipients. Firm conclusions on these points are, therefore, unattainable.

Date: Most interpreters who regard 2 Thessalonians as pseudonymous date it either late in the first or very early in the second century, C.E. (a) Neither Paul's associates and supporters nor his detractors and opponents would have had reason to produce a letter in his name while he was still alive. For this reason, the earliest likely date would be sometime after the early 60s, when Paul, according to tradition, was martyred in Rome. (b) Because the letter was well established as a second Pauline letter to Thessalonica by at least the middle of the second century (Marcion), a date later than the early second century is unlikely. (c) The author's apparent familiarity with several Pauline letters in addition to 1 Thessalonians suggests that some collection of them was being circulated, and the best evidence suggests that this did not happen until sometime in the 80s or 90s.

Some hold that any date after the destruction of the Jerusalem temple in 70 C.E. is precluded by 2 Thess 2:4, which refers to "the temple of God" as if it were still standing (e.g., Nicholl 2004, 220). But this is readily enough explained as part of the fiction created by the post-Pauline writer; it is understandable that he would adopt the time frame of the apostle's ministry.

Place of Writing and Destination: The address, "To the church of the Thessalonians" (1:1) should not be accepted uncritically as evidence for the destination of this letter. What little can be determined about the situation of the addressees could have been true of any Pauline congregation toward the end first century: they were experiencing the hostility of unbelievers, perplexed about the end-time, and troubled by disorderly conduct within their own community. The author may address the letter specifically to the Thessalonians for the same reason that he uses 1 Thessalonians as his model—because what the apostle had written to them about the day of the Lord is now in question. Presumably, he could have introduced 2 Thessalonians into circulation through almost any of the Pauline churches—although probably not through the church in Thessalonica, where a hitherto unknown letter from Paul might have aroused suspicions.

It is reasonable to suppose that this letter was produced within the same general region in which it was to be circulated. The place most often suggested is Asia Minor, on the grounds that (a) that is where Paul's letters may have been first collected for circulation; (b) there are indications that during the reign of the emperor Domitian (81–96 C.E.) the Christians of Asia Minor were persecuted; and (c) apocalyptic eschatology seems to have flourished among the Christians there. The latter is attested both by the Book of Revelation (the seer identifies Patmos, an island off the western coast, as the place of his visions) and the rise of the Montanist movement (with its realized eschatology) in the last quarter of the second century. But (a) remains a hypothesis, the evidence of Domitianic persecutions (b) is not as firm as often alleged, and (c) a perversion of Paul's apocalyptic eschatology could have arisen within any of his congregations, including those in Achaia and Macedonia.

THEOLOGICAL AND ETHICAL ORIENTATION

This author's understanding of God, Christ, the gospel, faith, salvation, and the moral life is deeply indebted to the apocalyptic-eschatological traditions of formative Judaism and early Christianity. It is clear that he has been in touch with these not only through 1 Thessalonians and the other Pauline letters known to him. Especially in 1:5-10, where he speaks of God's righteous judgment, and in 2:1-12, where he describes the events that must precede the eschatological day, he is drawing mainly on traditions that do not appear in the apostle's own letters.

In accord with 1 Thessalonians, believers are viewed as *God's chosen people* (1:11; 2:13-14), destined for life in God's kingdom (1:5). But the theological determinism that characterizes most apocalyptic thinking has influenced this writer's outlook much more than Paul's. Here, those whom God has designated for salvation are also understood to be destined to suffer, whereby they are made worthy of salvation (1:5, 11). Moreover, on those he has not chosen for salvation, God sends a "powerful delusion" that leads them to "believe what is false" (2:11). So their destiny is to be punished with "eternal destruction," which this writer visualizes as irreversible alienation from the Lord and his glory (1:9).

The *salvation* for which believers are destined will be conferred when, on the last day, "the Lord Jesus is revealed from heaven." At that time, he will wreak vengeance on those who have spurned the gospel and oppressed its adherents (1:7-8) and utterly destroy the "lawless one," whose satanic power will have been let loose in the world (2:8-10). For believers, salvation will mean relief from suffering (1:7a), reception into the kingdom (1:5), and the joy of glorifying the Lord Jesus and being glorified in him (1:9, 12; 2:14).

This understanding of salvation as belonging entirely to the future differs significantly from Paul's. According to the apostle, the decisive saving event has already taken place in Christ's death and resurrection (e.g., 1 Thess 1:10; 4:14; 5:9-10); but according to 2 Thessalonians, which makes no mention of Christ's death or resurrection, the saving event will be the Lord's return at the eschaton. Because this writer identifies the day of salvation with the coming "day of the Lord," it is not surprising that the designation "Lord" (*kyrios*) occurs in all but one of his nearly two dozen references to Jesus (R. F. Collins 1990, 436; the exception is "Christ," used alone in 3:5). *Kyrios* is not only a christological title in the combinations "Lord Jesus" and "Lord Jesus Christ"; even when it stands alone, it usually refers to Jesus rather than God (e.g., 1:9; 2:2). Moreover, in 2 Thess 3:5, 16 Paul's references to God (in

1 Thess 3:11; 5:23, respectively) are replaced by *kyrios* used as a christological title. This corresponds to the author's tendency to transfer God's attributes to Christ (see 1:7b-10a; 2:8, 13; cf. 3:3).

The author's radically "futurized" soteriology has consequences for what he says about the *present* and the *moral life*. Whereas Paul sees the present as graced and claimed by the saving power of God, so that believers already "belong to the day" (1 Thess 5:4-10), this writer views the present as the domain of lawlessness, which will continue to rule for as long as God has decreed (2:3b-12). Accordingly, when he speaks of the gospel that the elect have heard (1:8; 2:14), he does not identify it, as Paul does, with the saving, empowering presence of God's Spirit (1 Thess 1:5-6; 2:13). He identifies it, rather, with the "truth" (2:10; 12, 13) that is conveyed in the apostolic (specifically Pauline) tradition(s) (2:15; 3:6).

For the elect, therefore, the present is a time for proving themselves worthy of salvation by fearlessly adhering to the tradition, which mandates and is the norm for both right belief (orthodoxy; e.g., 1:8, 10; 2:13, 15) and right conduct (orthopraxis; e.g., 1:11; 2:17; 3:5). While the author also speaks of the grace and love of God and of the Lord Jesus (1:2, 12; 2:13, 16; 3:5, 18), he understands these to be experienced as "eternal comfort and good hope" (2:16), not yet as eschatological existence. This means that the "indicative" that underlies the doctrinal and moral imperatives of this letter is not God's saving act in Christ—which for this writer remains a *hope*—but the tradition as such.

COMMENTARY:
2 THESSALONIANS

PRESCRIPT (1:1-2)

The superscription (v. 1a) and adscription (v. 1b) of this letter are identical to those in 1 Thessalonians, except for the addition of the pronoun "our" (v. 1b). The salutation, however (v. 2), is more expansive than the one in 1 Thessalonians.

◊ ◊ ◊ ◊

In the adscription (v. 1a) and throughout, 2 Thessalonians is presented as written by Paul (see also 3:17). There are weighty reasons, however, to regard it as the work of a later Paulinist who was seeking to interpret and uphold the Pauline tradition (see Introduction). Accordingly, the present commentary will refer only to the "author" or "writer" of this letter. As in 1 Thessalonians, Silvanus and Timothy are named as the letter's co-senders (see commentary on 1 Thess 1:1). Unlike 1 Thessalonians, neither is mentioned again.

The identification of "God our Father and the Lord Jesus Christ" (v. 2b) as the sources of grace (cf. 1:12; 2:16; 3:18) and peace (cf. 3:16) is somewhat awkward, given the reference to God and Christ in the adscription (v. 1b). If, indeed, our letter is from a later writer who knows a number of Pauline letters, the duplication may reflect his wish to have this salutation conform to the usual Pauline form.

◊ ◊ ◊ ◊

From a theological standpoint, there is no reason to question the Pauline character of this prescript. As in 1 Thessalonians, the addressees are identified not by where they happen to be located geographically ("in Thessalonica") but as "Thessalonians" who have a relationship with God and the Lord Jesus Christ (v. 1b). The specification of God and Christ as the sources of "grace" and "peace" (v. 2) only makes explicit what is implicit in the briefer formulation of 1 Thessalonians (see commentary on 1 Thess 1:1). The present letter's closing benedictions strike the same note (3:16, 18).

THANKSGIVINGS, WARNING, AND INSTRUCTION (1:3–2:14)

Following the example of 1 Thessalonians, the author includes two thanksgiving paragraphs in the first section of the letter (1:3-12 and 2:13-14; cf. 1 Thess 1:2-10 and 2:13-16). The intervening paragraphs (2:1-12) offer instruction about the character of the present time to show why any claim that the day of the Lord has already arrived must be rejected as false.

First Thanksgiving (1:3-12)

Although the initial expression of thanks (vv. 3-4) and the promise to continue in prayer for the addressees (vv. 11-12) have been influenced by Paul's own thanksgivings (e.g., 1 Thess 1:2-10), they contain several new touches. An intervening paragraph (vv. 5-10), without parallel in the certainly Pauline letters, is quite distinctive. It offers instruction about the "righteous judgment of God" in order to console those now undergoing persecution. In doing so, it sets forth the first doctrinal claims of the letter.

In Greek, vv. 3-12 constitute just one sentence (grammatical analysis: Schmidt 1990), which at several points is syntactically unclear. Especially in vv. 5-10, there are numerous echoes of Jewish Scripture (notably, Isa 66) and apocalyptic traditions.

Thanksgiving Proper (1:3-4)

Probably echoing Jewish liturgical usage (Aus 1973), the author presents thanksgiving as an obligation (not an unusual idea in the ancient world; *EDNT* 2.551 [M. Wolter]): "We ought always to give thanks to God...as is fitting" (v. 3a, AT). This emphasis distinguishes the present thanksgiving from those in the certainly Pauline letters, including 1 Thessalonians, as well as from that in Colossians. In particular, the author expresses thanks for the congregation's growth in faith and love (v. 3b). Implicitly, he is commending the progress that has been made since the sending of 1 Thessalonians, where the opening thanksgiving also includes a reference to the converts' faith and love (1:3). Although the pairing of faith (*pistis*) with love (*agapē*) is Pauline (1 Thess 3:6; 1 Cor 13:2; 16:13-14; Gal 5:6; Phlm 5), in this case one would expect hope (*elpis*) to be mentioned, too, as it is in 1 Thess 1:3. Instead, that third member of the Pauline triad has been replaced by "steadfastness" (*hypomonē*), which in v. 4 is linked with a further reference to faith.

The faith that is commended in v. 3 is presumably faith in God (cf. 1 Thess 1:8), but elsewhere in this letter, even in this same passage, the noun and verb take on other meanings (see comments on vv. 4, 10b, 11; 2:11, 12, 13; 3:2). Although there are subsequent references to "love" (noun: 2:10; 3:5; verb: 2:13, 16), the love of believers for one another is in view only here. It is not surprising that this letter makes no mention at all of love toward unbelievers (contrast 1 Thess 3:12; 4:9-12; 5:15), for throughout unbelievers are depicted only as despising "the truth" and persecuting its adherents (1:5-10; 2:9-12; 3:2). In v. 4, where "steadfastness" refers to the endurance of "persecutions and...afflictions" (contrast 1 Thess 1:3, where it means persisting in hope for the Lord's return), "faith" connotes "faithfulness" in the midst of those (cf. the same pairing of terms in Rev 13:10).

For anyone who reads 2 Thessalonians as Paul's own letter, the statement that he himself has spoken highly of the congregation's endurance and faithfulness (v. 4) poses a difficulty. In 1 Thess 1:8, Paul has claimed that the faith of the Thessalonians "sounded forth...in every place" *without* his having to speak of it himself.

Why would he now say, and with such emphasis ("we ourselves"), that he *did* speak of it? It is easier to understand this as the comment of a later writer who wishes to enhance Paul's own compliment: the faith of the Thessalonian congregation has been attested by its founder, the great apostle himself (cf. Trilling 1980, 46). In locating this testimony simply "among the churches of God" (cf. 1 Cor 11:16) with no geographic reference (contrast 1 Thess 2:14), the writer uses hyperbole that is equivalent to the apostle's own "in every place" (1 Thess 1:8).

Here the addressees are praised, specifically, for enduring and remaining faithful despite the "persecutions and the afflictions" they are experiencing. The second of these terms (*thlipsis*, as in 1 Thess 1:6; 3:3, 4, 7) can be used of various types of affliction (see also vv. 6, 7), while the first (*diōgmos*) refers more specifically to persecution (cf. Mark 10:30; Acts 8:1; 13:50; only twice in the certainly Pauline letters, both in listings of hardships: 2 Cor 12:10; Rom 8:35). These terms are also paired in Mark 4:17 par. Matt 13:21 (the interpretation of the parable of the sower), which warns that those of shallow faith will fall away when confronted with "affliction and persecution" (AT). In contrast, the Thessalonian believers are praised for standing firm despite their suffering, which our author visualizes as present and ongoing ("that you are enduring," v. 4; see also vv. 5, 6).

Instruction: God's Righteous Judgment (1:5-10)

Thanksgiving turns into consolation, offered in the form of instruction about the significance of what the audience has been enduring. The topic is the "righteous judgment of God," but it is unclear what the author believes the "evidence" (*endeigma*) of divine justice to be (v. 5). If the word stands in apposition to "steadfastness and faith" in v. 4, which the syntax allows, then it is the believers' faithful endurance that proves God's justice (most interpreters). In this case, the thought would be akin to Paul's assurance to the Philippians that their "standing firm" despite opposition is evidence (*endeixis*) of their opponents' destruction and their own salvation (Phil 1:27-28). It is conceivable, however, that the author means to identify the persecutions themselves as the evidence (e.g., Bassler 1984; Wanamaker 1990, 220-23; Menken 1994, 85-86). If so, he could be espousing the view, found in certain Jewish texts of the period, that the *present* suffering of the faithful for their *few* sins will allow them to escape the fate of the wicked, whom God will severely punish in the world to come (Bassler 1984; see esp. 2 Macc 6:12-16; *Pss. Sol.* 13:6-12; *2 Bar.* 13:3-10; cf. 48:48-50; 52:5-7; 78:5).

Whatever the evidence to which the author refers, it is clear that he believes the present afflictions of the elect are making them worthy to be called into the kingdom of God (v. 5; cf. Acts 14:22). He does not mean that believers are to embrace suffering as their way into the kingdom. He means, rather—as he says explicitly in v. 11—that they are to understand their suffering as *God's* way of making them worthy of his kingdom. There are echoes in vv. 5, 11 of 1 Thess 2:12, where the apostle summons believers to live in a manner that is worthy of the God whose call has already qualified and claimed their lives in the world. In the present passage, however, the author focuses on the eschatological future, assuring believers that through their sufferings God is qualifying them to enter that coming kingdom.

The consolatory aim of this passage is achieved primarily through its statements about the ultimate fate of those who are afflicting believers (vv. 6, 8-9; cf. 2:10-12). The wording of the claim that God in his justice will "repay" the afflicters with affliction (v. 6) is likely influenced by Isa 66:6, 15 (cf. Deut 32:35, quoted by Paul in Rom 12:19). Here the ancient law of retaliation (Exod 21:23-25) has been "transposed to the level of divine, eschatological retribution" (Menken 1994, 86; cf. e.g., Matt 7:1-2).

By contrast (v. 7a), to "the afflicted" (lit. "to you who are being afflicted") God will grant "relief" from suffering. The notion of an eschatological "rest" (*anesis*) for the righteous is common in Jewish apocalyptic texts (Malherbe 2000, 398, cites *4 Ezra* 7:36, 38, 75, 85, 95; *2 Bar.* 73:1), although this particular term never has an eschatological reference in the certainly Pauline letters. The comment that relief from suffering will be—indeed, from this writer's standpoint *has been*—granted also to Paul ("as well as to us") is consistent with the supposition, evident elsewhere, that his audience reveres the apostle and is disposed to heed his instructions (e.g., 2:15; 3:6-10).

In vv. 7b-8a, the writer employs familiar apocalyptic images as he speaks of the eschatological day (v. 10a; cf. Isa 2:11, 17, 20) when the Lord Jesus will be "revealed from heaven with his mighty angels in flaming fire." The Lord's "revealing" (cf. *4 Ezra* 7:28; 13:22; 1 Cor 1:7) from heaven is the same as his "coming" (*parousia*, 2:1, 8b) from there (cf. God's descent from heaven, e.g., Ps 18:9; Isa 64:1). The accompanying angels (note the passages cited in the commentary on 1 Thess 3:13) will assist him in executing judgment. The "flaming fire" should probably be understood as both a manifestation of the divine presence (cf., e.g., Isa 64:1-2; Ps 18:6-12) and an instrument of divine judgment (cf., e.g., Isa 29:6; 66:15, 16; Dan 7:10; *2 Bar.* 48:39). Whereas our author started out by identifying the agent of the final judgment as God (vv. 5-7a), in vv. 7b-10a Jesus assumes that role. This accords with a tendency, throughout the letter, to attribute to Jesus the titles and functions ordinarily identified with God, both in Jewish apocalyptic traditions and in 1 Thessalonians (see Introduction).

The afflicters who will be "repaid" for persecuting believers (v. 6) are now (v. 8b) described as "those who do not know God" (cf. Jer 10:25; Wis 12:26-27; 1 Thess 4:5) and "who do not obey the gospel of our Lord Jesus" (cf. LXX Isa 66:4 and, esp., Rom 10:16; but the phrase "gospel of our Lord Jesus" occurs only here in the NT, and may be this author's own coinage). Arguments that two separate groups are in view (e.g., Richard 1995, 307-8) fail to take account of the synonymous parallelism employed here (correctly, Malherbe 2000, 401). Whether it is supposed that *all* of those who are ignorant of God and disobey the gospel have oppressed believers (Malherbe 2000, 401 thinks not) is beside the point. The claim is that *all of the oppressors* are ignorant of God and disobey the gospel (cf. 2:10, 12: "refused to love the truth...have not believed the truth").

The "vengeance" (v. 8b) with which the Lord will pay back these afflicters (cf. Isa 66:15; Deut 32:35; Ezek 25:14, 17) is described as "the punishment of eternal destruction" (v. 9a). As in 4 Macc 10:15, the adjective (*aiōnios*) suggests that this "destruction" (*olethros*; cf. 1 Thess 5:3) is to be understood as endless punishment and devastation, not summary annihilation. More particularly, this devastation will be experienced as separation "from the presence of the Lord and from the glory of his might" (v. 9b; divine vengeance is similarly described in Sir 18:24). Although this wording derives from LXX statements about separation from God (esp. Isa 2:10, 19, 21; cf. 26:10), our author is once more reading an originally *theo*logical statement *christo*logically. Here, "the Lord" is clearly "the Lord Jesus" (vv. 7, 8), and it is from his glorious presence that the wicked will forever be excluded.

For the afflicted, however, the eschatological day will bring not only deliverance from suffering (v. 7a) but *communion* with their Lord (v. 10a; cf. 1 Thess 4:17). The "saints" referred to are not (despite Richard 1995, 309) the "angels" who will accompany the Lord from heaven (v. 7b). They are believers who wait on earth for the Lord's return ("all who have believed" is parallel). The writer may refer to them as "saints" (lit. "holy ones") because God has chosen them "through sanctification by the Spirit" (2:13). The promise that the Lord Jesus will be "glorified among his saints" (AT; see also v. 12) and "marveled at . . . among all who have believed" (v. 10a) echoes the LXX wording of Isa 49:3; 66:5 and Pss 67:36; 88:8 [NRSV: Pss 68:35; 89:7]. Yet again, statements about God and Israel are adapted to characterize Christ and the church.

Parenthetically, but not incidentally, the faith and wonder with which the Lord will be greeted are attributed to Paul's preaching (v. 10b), which is described as "our testimony to you" (although "to *you*" stands in tension with "*all* who have believed"). For this author, Paul's "testimony" is the same as his "gospel" (2:14, AT; cf. 1:8b), and those "who have believed" in that testimony have believed in "the truth" (2:13b, AT; cf. 2:10-12). Consistent with this understanding of faith as unyielding adherence to the truth, only aorist (past tense) forms of the verb "to believe" occur in our letter (1:10; 2:11, 12). Missing is the more dynamic view of faith as "believing" (expressed with present tense forms) that is predominant in the certainly Pauline letters (e.g., 1 Thess 1:7; 2:10, 13, "those who are believing" [AT]; 4:14, "since we continue believing that Jesus died and rose again" [AT]).

Prayer-Pledge (1:11-12)

This pledge of continuing prayer for the congregation could well have followed vv. 3-4, thus concluding the thanksgiving before the consoling instruction of vv. 5-10. As it is, vv. 11-12 are connected with vv. 5-10 simply by the phrase "To this end," which introduces the content of the continuing prayer (v. 11). The prayer is that God (now again the subject, as in vv. 3-7a) will make believers worthy of "his call" by enabling them to accomplish "every good resolve and work of faith." God's "call" is parallel with "the kingdom of God" in v. 5. It therefore does not refer to the calling that believers received at their conversion (as in 2:14 and 1 Thess 2:12; 4:7), but to the invitation into God's kingdom (= salvation) that they hope to receive upon the Lord's return (Trilling 1980, 62-63; Marxsen 1982, 75; cf. Menken 1994, 92-93; for the contrary view: Marshall 1990, 272; Richard 1995, 365; Malherbe 2000, 410).

The expression "work of faith," which echoes 1 Thess 1:3, now refers generally to all the good that believers resolve to do in prospect of their Lord's return and the final judgment. In the Greek sentence, "with power" (AT; NRSV: "by his power") stands in an emphatic position, thereby underscoring God's role in making believers worthy of salvation (Malherbe 2000, 411). But neither here nor elsewhere does the author follow Paul (e.g., 1 Thess 1:5; 4:8) in viewing Christian conduct as informed and empowered by God's Holy Spirit (Furnish 2004, esp. 234-40).

In stating the purpose of the prayer (v. 12), the author speaks again (as in v. 10a) of believers glorifying "the name of our Lord Jesus" ("name" stands for the person himself, and NRSV's "in you" can be equally well translated "among you"). But now, going further, he speaks also of the glorification of believers "in him" (cf. the apostle's own statements about being "glorified *with* him [Christ]," Rom 8:17-18, and "conformed to the body of his [Christ's] glory," Phil 3:20-21; cf. Rom 8:30; 2 Cor 3:18; 4:4-6). It is unclear whether our author thinks of this glorification as occurring only upon the Lord's return (e.g., Best 1972, 270-71) or as beginning already in the present (e.g., Malherbe 2000, 412, 413). The former seems more likely, since the claim in v. 10a that the "saints" will glorify the Lord and a later one that believers will share in the Lord's glory (2:14) both concern the eschatological future. That future will be far different for the faithful than for their afflicters. Those who do not know God will be eternally excluded from the glory of the Lord, whereas the faithful will both experience his glory and be glorified in him (cf. *2 Bar.* 54:21; the wicked are destined for retribution, the faithful for glorification).

The final, stock phrase, "according to the grace of our God...," can be read as applying broadly to the whole thanksgiving (vv. 3-12). It also has the effect of reasserting the writer's expectation that God himself will make believers worthy of the kingdom (v. 11). The addition of a reference to the "Lord Jesus Christ" echoes the salutation (v. 2), where Christ and God are identified as the two sources of grace.

This thanksgiving serves, in part, to console and encourage believers who are experiencing persecution. Focusing on the expected return of the Lord, the writer explains what his "revealing" will mean for both the afflicted and, especially, their afflicters. To some degree, the description of "that day" is shaped by the need to refute the claim that it has already arrived, although that false notion becomes a specific topic only in chapter 2. Here, our author makes several notable theological claims.

(a) The afflictions that the addressees must endure have a theological interpretation. To be sure, viewed historically they have been maliciously perpetrated by "those who do not know God" and "do not obey the gospel of our Lord Jesus" (v. 8). But viewed theologically, as this writer urges, the afflictions are "evidence" of God's justice (v. 5). God is providing, on the one hand, an opportunity for believers to demonstrate their fidelity to the gospel and to be made worthy of salvation. And, on the other hand, God is exposing the afflicters as people who do not know him, are hostile to the gospel, and are therefore deserving of the "eternal destruction" for which they are destined (v. 9).

(b) The affliction with which God will repay the afflicters in the end-time (v. 6) matches in kind their present ignorance of God and refusal to accept the gospel of the Lord Jesus. Because of their unbelief, which is actualized in their persecution of believers, they will experience the "eternal destruction" of endless alienation from Christ and his glory (v. 9). There is no comparable statement about eternal damnation either in Paul's own letters or in other deutero-Pauline writings (Popkes 2004, 55).

(c) The "relief" that God will grant to the faithful (v. 7a) will be more than an existence without persecution. It will be life in the awesome presence of the Lord Jesus, to whom they can give glory without fear or hindrance, and in whom they themselves will be glorified (vv. 10, 12).

(d) The "gospel" is identified with Paul's authoritative "testimony," so that "faith" means embracing the truth disclosed in the apostle's preaching (see comments on vv. 9b, 10b). This writer is especially intent on establishing and safeguarding the truth about "the coming of our Lord Jesus," which is the subject of the warning in 2:1-3a.

(e) The decisive saving events will occur only "when the Lord Jesus is revealed from heaven" (2 Thess 1:7b). To be sure, the writer understands the present as a time for believers, with God's help, to remain steadfast in the "work of faith" despite afflictions. This endurance will qualify them to receive God's call into his kingdom, to glorify their Lord, and to be glorified in him (vv. 4-5, 10-12). Yet this call to persist in faith amounts to no more than an intimation that God is presently at work making believers worthy of salvation. For our author, salvation itself belongs strictly to the future (see also 2:13, 14), and the present is defined primarily by the working of "the mystery of lawlessness" (2:7a; cf. Trilling 1980, 50). Insofar as the eschatological future is seen as impinging on the present, it is only in the sense that what happens now will have consequences then. Nothing in this letter reflects the apostle's own view that believers are already endowed with an eschatological existence ("you are all children of light and children of the day") by reason of Christ's saving death (1 Thess 5:5, 9-10).

Warning and Instruction (2:1-12)

Here a verb of entreaty reinforced by direct address indicates the high importance that the writer attaches to the warning and instruction that follow (in Gk., "we beg you, brothers and sisters," v. 1, stands at the beginning of the sentence; cf. 1 Thess 5:12). The warning about claims that the day of the Lord has already arrived (vv. 1-3a) discloses his principal aim in this section of the letter. It is not to describe the end-time events (although there are allusions to those) but to refute the idea that they are already occurring. To accomplish this task, he offers a different characterization of the present time (vv. 3b-12), insisting that there are events that must still unfold in this age before the Lord returns. In making this case, he continues to rely on Jewish and early Christian apocalyptic traditions.

Warning (2:1-3a)

The author prefaces his warning with a reference to Jesus' anticipated eschatological return (v. 1a). He has previously spoken of the Lord's return as his "revealing" (1:7) on "that day" (1:10), but now he identifies it as his "coming" (*parousia*, as in 1 Thess 2:19, etc.). The expectation that believers will be "gathered together to him" is less comparable to Paul's notion of a "rapture" (1 Thess 4:17) than to Jewish expectations of an ultimate ingathering of the righteous (e.g., Isa 27:13; *Pss. Sol.* 17:26; *T. Naph.* 8:3; *T. Ash.* 7:7). An especially close parallel to our author's expectation appears in the Synoptic apocalypse, which identifies the returning Jesus (the "Son of Man") as the one who will gather together all of the elect (Mark 13:27 par. Matt 24:31).

The warning proper opens and closes in a way that communicates its importance ("we beg you ...," v. 1b; "Let no one deceive you ...," v. 3a). The focus is on the false claim "that the day of the Lord is already here" (v. 2). The perfect tense verb cannot mean "almost here" or "in the process of coming"; our author (whether rightly or wrongly) understands the claim to be that the day is actually present. He neither identifies the proponents nor provides details about their beliefs.

The writer himself may be uncertain about the way this claim has been propagated, for he seems to take account of several possibilities (see also v. 3a, "in any way"). Has it been promoted by means of an allegedly Spirit-inspired pronouncement ("by spirit"), someone's reasoned speech ("by word"), or a written communication ("by letter")? While it is conceivable that the phrase "as though from us" (v. 2) goes with all three of the preceding expressions (e.g., Best 1972, 278; Wanamaker 1990, 239; Malherbe 2000, 417), the only certain connection is with "by letter." If the phrase reflects a suspicion that 1 Thessalonians is being cited in support of the false claim (e.g., Trilling 1982, 76; Menken 1994, 32-35; Malherbe 2000, 416), it would mean: "as though what is alleged represents the view stated in our letter, which it does not." If, alternatively, the phrase reflects a suspicion that the false claim is made in a forged letter being represented as Paul's own (e.g., Jewett 1986, 184-85; Richard 1995, 325), it would mean: "as though the letter were from us, which it is not."

The ideological origin of the false claim remains obscure. That it reflects a gnostic spiritualizing of Paul's apocalyptic eschatology (e.g., Schmithals 1972, 202-8) is improbable, because the writer assumes that his apocalyptically framed refutation of it will have resonance with his audience (cf. Menken 1994, 98). One suggestion is that it originated as the claim of a messianic pretender (Menken 1994, 100-01) like those mentioned in Jewish sources from the period (see J. J. Collins 1995, esp. 195-214) and denounced in the Synoptic apocalypse (Mark 13:5-6, 21-22 and parr.). More frequently and plausibly, however, it is explained as due to a gross misunderstanding (or deliberate misrepresentation?) of Paul's declaration that believers already *belong* to the eschatological day (1 Thess 5:5, 8) even though it has not yet dawned (e.g., Malherbe 2000, 417).

The Mystery of Lawlessness (2:3b-7)

Over against those who declare that the day of the Lord has arrived, our author characterizes the present time as pervaded by a "lawlessness" that is "already at work" (v. 7a). Here, as elsewhere in the LXX and NT, "lawlessness" (*anomia*) refers broadly to all kinds of immorality (e.g., 1 John 3:4; also Rom 4:7—quoting Ps 32 [LXX 31]:1-2—and Rom 6:19, where NRSV translates *anomia* as "iniquity"). It may be that the working of lawlessness is called a "mystery" because, as the writer believes, the agent of this evil was still (when Paul supposedly wrote this letter) temporarily undisclosed (vv. 3b, 6b) and under restraint (vv. 6a, 7b). The power that is said to restrain evil is presented initially as an impersonal force or activity (*"what* is now restraining," v. 6a), but subsequently as a powerful human—or perhaps divine—being ("the *one* who now restrains," v. 7b).

The mysterious agent of lawlessness is, apparently, a human (not "supra-human") figure (otherwise, Best 1972, 284, 288), although our author does not explicitly identify him with any historical personage. The characterization of him as "the lawless one" who is "destined for destruction" (lit. "the man of lawlessness . . . the son of perdition," v. 3b) is reminiscent of LXX Isa 57:3-4, where the wayward Israelites are referred to as "sons of lawlessness" and "children destined for destruction, a lawless seed" (AT). The variant text, "man of sin" (NRSV alt.) is widely attested but almost certainly secondary, for vv. 7, 8 seem to presuppose an association of this mysterious figure specifically with "lawlessness" (cf. B. Metzger 1994, 567).

Whether the writer means that this figure is more particularly identifiable when he is "revealed" (vv. 3b, 6, 8a) is doubtful. The critical point is that the present time continues to be defined by lawlessness. The aim is neither to describe the end-time events nor to forecast when they will take place. It is to show that the day of the Lord cannot possibly have arrived, because the lawless one remains at work. The scenario sketched out here has no certain parallels in either Jewish or other Christian sources of the day, and may therefore be of this writer's own devising. In creating it, however, he has employed various apocalyptic traditions.

One of these was the expectation that the eschatological day would be preceded by evils and terrors of cosmic proportions (e.g., *Jub.* 23:14-21; *1 En.* 91:5-7; *4 Ezra* 5:1-12; cf. Mark 13:5-9 and parr.; 1 Tim 4:1-2; 2 Tim 3:1-5; Jude 17-18). The writer identifies those, collectively, as "the rebellion" (*apostasia*, v. 3b; in LXX Josh

22:22; Jer 2:19, rebellion against God), to which he refers as if it were imminent. The rebellion will begin when the lawless one, no longer under restraint, starts wreaking havoc in the form of wicked deceptions and erroneous beliefs (vv. 7-8a, 9-10).

Jewish apocalyptic traditions yield several possible prototypes for depicting the "lawless one" as desecrating God's temple and claiming divine status (v. 4; the reference here to the temple is of no help in dating this letter—see Introduction). The most notable is Antiochus IV ("Epiphanes"), whose outrages against the Judeans and the Jerusalem temple provoked the Maccabean revolt of 166–60 B.C.E. (e.g., Dan 8:24-25; 9:26-27; 11:31-39). Other possible models include the Roman general Pompey, who was denounced as "the lawless one" (*ho anomos*) for besieging Jerusalem (63 B.C.E.) and personally violating the sanctity of the temple's "holy of holies" (e.g., *Pss. Sol.* 17:11-18), and the Roman emperor Gaius ("Caligula," 37–41 C.E.), who sought to be hailed as a god and planned to install statues of himself in the Jerusalem temple (e.g., Josephus, *J. W.* 2.184-86, 192-97 [in Boring 1995, no. 826]; Philo, *Embassy* 186-89, 263-68).

It has proved especially difficult to determine what the author means when he refers to a restraining force or figure (vv. 6a, 7b; for surveys of various proposals, see Wanamaker 1990, 249-52; Richard 1995, 337-40; Malherbe 2000, 432-33; Nicholl 2004, 228-32). Because he portrays this power as restraining evil, many interpreters hold that he must regard it as essentially good. Accordingly, some propose that he is thinking of Paul as the *person* who restrains evil and of Paul's preaching to the Gentiles as the restraining *activity* (e.g., Cullmann 1950, 164-66; Munck 1959, 36-42). Others suggest that these are, respectively, God (or God's Holy Spirit or angel) and the divine plan of salvation (e.g., Menken 1994, 108-13). But a quite different interpretation, and one of the most ancient (e.g., Tertullian, *Apology* 32.1-2; *The Resurrection of the Flesh* 24.18; John Chrysostom, *Homilies on 2 Thessalonians* 4.1), identifies the restraining power with the Roman emperor and political institutions (e.g., Wanamaker 1990, 256-57; Richard 1995, 337-40). In this case, our author would be attributing a role in God's plan to a power that he regards as in itself hostile to God and the gospel (the strongest evidence and arguments for this interpretation are provided by P. Metzger 2005, esp. 92-131, 271-95).

Perhaps the writer has deliberately left much unclear (e.g., Marxsen 1982, 84-85; Koester 1990, 457). By making it more difficult to identify any specific event as an eschatological sign he would be serving his primary aim. He wants his audience to understand that the present is dominated by lawlessness and that the evils now experienced foreshadow the still greater lawlessness that must occur before the Lord returns.

The reminder in v. 5, formulated (unlike 1 Thess 2:9; 3:4) as a rhetorical question, is also part of this writer's strategy. He seeks to reinforce his present teaching about the lawless one ("these things," probably referring to vv. 3b-4) by identifying it as already a component of Paul's missionary preaching in Thessalonica. The momentary switch to the first person singular (elsewhere in the letter, only at 3:17) and use of the imperfect tense (lit. "I *was telling* you") accentuate the authority and constancy of the Pauline tradition. Yet the author's claim is not easily reconciled with 1 Thessalonians, which contains no stipulation that the restraint and release of a lawless one must precede the Lord's return. To the contrary, in that letter Paul says that his congregation already knows "very well" (which must mean through his own missionary preaching) that the Lord will come suddenly and without warning, "like a thief in the night" (5:1-2).

The Revealing of the Lawless One (2:8-12)

The author maintains that when the lawless one is no longer being restrained (v. 7b)—because his "time" has come (v. 6b)—he is "revealed" (v. 8a; cf. v. 3b) as the agent through whom Satan's power operates in this age (v. 9). What was once a "mystery" (v. 7a) is so no longer, for the satanic origins of lawlessness are disclosed and lawlessness escalates into open, full-scale "rebellion" (v. 3b).

Before describing this rebellion, however, our author interjects another assurance (see earlier, v. 3b) that the lawless one will not prevail in the end (v. 8b). He is confident that the Lord Jesus, when he comes again, will do away with that agent of Satan. Linking two terms not used in combination elsewhere, he refers to the Lord's anticipated return as "the manifestation [*epiphaneia*] of his coming [*parousia*]." This could be just another instance of the author's characteristically fulsome style (e.g., 1:4, "all your persecutions and the afflictions that you are enduring"; 3:2, "wicked and evil people"; 3:12, "we command and exhort"; 3:16, "at all times in all ways"). More likely, however, he employs *epiphaneia* (the only other NT occurrences are in the Pastoral Epistles) to emphasize that the Lord's *parousia* will be a compelling manifestation of divine power (esp. in 2 Macc 3:24; 14:15; 3 Macc 3:8, *epiphaneia* is associated with powerful interventions by God).

The writer's main point is clear: the "Lord Jesus" at his coming will slay the lawless one with the "breath [*pneuma*] of his mouth." Even without the name "Jesus," which is lacking in some ancient manuscripts, the present context requires us to read "Lord" as a christological title. Here again, the writer applies an image to Jesus that is used of God in the Jewish Bible. In this case, he has contracted two parallel images present in LXX Isa 11:4, where the prophet declares that God will "strike the earth with the rod of his mouth, and destroy the wicked with the breath of his lips" (AT; see also Ps 33 [LXX 32]:6; Job 4:9). The suggestion that *pneuma* refers to the (Holy) "Spirit" emanating from Jesus (Giblin 1967, 91-95) is not convincing, for it discounts the traditional character and use of the imagery in this passage (cf. Fee 1994, 75-76).

In v. 9 our author continues with his primary topic, which is the "rebellion" that characterizes this present time before the end. Picking up the narrative that he had begun in v. 8a, he proceeds to speak of the apostasy that the unleashing of the lawless one sets in motion. In contrast to the "revealing" (1:7) and "coming" (2:1, 8b) of the Lord, the "revealing" (2:3, 6, 8a) and "coming" (2:9) of this agent of Satan is demonstrated by *deceptive* signs and wonders (2:9) that spawn confusion about the truth and outright unbelief (2:10-11).

The lawless one is presented here as a pseudo-prophet (Trilling 1980, 104 rightly contrasts the description in v. 4), who with potent "signs" and "wonders" will lure people into believing what is false. The expectation that such deceivers will appear immediately before the end-time is found in both Jewish and Christian apocalyptic traditions of the writer's day (e.g., *Sib. Or.* 2.154-73; Mark 13:22 par. Matt 24:24). These traditions are also echoed, although in subdued tones, in what the author says about the terrible consequences of the deceits that are perpetrated. As truth is abandoned and falsehood embraced (vv. 10b-11; cf. *4 Ezra* 5:1; 14:16-18), unrighteousness flourishes (v. 12; cf. *1 En.* 91:5-7a; 99:8-9a; *4 Ezra* 5:2, 10-11; cf. *2 Bar.* 27) and those who have joined in the apostasy will experience God's condemnation (v. 12; cf. *1 En.* 91:7b; 99:9b; *4 Ezra* 7:113-15).

The apostates that our author has in view are not believers who have renounced their faith but unbelievers who have never accepted the gospel. Having succumbed to the satanic deceits of the lawless one, "those who are perishing" have "refused to love the truth and so be saved" (2:9-10; perhaps echoing Paul's own contrast between "those who are perishing" and "[we] who are being saved," 1 Cor 1:18; 2 Cor 2:15; cf. 4:3). Best's suggestion that our author is thinking specifically of Jewish unbelievers (1972, 308) is not supported by anything in this context or in the letter overall. If particular unbelievers are in mind, it would be those who, no matter their ethnic origin, are engaged in persecuting the church (cf. 1:6, 8).

The claim that unbelievers "refused to love the truth" (v. 10b) corresponds to the author's earlier assertion that those who are afflicting the believing community "do not obey the gospel of our Lord Jesus" (1:8). The use of the aorist (past) tense of the verb ("refused") suggests that their rejection of the gospel is now viewed from the standpoint of the end-time. For this writer, "truth" includes everything that the Pauline gospel declares and requires, and "loving" the truth (a phrase found nowhere else in the NT) means, like "obeying" the gospel, adhering to the apostle's teaching (see comments on vv. 13-14 and 15, where "the truth," "the gospel" [NRSV: "the good news"] and "the traditions" are closely related terms).

It is the writer's conviction that those who fail to adhere to the truth will not "be saved" (v. 10b; cf. v. 13, where "salvation" is linked to "belief in the truth"). What he means by salvation (his explicit references are confined to vv. 10b, 13) must be surmised from several more or less incidental remarks. Together, these suggest that he views the destiny of the faithful as admission into the kingdom of God (1:5), where they will find "relief" from persecution (1:7) and be in the presence of the Lord Jesus (1:9, 10; cf. 2:1). In that realm, the Lord will be glorified in them and they in him (1:10, 12; 2:14). The apostle's own dialectical view of salvation as "already" gracing and claiming the present but "not yet" fulfilled (e.g., 1 Thess 5:4-8) is not evident here. For this writer, salvation is present only by anticipation, as the "good hope" (v. 16) that is held by those who "love the truth" of the apostolic gospel.

The principal topic in these verses, however, is not the salvation that awaits believers but the horrible fate of those who do not accept the truth. The author declares that in consequence of their initial disobedience, "God sends them a powerful delusion" that corrupts both their thinking and their conduct and guarantees their condemnation (vv. 11-12). Once overcome by this delusion, unbelievers will be plunged into the absolute apostasy of believing "what is false." Our author likely has in mind the idolatry of accepting the claim of the lawless one to be God (v. 4; Malherbe 2000, 427; cf. Paul's own comment that idolaters have "exchanged the truth about God for a lie," Rom 1:25). Mention of the attendant "unrighteousness" (v. 12) lends plausibility to this interpretation, for the Jewish and Christian traditions that have shaped this writer's thinking often link wickedness (esp. sexual immorality) to idolatry (e.g., Wis 14:12, 22-29; 1 Thess 4:3-5; 1 Cor 10:6-11). Similarly, the naming of God as responsible for the "powerful delusion" that overcomes unbelievers is in line with such scriptural passages as 3 Kgdms [1 Kgs] 22:23, where Micaiah declares that God has given the prophets "a lying spirit" (cf. Ezek 14:9), and Isa 6:10-13, where God commissions Isaiah to dull the minds, stop the mouths, and shut the eyes of unfaithful Israel until it is utterly destroyed (cf. Mark 4:10-12; John 12:39-41).

◊ ◊ ◊ ◊

The writer has marshaled various apocalyptic traditions to instruct his audience about the true character of the present time. It is impossible to know the extent to which the recipients of this letter would have been able to correlate the figures and events that he mentions with actual persons and circumstances, or even whether the writer himself intended precise correlations. His thesis, however, is generally clear, and so is his theological and ethical point of view.

As explained here, the present time is under the dominion of "lawlessness" even though its working remains a "mystery" until the "lawless one" is "revealed"—which, one may infer, is to be very soon. Thus, where Paul himself (e.g., in 1 Thessalonians) anticipated the imminent *parousia* ("coming") of the Lord, the present writer represents the apostle as anticipating the imminent *parousia* of the lawless one, and of the consequent apostasy ("rebellion"). In fact, of course, this writer and his audience share a position in time subsequent to the apostle's death. So from their standpoint, presumably, the revealing of the lawless one has already occurred and the initial apostasy has already commenced (vv. 3b, 6-8a, 9-10; cf. Popkes 2004, 62-63).

The writer's further claim that God himself will lead unbelievers into yet deeper apostasy and the certainty of condemnation (vv. 11-12) has no real parallel in the apostle's own letters. Some interpreters compare Rom 1:24-32, where Paul speaks of God "giving up" idolaters to "impurity," "degrading passions," and "a debased mind" (vv. 24, 26, 28). The apostle, however, does not claim (like the author of 2 Thessalonians) that God is himself leading such people inexorably and irrevocably toward condemnation and eternal punishment (note Rom 2:5, "*storing up wrath for yourself* on the day of wrath, when God's righteous judgment will be revealed"). Rather, what he says about sin in Rom 1 and 2 prepares the way for his conclusion about salvation in Rom 3: that precisely because "all have sinned and fall short of the glory of God," humanity can only be rectified "by [God's] grace as a gift" (Rom 3:23-24; similarly, Rom 9:18, 22 must be read in the light of Rom 11:32). The author of 2 Thessalonians offers no such hope for those who reject the truth and believe in a falsehood.

Neither, however, does he consider them *arbitrarily* predestined for destruction. While he does say that God sends the "powerful delusion" that will overcome them, he regards this as God's response to their own willful disobedience (note "for this reason," v. 11). He can therefore interpret their condemnation and everlasting ruin as the outworking of divine justice (1:6).

There is no indication that the writer contemplates a prolonged period of apostasy before the Lord's return. His argument, however, concerns not the duration but the character of the present: the day of the Lord has not yet arrived, for the present is ruled by lawlessness, which causes gross apostasy and unrighteousness to flourish. These are the circumstances, according to our author, in which the believing community must endure manifold afflictions, and in which believers must prove themselves worthy of the kingdom by remaining faithful to apostolic teaching (1:4, 5, 10, 11).

Second Thanksgiving (2:13-14)

Formally, these verses constitute a thanksgiving, the second in this letter (cf. 1:3-12). Placed here, it serves to remind the addressees of their commitment to the gospel and to lay a foundation for the appeals and commands that will follow in 2:15–3:16.

◊ ◊ ◊ ◊

The opening words (v. 13a) are almost identical to those of the first thanksgiving (1:3a). One difference is the emphatic "But we," which contrasts the situation of those who have believed the truth and are destined for salvation with that of the unbelievers who have just been described as doomed to condemnation (vv. 10-12). A second difference is the addition of "beloved by the Lord" to the direct address, "brothers and sisters." Here the writer seems to have been influenced by a similar phrase that appears in the initial thanksgiving in 1 Thessalonians. As in other instances, however, he has replaced Paul's reference to God ("brothers and sisters beloved by God," 1 Thess 1:4) with a reference to "the Lord" (see also 3:3, 5, 16). To be sure, "Lord" could still refer to God, for the focus is on God's actions in the immediate context (vv. 11-12,

13b-14; Malherbe 2000, 436). More likely, however, our author is once again using "Lord" as a christological title (see Introduction); it does not appear in a statement but in a descriptive phrase, and in most if not all other occurrences in this letter, "the Lord" stands for "the Lord Jesus [Christ]."

Even if the writer means that believers have been loved by Christ, nothing indicates that he is thinking of Christ's saving death, which he mentions nowhere in this letter. Rather, his stated reason for giving thanks is God's election of believers for the coming salvation (v. 13b; similarly, 1 Thess 1:4; for the future reference of salvation in 2 Thessalonians, see comments on v. 10). Interpreters are divided on whether the original text referred to believers as chosen to be "the first fruits [*aparchēn*] for salvation" (NRSV; Fee 1994, 177 n. 142; Malherbe 2000, 437, et al.) or to their election "from the beginning [*ap' archēs*] for salvation" (NRSV alt.; NEB; Rigaux 1956, 682; Richard 1995, 356, *et al.*). These two readings are about equally attested by the ancient textual witnesses.

Some favor "first fruits" because this word is found in Paul's own letters and "from the beginning" is not. This means little, however, because our author employs many non-Pauline terms. A more important consideration is that the identification of believers as "the first fruits for salvation" seems unrelated to the thought in vv. 13b-14, whereas the statement that election was God's purpose "from the beginning" specifically enriches it. Moreover, one can readily understand how *aparchēn* ("first fruits") might have come to be substituted for *ap' archēs* ("from the beginning"), either as a scribal error (in Gk., the two expressions look very much alike) or as a scribe's deliberate "correction" of an expression that was presumed to be wrong because it occurred nowhere else in Paul's letters. In this context, "from the beginning" would almost certainly refer to what has obtained "from eternity" or "since the beginning of creation" (cf. von Dobschütz 1909, 298; Best 1972, 314; Gundry Volf 1991, 16-17). This meaning is found both in the LXX (e.g., Wis 6:22; 9:8; Sir 16:26; 24:9; Isa 63:16) and in early Christian apocalyptic traditions (e.g., Mark 13:19 par. Matt 24:21; 2 Pet 3:4).

In describing election to salvation as "through sanctification by the Spirit," our author mentions God's Spirit for the first and only time (Furnish 2004, esp. 232-40); and apart from one reference to believers as "saints" (1:10), this is the only place he has used the vocabulary of "holiness" and "sanctification." He seems to be drawing on 1 Thess 4:7-8, where a statement about God's call "in holiness" is followed by a reference to the giving of the Holy Spirit. But unlike Paul, who views the Spirit as a continuing, sanctifying presence with believers, empowering and guiding their lives (see commentary on 1 Thess 4:1-8), this writer associates "sanctification by the Spirit" strictly with the believer's conversion.

Arguments for reading *pneuma* even in the present case as a reference to the human spirit (thus Mof., "by the consecration of your spirit"; Findlay 1911, 189-90) are not persuasive. The same unusual phrase, which may derive from a baptismal tradition, is also associated with the idea of election in 1 Pet 1:2, where it is clear that *pneuma* can refer only to the Spirit of God (Elliott 2000, 318-19). In both instances, the claim is that election has been carried out through the sanctifying power of the Spirit. Although the author of 1 Peter may associate this with the baptismal rite, which he mentions elsewhere in his letter (1 Pet 3:21), our author's silence about baptism makes it impossible to know whether he, too, would make such a connection.

According to this author, election comes about not only through the working of the Spirit but also "through belief in the truth [*pistis alētheias*]." The word *pistis*, which NRSV renders as "faith" in 1:3, 4, 11, is in this instance appropriately translated as "belief." In this phrase the object of *pistis* is "truth," and in this context "truth" refers to "*what* is true" as opposed to "*what* is false" (vv. 11-12). The expression *pistis alētheias* is therefore to be understood as "assent to what is true." Our author offers no comment and seems not to have reflected on how, or even whether, such belief is related to God's acting through the Spirit. His point is only that both are required for salvation. As noted earlier (comments on v. 10), for this writer the "truth" that must be affirmed is the apostolic teaching conveyed by Paul; "believing the truth" and "believing [Paul's] testimony" (1:10) are parallel expressions.

This interpretation is confirmed in v. 14, where Paul's gospel (NRSV: "good news") is identified as the means through which God "called" believers to "obtain the glory of our Lord Jesus Christ." Those who have accepted that gospel have believed the truth, and in so doing have fulfilled their status as God's elect. Although the writer is here drawing on Paul's statements in 1 Thess 1:4, 5, he is going substantially beyond them. The apostle himself says that he is confident of the Thessalonians' election because the gospel did not come to them simply as his word. It came "also in power and in the Holy Spirit," which is to say, "not as a human word but as what it really is, God's word" (1 Thess 2:13). Nowhere in the certainly authentic letters does Paul represent God's call as mediated, either through his gospel or even through Christ. He affirms that call to be accomplished in no other way than through God's own working (Trilling 1980, 122; Richard 1995, 357). Despite Wanamaker (1990, 267), Gal 1:6-7 does not "imply" that the call comes through Paul's gospel; precisely in that passage the apostle refers to God as "the one who called you" (see Martyn 1997, 108-9).

In declaring that God has summoned believers to "obtain the glory of our Lord Jesus Christ," the author draws on and modifies two further statements in 1 Thessalonians. One is Paul's declaration that God calls believers "into his own kingdom and glory" (1 Thess 2:12). Now this writer, resuming a thought he has already advanced (1:12), speaks of God's call as giving access to the glory that belongs to the coming Lord. Typically, he has changed a reference to God into a reference to Christ.

There is also an echo here of 1 Thess 5:9-10, where Paul affirms that God "has destined us . . . for obtaining salvation through our Lord Jesus Christ." Our author, like the apostle, speaks of believers as "obtaining" their destiny, an expression that suggests but does not emphasize a role for human effort (see commentary on 1 Thess 5:9-10). His substitution of "glory" for "salvation" is inconsequential (he has just used the latter term, v. 13b), but his change of a preposition is telling. Where Paul says that salvation comes "*through* our Lord Jesus Christ, who died for us," this writer speaks of the glory "*of* our Lord Jesus Christ," with no mention of Christ's death (Trilling 1980, 123). As throughout the letter, and in accord with its aims, he speaks of Jesus only as an eschatological figure, never of his past or present saving work. He is presented as the Lord who will return at the last day, and in whose glorious presence believers may hope to spend eternity.

◊   ◊   ◊   ◊

With this second thanksgiving, the author shifts his focus from the character of the present time, which he has portrayed as still dominated by lawlessness, to the status of believers as God's elect, assured of salvation. Their election was God's purpose "from the beginning" and has been accomplished through the working of God's Spirit and their own assenting to the truth (v. 13). Having set them apart (sanctified them) for salvation, God "called" them through Paul's gospel to embrace their identity as the elect, and to live in hope of future glory (v. 14).

As many interpreters point out, this thanksgiving is dominated by the ideas of *election, calling*, and *glory*. Election and calling are presented as actions that God has already taken, while "glory" stands for the future salvation that God will bestow with the coming of the Lord Jesus (cf. Marshall 1990, 273). These three themes are present as well in Rom 8:28-30, but there the mention also of justification reflects Paul's view that God's saving work has already been inaugurated through Christ's death (vv. 31-34). The author of 2 Thessalonians, however, conceives salvation as wholly future, as given only with the coming of the day of the Lord. As he sees it, what defines the present lives of believers is their status as God's elect who have been *destined* for that coming salvation. By assuring them of this, he seeks to strengthen their "belief in the truth" (the apostolic tradition) and their resolve to withstand the lawlessness that prevails at the present time.

APPEALS, COMMANDS, AND PRAYERS (2:15–3:16)

This second part of the body of the letter, which is somewhat loosely arranged, contains several general appeals (2:15; 3:13-

15) and a longer section of "commands" about dealing with unruly believers (3:6-12). It includes, as well, three prayers for the faith and well-being of those addressed (2:16-17; 3:5; 3:16a), and a request that they pray for Paul and his preaching of the gospel (3:1-2). The writer's dependence on 1 Thessalonians continues to be evident, as do his modifications of what Paul himself had said.

Many interpreters regard the admonition and prayer in 2:15-17 as part of the preceding thanksgiving (2:13-14), and see a new section as beginning only in 3:1 (e.g., Best 1972, 316-17; Richard 1995, 361). A number of others regard 2:13 through 3:5 as a unit, with 3:6 as the beginning of a new section (e.g., Findlay 1911, 187; Rigaux 1956, 680-81; P.-G. Müller 2001, 279-80). There is much to be said, however, for the view that a new section begins already with the admonition in 2:15. This is the judgment of both Trilling (1982, 124-26), who identifies the new section as extending through 3:16, and Malherbe (2000, 439), who has it extending only through 3:5.

Trilling's proposal, which is the one adopted here, has several things in its favor. (a) The phrase that opens 2:15, "So then, brothers and sisters" (*ara oun, adelphoi*), marks a transition; the audience will next be shown some consequences of what has just been said (*adelphoi* also marks transitions in 1:3; 2:1; and 2:13). (b) The varied contents of 2:15–3:16 are framed, and thereby gain a certain coherence, by an admonition to "hold fast" to the "traditions" that Paul has taught (2:15) and the complementary instruction about dealing with believers who do not "obey" what he says (3:14-15). (c) Within this section, the term *adelphoi* ("brothers and sisters") occurs four times in direct address (2:15; 3:1, 6, 13), each occurrence signaling a new appeal or instruction. (d) In each of the four paragraphs thus introduced there is some specific reference to Paul's singular authority for believers. Thus, 2:15-17: he has taught the traditions to which they should adhere (cf. 3:6); 3:1-5: what he "commands" them they are to do; 3:6-12: his commands are given "in the name of our Lord Jesus Christ," and his personal example is part of the apostolic tradition; 3:13-16: what he says in this letter must be obeyed.

Appeal to Adhere to the Traditions (2:15-17)

The appeal in v. 15 is formulated so broadly that it serves all of the author's aims in this letter (Trilling 1980, 127). He urges the addressees to "stand firm" by "hold[ing] fast to the traditions" that they have been "taught," whether "by word of mouth or by our letter." This appeal supports both the preceding instruction about the end-time (2:1-12) and the following directives about church order (3:6-12). Thus, the "traditions" most directly in view here are eschatological (2:1-12) and ecclesiastical (3:6-12).

If "our letter" refers to 1 Thessalonians (most interpreters), the audience is being asked to understand the teaching of that letter and this one as fully consistent, no matter what the false teaching claims. A reference to the present letter (e.g., Lindemann 1999, 230, 232; for different reasons, Wanamaker 1990, 269) is not impossible, but unlikely. A third possibility is to understand the phrase "by word of mouth or by our letter" as a general reference to the whole body of Paul's teaching both in the oral and written tradition (cf. Trilling 1980, 128-29; Richard 1995, 359). Whatever the case may be, it is clear that our author wants the present instruction to be accepted as a constituent part of that tradition.

However, the writer appears to reject in principle any notion that the apostolic tradition is open to changes or additions. He has warned earlier that false teaching may be promoted "by spirit or by word or by letter" (2:2). Now, referring to the teaching that believers must "hold fast" (*krateō*, also of tradition in Mark 7:3, 4, 8), he mentions only "word" and "letter." The omission of "spirit," which can hardly have been an oversight, implicitly excludes from the tradition any teachings that have originated as Spirit-inspired utterances or prophecies (Holland 1988, 49; Richard 1995, 359).

This idea of a fixed Pauline tradition to which believers must adhere surfaces again in 3:6. There "the tradition" received from Paul is mentioned as the norm according to which believers must conduct their lives. For this author, holding fast to the apostolic "tradition(s)," obeying "the gospel of our Lord Jesus" (1:8; cf. 2:14), believing Paul's "testimony" (1:10b), and believing "the truth" (2:12, 13b; cf. 2:10) are overlapping ideas, even if these expressions are not entirely interchangeable.

The appeal is reinforced by a benedictory prayer (vv. 16-17) that seems to be modeled in part on the one in 1 Thess 3:11-13, although naming "the Lord Jesus Christ" before "God our Father" reverses the order in the earlier letter. The reversal serves to identify God more directly than Christ as the one who has "loved us" and bestowed "eternal comfort and good hope" (v. 16). The phrase "with grace" (AT), which (in Gk.) occurs at the end of the verse, should probably be construed (adverbially) with both "loved" and "gave." As in 1:12, it refers to God's beneficence in providing for the salvation of the elect (Richards 1995, 359). The aorist (past tense) verb, "loved," may refer more particularly to God's electing love (cf. 2:13). Nothing here or elsewhere in the letter supports the view (held, e.g., by Menken 1994, 123 and Richard 1995, 359) that the author is thinking of the saving event of Christ's death.

As beneficiaries of God's love, the elect are already graced with "eternal comfort" and "good hope." The words "comfort" and "hope" do not appear in 2 Thessalonians apart from this prayer. Moreover, they have a more general reference here than in 1 Thessalonians, where Paul offers pastoral counsel and instruction concerning the congregation's experience of afflictions and grief. In the present context, both phrases point ahead to the coming day of the Lord, when God's punishment of the wicked and vindication of the righteous will be the ultimate "comfort" for those who are now being persecuted (see esp., 1:5-10; 2:7-12). Both Hellenistic and Hellenistic-Jewish sources attest to the use of the expression "good hope" with reference to life after death (BDAG, 320 *s.v. elpis,* §1bβ).

In praying that the addressees' "hearts" (see commentary on 1 Thess 3:13) may continue to be "encouraged" (AT) and "strengthened" (v. 17), the author is echoing both 1 Thess 3:2 (Timothy had been sent to "strengthen and encourage" the Thessalonians) and 1 Thess 3:13 (Paul prays that God may "strengthen [the Thessalonians'] hearts in holiness"). The mention of being strengthened "in every good work and word" adds weight to the call for fidelity to the traditions (both ethical and doctrinal), and also anticipates the more specific directives in

3:6-12, 13-15. The expression "in deed[s] and word[s]" (either in this or the reverse order) is widely attested (BDAG, 390 *s.v. ergon*, §1a), and found elsewhere in the NT (e.g., Rom 15:18; 2 Cor 10:11 [NRSV: "what we say... we... do"]; Col 3:17).

◊ ◊ ◊ ◊

The call to "hold fast" to the apostolic tradition(s) is one of the most fundamental appeals in this letter. It presupposes that the "truth" one must believe in order to be saved (2:10-12; cf. 1:10) is definitively conveyed in what Paul preached and wrote. Therefore, all novel beliefs, like the claim that the day of the Lord has already arrived (2:2), are to be rejected.

In 1 Thessalonians, using a technical term (*paralambanō*) for the reception of a tradition that is handed on, the apostle himself writes of what the Thessalonians had "received" from him about conduct that is pleasing to God (4:1, AT; NRSV: "learned"). He also makes it clear, however, that the "instructions" he gave them were not his own, but came "through the Lord Jesus" (4:2; see also 1 Cor 11:23, and cf. 1 Cor 15:1, 3). Significantly, the present writer offers no such indication of the origin of the traditions. This, along with his asserting that the traditions were "taught" through the apostle's preaching and letter(s) (2:15), opens the door to conceiving of them as specifically *Pauline*. It is consistent with this modification that, while Paul himself summons the Thessalonians to "stand firm *in the Lord*" (*stēkete en kyriō*, 1 Thess 3:8), our author summons his audience to "stand firm and hold fast *to the traditions*" that the apostle had taught them (*stēkete, kai krateite tas paradoseis*, 2:15; cf. Koester 1980, 294).

Request for Prayer (3:1-5)

The expression "Finally" (v. 1a) does not signal the author's closing thought but simply takes over the term found in 1 Thess 4:1, which follows a paragraph (1 Thess 3:11-13) from which our author has just drawn (2 Thess 2:16-17). Although the apostle was introducing a series of ethical appeals (1 Thess 4:2-12), this writer is, in the first instance, introducing a request for prayer.

Unlike the open-ended request in 1 Thess 5:25, this one initially specifies prayer for the unhindered progress and success of "the word of the Lord" (Paul's gospel), that it may "run forward and be glorified as it is among you" (v. 1b, AT; "everywhere" [NRSV] has no counterpart in the Gk. text). The striking image of a word running (swiftly) forward echoes Ps 147:15 (LXX: 147:4), and hints that the gospel is propelled with a power of divine origin. The verb *doxazō* (to "glorify") is used, as in Acts 13:48 (NRSV: "praised"), to indicate the acceptance of the Lord's word by those to whom it is proclaimed (cf. 2 Thess 1:10a, 12).

The audience is asked to pray, as well, that Paul "may be rescued from wicked and evil people" (v. 2a). No specific threat is in view here, and the wording is scriptural (cf. Ps 140:1 [LXX: 139:2], "Deliver me, Lord, from the evil person; rescue me from the unjust man" [AT]; Isa 25:4, "you will rescue them from evil persons" [AT]). The generality of the requested prayer is confirmed in the appended comment that "not all have faith" (v. 2b). This is an example of *litotes* (understatement for the sake of emphasis), and supports both parts of the prayer request (vv. 1b, 2a): there are still many unbelievers who need to hear the gospel, and many who pose a threat to those who proclaim it.

With the affirmation that "the Lord is faithful" (v. 3a), the author abruptly shifts attention from Paul's welfare and the gospel's (vv. 1-2) to that of the addressees. His affirmation may have been prompted by the statement in 1 Thess 5:24 about God's faithfulness ("The one who calls you is faithful"). His particular formulation of it has scriptural as well as Pauline roots (note Deut 7:9; 32:4; Ps 144:13a [only in LXX]; Isa 49:7; 1 Cor 1:9; 10:13; 2 Cor 1:18). In the present context, it supports the following assurance that God "will strengthen" the addressees and "guard [them] from evil" (v. 3b, NRSV alt.; cf. esp. Pss 12:7 [LXX 11:8]; 121:7 [LXX 120:7]). If the words *tou ponērou* in the last phrase are interpreted as masculine instead of neuter, then the reference would not be to "evil" but to "the evil one" (NRSV), meaning Satan (see 2:9 and 1 Thess 2:18; 3:5). Either way, the letter's recipients are being assured that God will keep them safe during the course of this present time when lawlessness is loose in the world (cf. 2:8-10).

In expressing his confidence that the addressees will do what Paul commands (v. 4), the author is issuing an indirect appeal for their obedience. The statement primarily anticipates the commands that will be specified in vv. 6-12. The verb to "command" (Gk. *parangellō*) is the same one Paul uses in 1 Thess 4:11, where the context requires some translation like to "instruct" or "direct" (see comments about the corresponding noun in 1 Thess 4:2). But in the present context, where the authority of the Pauline tradition is repeatedly stressed (vv. 6, 7-9, 10, 12, 14), it has the harsher sense of "ordering" or "commanding." The "Lord" in whom this author's confidence about the addressees resides is probably "the Lord Jesus" (see v. 12), as in the apostle's own similar formulation, Gal 5:10 (cf. Rom 14:14; Phil 2:24).

The benedictory prayer in v. 5 corresponds in function to the one in 2:16-17, but is even more general. Although our author, like Paul in 1 Thess 3:11, employs the verb to "direct" (*kateuthynō*), he uses it differently. The apostle's prayer is that God and the Lord Jesus "direct" his way back to Thessalonica. When the present letter was written, however—sometime after Paul's death (see Introduction)—that was a historical impossibility. So now this author links the verb to the word "hearts" (which appears in 1 Thess 3:13), praying that "the Lord direct [the addressees'] hearts to the love of God and to the steadfastness of Christ." To "direct the heart" is in fact a LXX expression (found nowhere else in the NT) for earnestly seeking God (e.g., 1 Chr 29:18; 2 Chr 12:14; 19:3; Sir 49:3). Here, it is unclear whether "the Lord" refers to God (as in the LXX passages) or to the Lord Jesus. The two genitives, "of God" and "of Christ," are also open to different interpretations. If they are objective, the references are to love for God and patience in waiting for Christ (e.g., Menken 1994, 129); if they are subjective, they refer to God's own love (as in 2:16) and Christ's own steadfastness (e.g., Malherbe 2000). It is also possible that one is subjective and the other is objective.

◊ ◊ ◊ ◊

This paragraph is so general in outlook that it could stand as the conclusion of the body of the letter. As it is, these verses provide a transition between the preceding call to adhere to the Pauline traditions (2:15) and the specific commands that are issued in vv. 6-12. The request for prayers for the success of the Pauline mission (v. 1b) draws attention to the critical importance, and hence authority, of the Pauline tradition. And the request for prayers that the apostle be "rescued [*rhysthōmen*] from wicked and evil people" (v. 2b) highlights Paul's status as a heroic proclaimer of the gospel whose life is constantly at risk. In accord with this, the author's confidence that the addressees will do as the apostle commands (v. 4) is based not on the new life they presently experience as believers, but on their willingness to acknowledge the apostle's authority.

There are two places in Paul's own letters where he requests prayers for his safety. In 2 Cor 1:8-11, referring to a recent close call in Asia (v. 8), he asks that the Corinthians pray for God's continuing rescue (*rhyomai*, v. 10) of him; and in Rom 15:30-31, in advance of a trip to Jerusalem, he asks that the Romans join him in prayers that he "may be rescued [*rhysthō*] from the unbelievers in Judea." In contrast to those requests, the present one has no particular historical context. In its generality, it corresponds to the image of an idealized Paul that is presented in other post-Pauline writings. The parallel with 2 Tim 4:16-18 is particularly striking, for there, too, the writer has in view both the success of the apostle's mission and his need for rescue (*rhyomai*, vv. 17, 18) from evil people (cf. 2 Tim 3:10-13 [*rhyomai*, v. 10]).

Commands Regarding the Disorderly (3:6-12)

As in 2:15 and 3:1, "brothers and sisters" (v. 6; NRSV: "beloved") marks the opening of a new subsection, the longest one in this part of the letter. The passage is framed by two christological references ("in the name of our Lord Jesus Christ," v. 6; "in the Lord Jesus Christ," v. 12), which add weight to the directives that are conveyed.

Here the author's particular concern is that some believers are unwilling to support themselves. Yet despite extended discussion of this matter—which is second only to the attention given to false doctrine in chapter 2—the comments remain rather general and the argument is somewhat loosely organized. An initial command (v. 6) is supplemented with a reference to Paul's personal example (vv. 7-9) and reinforced by a further command, this one attributed to Paul when he was in Thessalonica (v. 10). But the statement in v. 11 ("For we hear that . . .") sounds more like an introduction to the issue than a summation of it, and the command with which the passage concludes (v. 12) is not entirely consistent with the command with which it opens (v. 6).

The author's use of various statements and expressions found in 1 Thessalonians (most notably: 1 Thess 1:6; 2:9; 4:10b-12; 5:14) is especially evident in these verses.

Initial Command (3:6)

Paul's authority to ask for obedience to his directives (v. 4) is demonstrated in a series of three commands about dealing with fellow believers who are "acting irresponsibly" (vv. 6, 11, AT [Gk. *ataktōs peripatountos*]). When our author issues these orders "in the (name of our) Lord Jesus Christ," he is endowing them also with the authority of Christ himself (the same or similar expressions with the same intent occur in 1 Cor 1:10; 5:4; cf. 7:10).

Later in this discussion there are references to believers who are unwilling to work for a living (e.g., vv. 10-12), and the NRSV anticipates this by translating the Greek adverb (*ataktōs*, vv. 6, 11) as "in idleness." The root meaning of the term, however, is "out of line"—hence "disorderly" or "unruly" (see commentary on 1 Thess 5:14)—and in the first instance the writer characterizes such conduct as not conforming to "the tradition that they received from us." The use here of the third person plural is unexpected, because the second person plural predominates in the passage as a whole. The third person is almost certainly original (B. Metzger 1994, 569), however, and indicates that the author visualizes a certain division among those for whom he is writing (confirmed in v. 12).

The command to "keep away" from unruly believers draws on 1 Thess 5:14, but it is more severe than Paul's counsel there to "admonish" and "be patient" with such people. Whether the present writer means that they should be summarily and permanently excommunicated, however, is uncertain. It is possible that he is calling for their exclusion only from designated congregational activities, or only until such time as they have been shamed into changing their irresponsible conduct (see comments on 3:14b-15).

Mandate to Follow Paul's Example (3:7-9)

To supplement and thereby support the opening command, our author turns again to 1 Thessalonians. His comments about "toil and labor" and "[working] night and day" (v. 8b) are taken over almost verbatim from 1 Thess 2:9. There the apostle points out that during his time in Thessalonica he sought to earn his own living in order "not [to] burden any of you while we proclaimed to you the gospel of God" (cf. 2 Cor 11:7-9). The present writer, however, passing over the apostle's wish not to place a burden on his converts, emphasizes that he wanted to provide them with "an example to imitate" (v. 9b).

When the apostle himself refers to believers who imitate him, he does not mean that they have accepted his day-to-day conduct as a model for their own. Rather, he refers to his converts as having become "imitators of us and of the Lord" by accepting the word of God in spite of the suffering that they experienced as a consequence (see comments on 1 Thess 1:6-7). Moreover, the idea that one imitates Paul in the way that he himself imitates *Christ*, which is a critical point in 1 Thess 1:6 ("*and of the Lord*") and other Pauline letters (1 Cor 11:1; Phil 3:17), is completely missing from 2 Thessalonians. Here, Paul's conduct is represented as in itself normative for believers. Accordingly, where the apostle speaks of "how [the Thessalonians] ought to live and to *please God*" (1 Thess 4:1), our author speaks of "how [they] ought to *imitate us*" (v. 7a), and claims their prior familiarity with this obligation ("you yourselves know," v. 7a—an expression drawn from 1 Thess 2:1; 3:3; 5:2, etc.).

The mention of Paul's "right" (*exousia*) to be supported by others (v. 9a) seems to assume that this apostolic privilege was already acknowledged by those who would be receiving 2 Thessalonians, even though 1 Thessalonians had been silent on the matter. It would appear that our author, and perhaps his audience, were also acquainted with 1 Corinthians, where Paul argues that this right is mandated by both the Law of Moses (9:9, citing Deut 25:4) and Jesus (9:14; cf. Matt 10:10; Luke 10:7). But consistent with 1 Thess 2:9, Paul tells the Corinthians that he waives the right to be supported by them in order to avoid hindering the advancement of the gospel (1 Cor 9:12b, 15-23). Unlike the author of 2 Thessalonians, he says nothing about having wanted to provide an example for his converts to follow.

Second Command (3:10)

In addition to Paul's personal example, the writer invokes an apostolic command that he dates to the time of the founding of the Thessalonian congregation (v. 10a, "when we were with you"; cf. 1 Thess 3:4). He conveys this as a rule of fundamental importance (note the emphatic "this" and the imperfect tense [= continuing past action]): "This is what we were commanding you: 'If someone is not willing to work, let him not eat'" (v. 10b, AT). Formally, this command is typical of regulations that stipulate how particular situations should be dealt with in the life of a particular community ("If . . . let" [*ei* + a third person imperative]; see, e.g., 1 Cor 7:9, 15; 11:6, 34; 14:35; 1 Tim 5:4, 16). Moreover, its linking of eating to work reflects the view, expressed in many ancient sources, that providing for one's own livelihood is a responsibility that must not be shirked, and that there will be serious consequences when it is (e.g., Prov 6:6-11; cf. 10:4; 12:11; Pseudo-Phocylides, *Sent.* 153-54; Dio Chrysostom *Or.* 7 [discussed by Hock 1980, 44-45]).

It is important to recognize that the rule mentioned here does not pertain to those who for some reason are *unable* to support themselves (e.g., due to the lack of opportunity, a particular infirmity, or their age). Rather, it concerns those who specifically *refuse* to earn their own living, and thus become dependent on others.

Several further matters are less clear. Does our author know of believers who actually are disrupting the church's life by refusing to support themselves? If so, what motivates their refusal? And from what sort of eating are they to be excluded? From participation in ritual celebrations of the Lord's Supper, or from all table fellowship within the community of believers?

Most interpreters regard the attention given to disruptive idleness as evidence that our author knows it to be a problem in Christian circles (cf. Trilling 1980, 152). There is less agreement, however, about why certain believers were no longer willing to work. Some offer a theological explanation, attributing it to the (perhaps fanatical) belief that the day of the Lord had already arrived, from which it was concluded that mundane responsibilities were no longer important (e.g., P.-G. Müller 2001, 294). A variation of this view holds that those who regarded the Kingdom as Paradise restored were rejecting as obsolete the decree of Gen 3:17-19 that humanity must sustain itself through the arduous tilling of the soil (Menken 1994, 137-41). In fact, however, the author himself neither specifies nor even implies that the problem of idleness has its roots in an erroneous eschatology.

Sociological explanations of the problem, even when they are plausible, are also hard to substantiate from what is actually said. Were some believers seeking to be supported by wealthy Christian (or non-Christian) patrons, thus lapsing back into the patron-client relationships that they had abandoned at their conversion (Winter 1989; cf. Russell 1988)? Or were some believers simply taking unfair advantage of the generosity of others, thereby putting a strain on the ties that bound the believing community together as a "family" (Nicholl 2004, 166-75; cf. Wanamaker 1990, 287; Malherbe 2000, 455-57)? Or was the problem not that certain believers refused to support themselves, but that urban assemblies of believers were organized as communes, and that some members were failing to contribute their fair share (Jewett 1993)?

Because the author's whole discussion of this matter is couched in such general terms, it is impossible to draw any firm conclusions about the situation that may have evoked it. Indeed, some have questioned whether the author even had a specific situation in view (e.g., Marxsen 1982, 100). Perhaps he has simply *imagined* a situation that allows him to emphasize very concretely—by invoking an allegedly Pauline rule—the vital importance of adhering to the apostolic tradition.

Third Command (3:11-12)

A third command (v. 12) is introduced by a further characterization of those who are "acting irresponsibly" (AT, v. 11; cf. v. 6). The phrase "we hear" (v. 11), which would ordinarily introduce rather than conclude a discussion (see, e.g., 1 Cor 5:1 [lit. "it is heard"]; 11:18), suggests that the problem of disorderliness has only recently come to light. Moreover, the unruly are now described (with wordplay that English cannot capture) as not only "not working" (AT; Gk. *mēden ergazomenous*) but also "mere busybodies" (Gk. *periergazomenous*; cf. REB: "minding everybody's business but their own"). The latter expression has a fairly wide range of meaning, which includes idle curiosity (e.g., Plutarch, *On Being a Busybody*; Philo, *On Drunkenness* 135, 167), pointless busy-ness (e.g., Philo, *Names* 72), and intruding where one does not belong (e.g., Sir 3:23; 41:22). Once again, no particulars are offered about the conduct that may be in view.

As he had at the beginning of this passage (v. 6), our author invokes the authority of the "Lord Jesus Christ" for the command that he issues (v. 12). Unlike the opening command, this one is not directed to all of the addressees, but formulated specifically for those ("such persons") whom the writer has just characterized as not working and "mere busybodies." (The use of two verbs, "command and exhort," perhaps echoes 1 Thess 4:1-2, 10-11.) He has previously urged believers to stay away from the disorderly (v. 6) and to exclude them from eating (v. 10b); now he commands the disorderly to "work quietly" (i.e., not to be "busybodies"; ancient parallels in Malherbe 2000, 454) and "earn their own living." The pairing of these directives reflects Paul's own call for believers to "live quietly" and "work with [their] hands" (1 Thess 4:11). But where the apostle was concerned about how believers would be viewed by outsiders (1 Thess 4:12), this author, whose stance toward unbelievers is unrelentingly negative (e.g., 2:9-12; 3:2), is concerned about relationships within the believing community itself.

Here, as earlier in the letter, our author stresses the importance of adhering to the apostolic—which, for him, means Pauline—

tradition. He has already appealed to the tradition as normative for what one must *believe* (2:15); now he appeals to it as also the norm for what one must *do*. Moreover, it is now apparent that he understands Paul's own exemplary conduct to be a constituent part of that tradition (vv. 7-9). As a consequence, and as in other writings of the post-Pauline period, the apostle is viewed here less as a *historical* than as a *heroic* figure (cf. the comments on vv. 2, 4). Along with his gospel, Paul himself has been enshrined in the church's tradition, which extols him as the perfect model of Christian faith and conduct (e.g., Acts 20:17-35 [esp. vv. 33-35]; 1 Tim 1:16; 2 Tim 1:13; *1 Clem.* 5:5-7; Ign. *Eph.* 12:2). Accordingly, imitating Paul is not simply commended as advisable; it is commanded as absolutely imperative (v. 7a, "how one *must* [*dei*] imitate us," NAB).

The writer's emphasis on the importance of obeying what the tradition mandates may help explain why he offers few particulars about the situation he is ostensibly addressing. He says nothing specific about the harm that the disorderly are inflicting (or could inflict) on their fellow believers, or on the cause of the gospel; and nothing, either, about the particular characteristics that distinguish a community as Christian. Instead of pastoral advice and encouragement he issues commands, which in the end amount to just the one command to adhere to the tradition.

Final Advisories (3:13-16)

These final advisories conclude the second part of the letter, and thus the letter-body as a whole. The author no longer speaks of "commanding" as he has in vv. 6-12, but takes a somewhat more pastoral stance, perhaps influenced by the tone of Paul's counsels in 1 Thess 5:12-22, some of which are echoed here. Yet the writer is no less insistent than he has been all along (see esp. 2:15-17) that the addressees must obey the doctrines and directives that are conveyed in this letter (note v. 14a).

◊ ◊ ◊ ◊

The emphatic "Now *you*" (*hymeis de*, v. 13; not translated by NRSV) distinguishes the "brothers and sisters" who are now addressed from the unruly who have just been in view (vv. 6-12).

In fact, nothing in vv. 13-16 connects specifically with the preceding topic. The appeal not to tire in "doing what is right" (or: "doing good") is simultaneously an encouraging word, and it is stated broadly enough to apply to all types of good conduct (cf. 1:11, "every good resolve and work of faith"; 2:17, "every good work and word"). Although it may reflect Paul's own exhortations about "the good" in 1 Thessalonians (5:15, 21), there is actually a closer parallel in Gal 6:9. In the context of 2 Thessalonians, however, the appeal has a special aspect. For our author, persistence in doing good requires continuing fidelity to what the tradition teaches and commands.

It is also evident that this writer wants his letter to be accepted as an authentic part of that apostolic tradition. Accordingly, he urges the "brothers and sisters" to take action against those "who do not obey what we say in this letter" (v. 14a). He refers not just to the disorderly believers who have been the subject of vv. 6-12, but to *all* who embrace false doctrines or act irresponsibly. It is uncertain whether he is calling for such people to be identified (and perhaps rebuked) in some formal way (cf. Matt 18:17a; 1 Tim 5:10). The call to "take note" (*sēmeiousthe*) of them could simply mean that the community should be on the lookout for disobedience (Richard 1995, 384, compares Rom 16:17, where the verb *skopeō* [to "keep an eye on"] is used in a similar context).

The instructions for dealing with the disobedient are also ambiguous. The author first charges the community to "have nothing to do with them, so that they may be ashamed" (v. 14b). While this is consistent with his earlier command to "keep away from" the disorderly (v. 6), the two directives are equally vague on whether such offenders are to be excluded from the community or somehow isolated within it. A further question is whether he intends that the disciplinary action will shame them into *repenting*, so that they may be forgiven and restored to full fellowship (note the apostle's own counsel in 2 Cor 2:5-11).

Uncertainties only increase with the addition of a directive not to treat the disobedient "as enemies" (= outsiders) but to "admonish (*noutheteite*) them as brothers and sisters" (v. 15, AT; cf. 1 Thess 5:14, "admonish [*noutheteite*] the unruly," AT). How can someone who has been isolated within or excluded from the community still be admonished as a fellow believer? Or does the writer intend that disobedient members be *first* admonished and only isolated or excluded if they nevertheless continue to offend? If the latter course of action is the one envisioned, it would be similar to the procedures set forth in Matt 18:15-17 and Titus 3:10-11—both of which, however, are more specific about the disciplinary steps that a congregation should take.

The benedictory prayer in v. 16a is an adaptation of a prayer in 1 Thess 5:23, which directly follows some counsels on which this writer has just been drawing (echoes in vv. 6, 11, 13, 15). His invoking of "the Lord of peace" where Paul has "the God of peace" (see also Rom 15:33; 2 Cor 13:11; Phil 4:9) is another example of his inclination to replace *theos* ("God") with *kyrios* ("Lord"), which he almost always employs as a christological title. Moreover, where the apostle prays for the fulfillment of sanctification "at the coming of our Lord Jesus Christ," our author prays for the granting of the Lord's peace "at all times in all ways." These adverbial expressions suggest that "peace" is used quite comprehensively here, for the fullness of divine blessings through which the believing community is enabled, despite adversity, to live in faith and hope (cf. 2:16).

The invocation of the Lord's presence (v. 16b) echoes a traditional Jewish greeting (e.g., 2 Chr 15:2; Judg 6:12; Ruth 2:4) and anticipates the letter's closing benediction (v. 18). There is no such invocation in Paul's own letters, unless one counts Rom 15:33, "The God [!] of peace be with all of you" (cf. 2 Cor 13:11; Phil 4:9).

◊ ◊ ◊ ◊

The author's chief aim in this passage is to emphasize that the teaching of the present letter is definitive of the Pauline tradition (see also 1:1-2; 3:17) and must be obeyed as such. He remains concerned to establish the point that any contrary teaching must be rejected, even if it has been conveyed in a letter that is claimed to be Paul's or through utterances that are claimed to be inspired (cf. 2:2, 15). The instructions for dealing with those who fail to heed this letter are too general and ambiguous to be practical. In fact, they seem intended only to bolster the author's claim that everything he has written is fully and authentically apostolic.

LETTER-CLOSING (3:17-18)

Formally, this letter closes much like 1 Thessalonians, with a "greeting" (v. 17a; cf. 1 Thess 5:26) and a benediction (v. 18; cf. 1 Thess 5:28). The greeting, however, is almost eclipsed by appended claims that intend to certify this letter's authenticity. It is not surprising that there is no request for prayer (1 Thess 5:25), because that has been included earlier (3:1-2).

◊   ◊   ◊   ◊

In a closing greeting (v. 17), the author employs the first person singular for only the second time in the letter (see also 2:5). The greeting proper—"I, Paul, write this greeting with my own hand" (v. 17a)—is identical to one that appears in both 1 Cor 16:21 and Col 4:18. In the present case, however, the greeting is overshadowed by the writer's concern to certify this letter as Paul's. He offers as evidence the autograph greeting itself, alleging that it exhibits the distinctive characteristics of the apostle's handwriting ("it is the way I write," v. 17c).

The claim that this authenticating "mark" (*sēmeion*; see BDAG, 920 *s.v.*, §1) is present in "every letter" that Paul wrote (v. 17b) is problematic. In fact, the very letter on which our author is so dependent, 1 Thessalonians, does *not* contain any such identifying mark. Even though the apostle may have written at least one of the closing sentences of that letter in his own hand (see commentary on 1 Thess 5:27), he does not actually say so. Moreover, in the letters where Paul does specify that the handwriting is his own, not a scribe's (1 Cor 16:21; Gal 6:11; Phlm 19), his aim is to personalize the letter, not to certify its authenticity.

A closing benediction (v. 18) repeats the one in 1 Thess 5:28, except that the adjective "all" has been added. This addition conforms it to the rhetoric of the invocatory prayer in v. 16b ("with all of you"), but otherwise has no particular significance (the same addition occurs in two of Paul's own benedictions, 1 Cor 16:24; 2 Cor 13:13).

◊ ◊ ◊ ◊

None of the letters that can be attributed with certainty to Paul himself contains anything like the claim of authenticity that stands in v. 17. Placed strategically, at the close of the letter, it serves the vital function of certifying that what has been taught and commanded here belongs to the genuine apostolic tradition and must therefore be believed and obeyed. Paradoxically, this emphatic assertion of Pauline authorship may itself be cited as one reason to question the letter's authenticity (see Introduction).

SELECT BIBLIOGRAPHY

COMMENTARIES ON 1 AND 2 THESSALONIANS
(BOTH CITED AND NOT CITED)

Best, Ernest. 1972. *The First and Second Epistles to the Thessalonians.* HNTC. New York: Harper & Row. Still one of the most important commentaries in English; interprets 2 Thessalonians as Pauline.

Bruce, Frederick Fyvie. 1982. *1 & 2 Thessalonians.* WBC 45. Waco, Texas: Word. A moderately evangelical approach; interprets 2 Thessalonians as Pauline.

Dibelius, Martin. 1937. *An die Thessalonicher, I, II. An die Philipper.* 3d edition HNT 11. Tübingen: Mohr-Siebeck. A brief but still important older commentary; interprets 2 Thessalonians as Pauline.

Dobschütz, Ernst von. 1909. *Die Thessalonicher-Briefe.* 7th edition. KEK 10. Göttingen: Vandenhoeck & Ruprecht. [Repr. 1974, ed. by F. Hahn, with a Literaturverzeichnis by O. Merk.] A classic, widely cited commentary; interprets 2 Thessalonians as Pauline.

Findlay, George G. 1911. *The Epistles of Paul the Apostle to the Thessalonians.* CGTSC 13. Cambridge: Cambridge University Press. One of the more enduring of the older commentaries in English; interprets 2 Thessalonians as Pauline.

Frame, James Everett. 1912. *A Critical and Exegetical Commentary on the Epistles of St Paul to the Thessalonians.* ICC. New York: Scribner's. For many years the major English commentary on these letters; interprets 2 Thessalonians as Pauline.

Friedrich, Gerhard. 1981. "Der erste Brief an die Thessalonicher," and "Der zweite Brief an die Thessalonicher," in J. Becker, *et al., Die Briefe an die Galater, Epheser, Philipper, Kolosser, Thessalonicher und Philemon,* 202-76. 2d edition. NTD 8. Göttingen: Vandenhoeck & Ruprecht. In a series for clergy and laity; regards 1 Thess 5:1-11 as a later, non-Pauline addition; interprets 2 Thessalonians as deutero-Pauline.

Gaventa, Beverly Roberts. 1998. *First and Second Thessalonians.* IBC. Louisville: John Knox. Like the series in which it appears, focused on the teaching and preaching of these letters in the church; interprets 2 Thessalonians as deutero-Pauline.

Holtz, Traugott. 1998. *Der erste Brief an die Thessalonicher.* 3d edition. EKKNT 13. Zürich and Braunschweig: Benziger Verlag; Neukirchen-Vluyn: Neukirchener Verlag. One of the most important German commentaries on this letter; includes brief comments on its reception-history.

Malherbe, Abraham J. 2000. *The Letters to the Thessalonians. A New Translation with Introduction and Commentary.* AB 32B. New York: Doubleday. Accents the pastoral aims of both letters, giving particular attention to the Greco-Roman setting of Paul's ministry and thought; interprets 2 Thessalonians as Pauline.

Marshall, I. Howard. 1983. *1 and 2 Thessalonians.* NCBC. Grand Rapids: Eerdmans. A brief but substantial evangelical commentary; interprets 2 Thessalonians as Pauline.

Marxsen, Willi. 1979. *Der erste Brief an die Thessalonicher.* ZBK/NT 11.1. Zürich: Theologischer Verlag. Brief, intended primarily for clergy and laity; the approach is at once determinedly historical and theologically provocative.

———. 1982. *Der zweite Brief an die Thessalonicher.* ZBK/NT 11.2. Zürich: Theologischer Verlag. A companion volume to the preceding (see comments); interprets 2 Thessalonians as deutero-Pauline.

Menken, Maarten J. J. 1994. *2 Thessalonians.* NTR. London and New York: Routledge. Influenced in many respects by the work of W. Trilling (see below); interprets 2 Thessalonians as deutero-Pauline.

Milligan, George. 1908. *St. Paul's Epistles to the Thessalonians: The Greek Text with Introduction and Notes.* London: Macmillan. Still worth consulting on particular points; interprets 2 Thessalonians as deutero-Pauline.

Morris, Leon. 1991. *The First and Second Epistles to the Thessalonians.* Revised edition. NICNT. Grand Rapids: Eerdmans. A conservative evangelical approach; interprets 2 Thessalonians as Pauline.

Müller, Paul-Gerhard. 2001. *Der Erste und Zweite Brief an die Thessalonicher.* RNT. Regensburg: Pustet. Appears in an important Catholic series; interprets 2 Thessalonians as deutero-Pauline.

Reinmuth, Ekart. 1998. "Der erste Brief an die Thessalonicher," and "Der zweite Brief an die Thessalonicher," in Nikolaus Walter, *et al.*, *Die Briefe an die Philipper, Thessalonicher und an Philemon*, 105-202. NTD 8/2. Göttingen: Vandenhoeck & Ruprecht. Replaces

Friedrich's earlier commentary in this series; interprets 2 Thessalonians as deutero-Pauline.

Richard, Earl J. 1995. *First and Second Thessalonians.* SP 11. Collegeville, Minn.: Liturgical Press. Argues that 1 Thessalonians combines two originally separate letters; interprets 2 Thessalonians as deutero-Pauline.

Rigaux, Beda. 1956. *Saint Paul: Les Épîtres aux Thessaloniciens.* EBib. Paris: Gabalda. Hardly rivaled for its detail, a classic commentary with important chapters on the Greek texts and the history of exegesis; interprets 2 Thessalonians as Pauline.

Smith, Abraham. 2000. "The First Letter to the Thessalonians" and "The Second Letter to the Thessalonians," in L. E. Keck, *et al.*, eds., *The New Interpreter's Bible,* 11.671-772. Nashville: Abingdon. Analyses the letters according to ancient rhetorical categories; tends to read 2 Thessalonians as deutero-Pauline, but downplays the issue.

Trilling, Wolfgang. 1980. *Der Zweite Brief an die Thessalonicher.* EKKNT 14. Zürich and Braunschweig: Benziger Verlag; Neukirchen-Vluyn: Neukirchener Verlag. One of the most influential of the commentaries that treats 2 Thessalonians as deutero-Pauline.

Wanamaker, Charles A. 1990. *The Epistles to the Thessalonians: A Commentary on the Greek Text.* NIGTC. Grand Rapids: Eerdmans. Analyses the letters according to ancient rhetorical categories; interprets 2 Thessalonians as Pauline and written before 1 Thessalonians.

OTHER WORKS CITED

Aasgaard, Reider. 2004. "My Beloved Brothers and Sisters!" *Christian Siblingship in Paul.* Early Christianity in Context. London: Clark.

Allison, Dale C. 1982. "The Pauline Epistles and the Synoptic Gospels: The Pattern of Parallels," *NTS* 28:1-32.

Arzt, Peter. 1994. "The 'Epistolary Introductory Thanksgiving' in the Papyri and in Paul," *NovT* 36: 29-46.

Ascough, Richard S. 2003. *Paul's Macedonian Associations: The Social Context of Philippians and 1 Thessalonians.* WUNT 161. Tübingen: Mohr-Siebeck.

Aune, David E. 2003. *The Westminster Dictionary of New Testament and Early Christian Literature and Rhetoric.* Louisville and London: Westminster John Knox.

Aus, Roger D. 1973. "The Liturgical Background of the Necessity and Propriety of Giving Thanks According to 2 Thess 1:3," *JBL* 92: 432-38.

Bailey, John A. 1978–79. "Who Wrote 2 Thessalonians?" *NTS* 25: 131-45.

Bammel, Ernst. 1984. "Romans 13," *Jesus and the Politics of His Day*, ed. by Ernst Bammel and C. F. D. Moule, 365-84. Cambridge: Cambridge University Press.

Barclay, John. 1993. "Conflict in Thessalonica," *CBQ* 55: 512-30.

Bassler, Jouette M. 1984. "The Enigmatic Sign: 2 Thessalonians 1:5," *CBQ* 46: 496-510.

———. 1995. "Σκεῦος: A Modest Proposal for Illuminating Paul's Use of Metaphor in 1 Thessalonians 4:4," *The Social World of the First Christians: Essays in Honor of Wayne A. Meeks*, ed. by L. M. White and O. L. Yarbrough, 53-66. Minneapolis: Fortress.

Becker, Jürgen. 1993. *Paul. Apostle to the Gentiles.* Louisville: Westminster John Knox. Originally published in German, 1991.

Betz, Hans Dieter. 1989. "The Foundations of Christian Ethics According to Romans 12:1-2," *Witness and Existence. Essays in Honor of Schubert M. Ogden*, ed. by P. Devenish and G. Goodwin, 55-72. Chicago and London: University of Chicago Press.

Bockmuehl, Markus. 2000. *Jewish Law in Gentile Churches. Halakhah and the Beginning of Christian Public Ethics.* Edinburgh: T & T Clark, 2000.

———. 2001. "1 Thessalonians 2:14-16 and the Church in Jerusalem," *TynBul* 52: 1-31.

Boring, M. Eugene, Klaus Berger, and Carsten Colpe. 1995. *Hellenistic Commentary to the New Testament.* Nashville: Abingdon.

Brocke, Christoph vom. 2001. *Thessaloniki—Stadt der Kassander und Gemeinde des Paulus. Eine frühe christliche Gemeinde in ihrer heidnischen Umwelt.* WUNT 125. Tübingen: Mohr-Siebeck.

Burke, Trevor J. 2003. *Family Matters. A Socio-Historical Study of Kinship Metaphors in 1 Thessalonians.* JSNTSup 247. London and New York: Clark.

Byrskog, Samuel. 1996. "Co-Senders, Co-Authors and Paul's Use of the First Person Plural," *ZNW* 87:230-250.

Charlesworth, M. P. 1926. *Trade-Routes and Commerce of the Roman Empire.* 2d edition, rev. Cambridge: Cambridge University Press.

Collins, John J. 1993. *Daniel. A Commentary on the Book of Daniel.* Hermeneia. Minneapolis: Fortress.

————. 1995. *The Scepter and the Star: The Messiahs of the Dead Sea Scrolls and Other Ancient Literature.* ABRL. New York: Doubleday.

Collins, Raymond F. 1979. "Apropos the Integrity of 1 Thess," repr. 1984 in *Studies on the First Letter to the Thessalonians*, 96-135. BETL 66. Leuven: Leuven University Press.

————. 1980a. "1 Thess and the Liturgy of the Early Church," repr. 1984 in *Studies on the First Letter to the Thessalonians*, 136-53. BETL 66. Leuven: Leuven University Press.

————. 1980b. "Tradition, Redaction and Exhortation in 1 Thess 4,13–5,11," repr. 1984 in *Studies on the First Letter to the Thessalonians*, 154-71. BETL 66. Leuven: Leuven University Press.

————. 1980–81. "Paul, as seen through his own eyes," repr. 1984 in *Studies on the First Letter to the Thessalonians*, 175-208. BETL 66. Leuven: Leuven University Press.

————. 1984. "Paul's Early Christology," *Studies on the First Letter to the Thessalonians*, 253-84. BETL 66. Leuven: Leuven University Press.

————. 1988. *Letters That Paul Did Not Write: The Epistle to the Hebrews and the Pauline Pseudepigrapha.* GNS 28. Wilmington, Delaware: Glazier.

————. 1990. "'The Gospel of Our Lord Jesus' (2 Thes 1,8): A Symbolic Shift of Paradigm," *The Thessalonian Correspondence*, ed. by R. Collins, 426-40. BETL 87. Leuven: Leuven University Press/Peeters.

————. 1998. "The Function of Paraenesis in 1 Thess 4,1-12; 5,12-22," *ETL* 74:398-414.

Cullmann, Oscar. 1950. *Christ and Time. The Primitive Christian Conception of Time and History.* Philadelphia: Westminster. Originally published in German, 1946.

Davies, W. D. 1999. "Paul: from the Jewish point of view," *The Cambridge History of Judaism. Vol. 3: The Early Roman Period,* ed. by W. Horbury, *et al.*, 678-730. Cambridge: Cambridge University Press.

de Vos, Craig Steven. 1999. *Church and Community Conflicts. The Relationships of the Thessalonian, Corinthian, and Philippian Churches with Their Wider Civic Communities.* SBLDS 168. Atlanta: Scholars Press.

Donfried, Karl P. 1985. "The Cults of Thessalonica and the Thessalonian Correspondence," repr. 2002 in *Paul, Thessalonica, and Early Christianity*, 21-48. Grand Rapids: Eerdmans.

————. 1993. "The Theology of 1 Thessalonians," in Karl P. Donfried and I. H. Marshall, *The Theology of the Shorter Pauline Letters,*

1-79. New Testament Theology. Cambridge and New York: Cambridge University Press.

———. 2000a. "The Epistolary and Rhetorical Context of 1 Thessalonians 2:1-12," *The Thessalonians Debate: Methodological Discord or Methodological Synthesis?*, ed. by K. Donfried and J. Beutler, 31-60. Grand Rapids: Eerdmans.

———. 2000b. "Paul and Qumran: The Possible Influence of סדרך on 1 Thessalonians," repr. 2002 in Karl P. Donfried, *Paul, Thessalonica, and Early Christianity*, 221-31. Grand Rapids: Eerdmans.

———. 2002. "Was Timothy in Athens? Some Exegetical Reflections on 1 Thess. 3.1-3," *Paul, Thessalonica, and Early Christianity*, 209-19. Grand Rapids: Eerdmans. Originally published in German, 1991.

Edson, Charles. 1948. "Macedonia, III: The Cults of Macedonia," *HTR* 41:153-204.

Elliott, John H. 2000. *1 Peter. A New Translation with Introduction and Commentary.* AB 37B. New York: Doubleday.

Ernst, Michael. 1998. *Distanzierte Unpersönlichkeit. Analyse von Sprache und Stil des Zweiten Thessalonicherbriefes im Vergleich mit paulinischen Texten.* Salzburg: Institut für Neutestamentliche Bibelwissenschaft.

Fatum, Lone. 1997. "Brotherhood in Christ: A gender hermeneutical reading of 1 Thessalonians," *Constructing Early Christian Families: Family as Social Reality and Metaphor*, ed. by H. Moxnes, 183-97. London and New York: Routledge.

Fee, Gordon D. 1992. "On Text and Commentary on 1 and 2 Thessalonians," *SBLSP*, ed. by E. Lovering, 165-83. Atlanta: Scholars Press.

———. 1994. *God's Empowering Presence: The Holy Spirit in the Letters of Paul.* Peabody, Mass.: Hendrickson.

Fitzgerald, John T. 1988. *Cracks in an Earthen Vessel. An Examination of the Catalogues of Hardships in the Corinthian Correspondence.* SBLDS 99. Atlanta: Scholars Press.

Fredrickson, David E. 1996. "παρρησία in the Pauline Epistles," *Friendship, Flattery, and Frankness of Speech*, ed. by J. Fitzgerald, 163-83. Studies on Friendship in the New Testament World. NovTSup 82. Leiden: Brill.

———. 2003. "Passionless Sex in 1 Thessalonians 4:4-5," *WW* 23:23-30.

Friedrich, Gerhard. 1965. "Ein Tauflied hellenistischer Judenchristen, 1. Thess. 1,9f.," *TZ* 21:502-16.

———. 1973. "1. Thessalonicher 5,1-11, der apologetische Einschub eines Späteren," *ZTK* 70: 288-315.

Furnish, Victor Paul. 1989. "Der »Wille Gottes« in paulinischer Sicht," *Jesu Rede von Gott und ihre Nachgeschichte im frühen Christentum. Beiträge zur Verkündigung Jesu und zum Kerygma der Kirche. Festschrift für Willi Marxsen zum 70. Geburtstag,* ed. by D.-A. Koch, G. Sellin, and A. Lindemann, 208-21. Gütersloh: Mohn.

———. 2002. "Inside Looking Out: Some Pauline Views of the Unbelieving Public," *Pauline Conversations in Context: Essays in Honor of Calvin J. Roetzel,* ed. by J. Anderson, P. Sellew, and C. Setzer, 104-24. JSNTSup 222. Sheffield: Academic Press.

———. 2004. "The Spirit in 2 Thessalonians," *The Holy Spirit and Christian Origins. Essays in Honor of James D. G. Dunn,* ed. by G. Stanton, B. Longenecker, and S. Barton. 229-40. Grand Rapids and Cambridge, U.K.

———. 2005. "Uncommon Love and the Common Good: Christians as Citizens in the Letters of Paul," *In Search of the Common Good. Theology for the Twenty-first Century,* ed. by P. Miller and D. McCann, 58-87. New York and London: Clark.

Gamble, Harry Y. 1995. *Books and Readers in the Early Church: A History of Early Christian Texts.* New Haven: Yale University Press.

Gaventa, Beverly Roberts. 1990. "Apostles as Babes and Nurses in 1 Thessalonians 2:7," *Faith and History: Essays in Honor of Paul W. Meyer,* ed. by J. Carroll, C. Cosgrove, and E. Johnson, 193-207. Atlanta: Scholars Press.

———. 1996a. "Mother's Milk and Ministry in 1 Corinthians 3," *Theology and Ethics in Paul and His Interpreters: Essays in Honor of Victor Paul Furnish,* ed. by E. Lovering, Jr. and J. Sumney, 101-13. Nashville: Abingdon.

———. 1996b. "Our Mother St. Paul: Toward the Recovery of a Neglected Theme," *PSB* 17:29-44.

Giblin, Charles H. 1967. *The Threat to the Faith: An Exegetical and Theological Re-Examination of 2 Thessalonians 2.* AnBib 31. Rome: Pontifical Biblical Institute.

Gilliard, Frank D. 1989. "The Problem of the Antisemitic Comma between 1 Thessalonians 2.14 and 15," *NTS* 35:481-502.

Glancy, Jennifer A. 2002. *Slavery in Early Christianity.* Oxford and New York: Oxford University Press.

Gundry Volf, Judith M. 1991. *Paul and Perseverance. Staying In and Falling Away.* Louisville: Westminster John Knox.

Harland, Philip A. 2005. "Familial Dimensions of Group Identity:

'Brothers' (Ἀδελφοί) in Associations of the Greek East," *JBL* 124:491-513.

Harnack, Adolf von. 1910. "Das Problem des zweiten Thessalonicherbriefes," SPAW/Philosophisch-Historischen Klasse, 31:560-78.

Harrison, J. R. 2002. "Paul and the Imperial Gospel at Thessaloniki," *JSNT* 25:71-96.

Heil, John Paul. 2000. "Those Now Asleep (not Dead) Must be Awakened for the Day of the Lord in 1 Thess 5:9-10," *NTS* 46:464-71.

Hendrix, Holland Lee. 1991. "Archaeology and Eschatology at Thessalonica," *The Future of Early Christianity. Essays in Honor of Helmut Koester*, ed. by B. Pearson, *et al.*, 107-18. Minneapolis: Fortress.

———. 1992. "Thessalonica," *ABD*, ed. by D. N. Freedman, *et al.*, 6.523-27. New York: Doubleday.

Hock, Ronald F. 1980. *The Social Context of Paul's Ministry: Tentmaking and Apostleship*. Philadelphia: Fortress.

Hofius, Otfried. 1991. "Unknown Sayings of Jesus," *The Gospel and the Gospels*, ed. by P. Stuhlmacher, 336-60. Grand Rapids: Eerdmans.

Holland, Glenn Stanfield. 1988. *The Tradition That You Received from Us: 2 Thessalonians in the Pauline Tradition*. HUT 24. Tübingen: Mohr-Siebeck.

Holtz, Traugott. 1991. "Paul and the Oral Gospel Tradition," *Jesus and the Oral Gospel Tradition*, ed. by H. Wansbrough, 380-93. Sheffield: JSOT Press.

Hooker, Morna D. 1994. "Paul," *Not Ashamed of the Gospel: New Testament Interpretations of the Death of Christ*, 20-46. Grand Rapids: Eerdmans.

———. 1996. "1 Thessalonians 1.9-10: a Nutshell—but What Kind of Nut?" *Geschichte—Tradition—Reflexion. Festschrift für Martin Hengel zum 70. Geburtstag. III: Frühes Christentum*, ed. by H. Lichtenberger, 435-48. Tübingen: Mohr-Siebeck.

Hughes, Frank Witt. 1989. *Early Christian Rhetoric and 2 Thessalonians*. JSNTSup 30. Sheffield: JSOT Press.

Jewett, Robert. 1971. *Paul's Anthropological Terms: A Study of their Use in Conflict Settings*. AGJU 10. Leiden: Brill.

———. 1986. *The Thessalonian Correspondence: Pauline Rhetoric and Millenarian Piety*. Philadelphia: Fortress.

———. 1993. "Tenement Churches and Communal Meals in the Early Church: The Implications of a Form-Critical Analysis of 2 Thessalonians 3:10," *BR* 38:23-43.

Johanson, Bruce C. 1987. *To All the Brethren. A Text-Linguistic and Rhetorical Approach to 1 Thessalonians.* ConBNT 16. Stockholm: Almqvist.

———. 1995. "1 Thessalonians 2:15-16: Prophetic Woe-Oracle with ἔφθασεν as Proleptic Aorist," *Texts and Contexts: Biblical Texts in Their Textual and Situational Contexts. Essays in Honor of Lars Hartman,* ed. by T. Fornberg and D. Hellholm, 519-34. Oslo: Scandinavian University Press.

Kennedy, George A. 1984. *New Testament Interpretation through Rhetorical Criticism.* Chapel Hill, N.C. and London: University of North Carolina Press.

Koester, Helmut. 1979. "I Thessalonians—Experiment in Christian Writing," *Continuity and Discontinuity in Church History. Essays Presented to George Hunston Williams on the Occasion of his 65th Birthday,* ed. by F. Church and T. George, 33-44. SHCT 19. Leiden: Brill.

———. 1980. "Apostel und Gemeinde in den Briefen an die Thessalonicher," *Kirche. Festschrift für Günther Bornkamm zum 75. Geburtstag,* ed. by D. Lührmann and G. Strecker, 287-99. Tübingen: Mohr-Siebeck.

———. 1985. "The Text of First Thessalonians," *The Living Text. Essays in Honor of Ernest W. Saunders,* ed. by D. Groh and R. Jewett, 219-27. Lanham, Md., New York, and London: University Press of America.

———. 1990. "From Paul's Eschatology to the Apocalyptic Schemata of 2 Thessalonians," *The Thessalonian Correspondence,* ed. by R. Collins, 441-58. BETL 87. Leuven: Leuven University Press/Peeters.

Lampe, Peter. 1987. "Paulus—Zeltmacher," *BZ* 31:256-61.

Lindemann, Andreas. 1999. "Zum Abfassungszweck des zweiten Thessalonicherbriefes," *Paulus, Apostel und Lehrer der Kirche. Studien zu Paulus und zum frühen Paulusverständnis,* 228-40. Tübingen: Mohr-Siebeck. Originally published in 1977.

Malherbe, Abraham J. 1986. *Moral Exhortation, A Greco-Roman Sourcebook.* LEC 4. Philadelphia: Westminster.

———. 1987. *Paul and the Thessalonians: The Philosophic Tradition of Pastoral Care.* Philadelphia: Fortress.

———. 1988. *Ancient Epistolary Theorists.* SBLSBS. Atlanta: Scholars Press.

———. 1989. *Paul and the Popular Philosophers.* Minneapolis: Fortress.

————. 1995. "God's New Family in Thessalonica," *The Social World of the First Christians: Essays in Honor of Wayne A. Meeks,* ed. by L. M. White and O. L. Yarbrough, 116-25. Minneapolis: Fortress.

Manson, Thomas Walter. 1953. "St. Paul in Greece: The Letters to the Thessalonians," *BJRL* 35: 428-47; repr. in *Studies in the Gospels and Epistles,* 259-78. Philadelphia: Westminster.

Marshall, I. Howard. 1990. "Election and Calling to Salvation in 1 and 2 Thessalonians," *The Thessalonian Correspondence,* ed. by R. Collins, 259-76. BETL 87. Leuven: Leuven University Press/Peeters.

Martin, Dale B. 1995. *The Corinthian Body.* New Haven: Yale University Press.

————. 1997. "Paul Without Passion: On Paul's rejection of desire in sex and marriage," *Constructing Early Christian Families: Family as Social Reality and Metaphor,* ed. by H. Moxnes, 201-15. London and New York: Routledge.

Martyn, J. Louis. 1997. *Galatians. A New Translation with Introduction and Commentary.* AB 33A. New York: Doubleday.

Meeks, Wayne A. 1983. *The First Urban Christians: The Social World of the Apostle Paul.* New Haven and London: Yale University Press.

Metzger, Bruce M. 1992. *The Text of the New Testament.* 3d edition. New York: Oxford University Press.

————. 1994. *A Textual Commentary on the Greek New Testament.* 2d edition. Stuttgart: Deutsche Bibelgesellschaft/United Bible Societies.

Metzger, Paul. 2005. *Katechon. II Thess 2.1-12 im Horizont apokalyptischen Denkens.* BZNW 135. Berlin–New York: de Gruyter, 2005.

Mitchell, Margaret M. 1992. "New Testament Envoys in the Context of Greco-Roman Diplomatic and Epistolary Conventions: The Example of Timothy and Titus," *JBL* 111: 641-62.

Müller, Markus. 1998. "Der sogenannte 'schriftstellerische Plural'—neu betrachtet. Zur Frage der Mitarbeiter als Mitverfasser der Paulusbriefe," *BZ* 42:181-201.

Munck, Johannes. 1959. *Paul and the Salvation of Mankind.* Richmond: John Knox.

Murphy-O'Connor, Jerome. 1995. *Paul the Letter-Writer: His World, His Options, His Skills.* Collegeville, Minn.: Liturgical Press.

————. 1996. *Paul: A Critical Life.* New York: Oxford University Press.

Neirynck, Frans J. 1986. "Paul and the Sayings of Jesus," *L'Apôtre Paul: Personnalité, style et conception du ministère,* ed. by A. Vanhoye. 265-31. Leuven: Leuven University Press/Peeters.

Neyrey, Jerome H. 1980. "Eschatology in 1 Thessalonians: The Theological Factor in 1,9-10; 2,4-5; 3.11-13; 4,6 and 4,13-18," *SBLSP*, ed. by P. Achtemeier, 219-31. Chico, Ca.: Scholars Press.

Nicholl, Colin R. 2004. *From Hope to Despair in Thessalonica. Situating 1 and 2 Thessalonians.* SNTSMS 126. Cambridge and New York: Cambridge University Press.

Oakes, Peter. 2005. "Re-mapping the Universe: Paul and the Emperor in 1 Thessalonians and Philippians," *JSNT* 27:301-322.

Osiek, Carolyn, and David L. Balch. 1997. *Families in the New Testament World. Households and House Churches.* The Family, Religion, and Culture. Louisville: Westminster John Knox.

Pearson, Birger. 1997. "1 Thessalonians 2:13-16," *The Emergence of the Christian Religion: Essays in Early Christianity,* 58-74. Harrisburg, Pa.: TPI. Originally published in 1971.

Plevnik, Joseph. 1997. *Paul and the Parousia. An Exegetical and Theological Investigation.* Peabody, Mass.: Hendrickson.

———. 1999. "1 Thessalonians 4,17: The Bringing in of the Lord or the Bringing in of the Faithful?" *Bib* 80: 537-46.

———. 2000. "The Destination of the Apostle and of the Faithful: Second Corinthians 4:13b-14 and First Thessalonians 4:14," *CBQ* 62:83-95.

Popkes, Enno Edzard. 2004. "Die Bedeutung des zweiten Thessalonicherbriefs für das Verständnis paulinischer und deuteropaulinischer Eschatologie," *BZ* 48:39-64.

Reed, Jeffrey T. 1997. "The Epistle," *Handbook of Classical Rhetoric in the Hellenistic Period, 330 B.C.–A.D. 400,* ed. by S. Porter, 171-93. Leiden: Brill.

Rist, Martin. 1972. "Pseudepigraphy and the Early Church," *Studies in New Testament and Early Christian Literature. Essays in Honor of Allen P. Wikgren,* ed. by D. Aune, 75-91. NovTSup 33; Leiden: Brill.

Russell, Ronald. 1988. "The Idle in 2 Thess 3.6-12: an Eschatological or a Social Problem?" *NTS* 34:105-19.

Schlueter, Carol J. 1994. *Filling Up the Measure: Polemical Hyperbole in 1 Thessalonians 2.14-16.* JSNTSup 98. Sheffield: JSOT Press.

Schmidt, Daryl. 1983. "I Thess 2:13-16: Linguistic Evidence for an Interpolation," *JBL* 102:269-79.

———. 1990. "The Syntactical Style of 2 Thessalonians: How Pauline Is It?" *The Thessalonian Correspondence,* ed. by R. Collins, 383-93. BETL 87. Leuven: Leuven University Press/Peeters.

Schmithals, Walter. 1964. "Die Thessalonicherbriefe als Brief-kompositionen," *Zeit und Geschichte. Dankesgabe an Rudolf*

Bultmann zum 80. Geburtstag, ed. by E. Dinkler. 295-315. Tübingen: Mohr-Siebeck.

————. 1969. *The Office of Apostle in the Early Church.* Nashville and New York: Abingdon. Originally published in German, 1961.

————. 1972. "The Historical Situation of the Thessalonian Epistles," *Paul and the Gnostics*, 123-218. Nashville: Abingdon. Originally published in German, 1965.

Schnelle, Udo. 2005. *Apostle Paul: His Life and Theology.* Grand Rapids: Baker. Originally published in German, 2003.

Schoon-Janßen, Johannes. 2000. "On the Use of Elements of Ancient Epistolography in 1 Thessalonians," *The Thessalonians Debate: Methodological Discord or Methodological Synthesis?*, ed. by K. Donfried and J. Beutler, 179-93. Grand Rapids: Eerdmans.

Schrage, Wolfgang. 1989. "Heiligung als Prozeß bei Paulus," *Jesu Rede von Gott und ihre Nachgeschichte im frühen Christentum. Beiträge zur Verkündigung Jesu und zum Kerygma der Kirche. Festschrift für Willi Marxsen zum 70. Geburtstag*, ed. by D.-A. Koch, G. Sellin, and A. Lindemann, 222-34. Gütersloh: Mohn.

Schubert, Paul. 1939. *Form and Function of the Pauline Thanksgivings.* BZNW 20. Berlin: Töpelmann.

Schweizer, Eduard. 1945. "Der zweite Thessalonicherbrief ein Philipperbrief?" *TZ* 1:90-105; see also 282-89 and *TZ* 2 (1946): 74-75.

Smith, Abraham. 1995. *Comfort One Another: Reconstructing the Rhetoric and Audience of 1 Thessalonians.* LCBI. Louisville: Westminster John Knox.

Smith, Jay E. 2001. "1 Thessalonians 4:4: Breaking the Impasse," *BBR* 11: 65-105.

Söding, Thomas. 1992. *Die Trias Glaube, Hoffnung, Liebe bei Paulus. Eine exegetische Studie.* SBS 150. Stuttgart: Verlag Katholisches Bibelwerk.

Spicq, Ceslaus. 1965. *Agape in the New Testament.* Vol. 2: *Agape in the Epistles of St. Paul, the Acts of the Apostles and the Epistles of St. James, St. Peter, and St. Jude.* St. Louis and London: Herder. Abridgement of the French edition published in 1959.

————. 1994. *Theological Lexicon of the New Testament.* 3 vols. Peabody, Mass.: Hendrickson.

Still, Todd D. 1999. *Conflict at Thessalonica. A Pauline Church and Its Neighbours.* JSNTSup 183. Sheffield: Academic Press.

Stirewalt, M. Luther, Jr. 2003. *Paul, the Letter Writer.* Grand Rapids: Eerdmans.

Stowers, Stanley K. 1986. *Letter Writing in Greco-Roman Antiquity.* LEC 5. Philadelphia: Westminster.

Sumney, Jerry L. 1990. "The Bearing of a Pauline Rhetorical Pattern on the Integrity of 2 Thessalonians," *ZNW* 81: 192-204.

Trilling, Wolfgang. 1972. *Untersuchungen zum zweiten Thessalonicherbrief.* ETS 27. Leipzig: St. Benno-Verlag.

Tuckett, Christopher M. 1990. "Synoptic Tradition in 1 Thessalonians?" *The Thessalonian Correspondence,* ed. by R. Collins, 160-82. BETL 87. Leuven: Leuven University Press/Peeters.

Turner, Seth. 2003. "The Interim, Earthly Messianic Kingdom in Paul," *JSNT* 25:323-42.

Vos, Johan S. 2000. "On the Background of 1 Thessalonians 2:1-12: A Response to Traugott Holtz," *The Thessalonians Debate: Methodological Discord or Methodological Synthesis?,* ed. by K. Donfried and J. Beutler, 81-88. Grand Rapids: Eerdmans.

Walker, William O. 2001. *Interpolations in the Pauline Letters.* JSNTSup 213. Sheffield: Academic Press.

Ware, James. 1992. "The Thessalonians as a Missionary Congregation: 1 Thessalonians 1,5-8," *ZNW* 83:126-31.

Watson, Francis. 2000. *Agape, Eros, Gender: Towards a Pauline Sexual Ethic.* Cambridge: Cambridge University Press.

Weima, Jeffrey A. D., and Stanley E. Porter. 1998. *An Annotated Bibliography of 1 and 2 Thessalonians.* NTTS 26. Leiden and Boston: Brill.

Weiß, Wolfgang. 1993. "Glaube—Liebe—Hoffnung. Zu der Trias bei Paulus," *ZNW* 84:196-217.

Wenham, David. 1995. *Paul: Follower of Jesus or Founder of Christianity? A New Look at the Question of Paul and Jesus.* Grand Rapids: Eerdmans.

White, John L. 1986. *Light from Ancient Letters.* Philadelphia: Fortress.

Wilckens, Ulrich. 1963. *Die Missionsreden der Apostelgeschichte.* 2d edition. WMANT 5. Neukirchen-Vluyn: Neukirchener Verlag.

Wiles, Gordon P. 1974, *Paul's Intercessory Prayers: Significance of Intercessory Prayer Passages in the Letters of St. Paul.* SNTMS 24. Cambridge: Cambridge University Press.

Winter, Bruce W. 1989. "'If a Man Does Not Wish to Work . . .' A Cultural and Historical Setting for 2 Thessalonians 3:6-16," *TynBul* 40:303-15.

———. 1993. "The Entries and Ethics of Orators and Paul (1 Thessalonians 2:1-12)," *TynBul* 44:55-74.

Wischmeyer, Oda. 1981. *Der höchste Weg. Das 13. Kapitel des 1. Korintherbriefes.* SNT 13. Gütersloh: Mohn.

Witmer, Stephen. 2006. "Θεοδίδακτοι in 1 Thessalonians: A Pauline Neologism," *NTS* 52 (2006) 239-50.

Wrede, William. 1903. *Die Echtheit des zweiten Thessalonicherbriefes untersucht.* TU n.F. 9/2. Leipzig: Hinrichs'sche Buchhandlung.

INDEX